House of Suds

House of Suds

A History of Beer Brewing in Western Canada

William A. Hagelund

hancock

house

ISBN 0-88839-526-4
Copyright © 2003 William A. Hagelund

Cataloging in Publication Data
Hagelund, William A. (William Arnold), 1924–
    House of suds

    ISBN 0-88839-526-4

    1. Brewing industry—Canada, Western—History. 2. Beer
industry—Canada, Western—History. 3. Molson Capilano
Brewery. I. Title.
TP573.C3H33 2003   338.4'766342'09712   C2002-910951-5

Printed in China—Jade

Editor: Nancy Miller
Production: Irene Hannestad
Cover design: Ingrid Luters
Front cover photos: (Top photo) Sick's Fort Steele Brewerey, 1900, *B.C. Archives & Records
Service*; (bottom photo) Full kegs in racking cellar, Molson Capilano Brewery, Burrard St.,
1954, *Sicks/Molsons*; (bottle of beer) "Alberta Pride," first brew by Fritz Sick at Lethbridge,
1901, *City of Lethbridge Archives*.
Back cover photo: Molson Capilano Brewery, Burrard St., *A.G Pugh collection*.

*We acknowledge the financial support of the Government of Canada through the
Book Publishing Industry Development Program (BPIDP) for our publishing activities.*

Published simultaneously in Canada and the United States by

HANCOCK HOUSE PUBLISHERS LTD.
19313 Zero Avenue, Surrey, B.C. V3S 9R9
(604) 538-1114 Fax (604) 538-2262

HANCOCK HOUSE PUBLISHERS
1431 Harrison Avenue, Blaine, WA 98230-5005
(604) 538-1114 Fax (604) 538-2262
Web Site: www.hancockhouse.com *email:* sales@hancockhouse.com

Contents

Dedication

A.G. Pugh was in the forefront of the Molson Capilano Brewery's tremendous growth from 1952 up until 1992. His gift of photographs depicting this growth, and his personal assistance in reviewing my manuscript have ensured a degree of accuracy to this story that should bring enlightenment as well as pleasure to all who take the effort to peruse its pages. While Art was my boss for most of these years, I considered him a friend and enjoyed his company on other projects not of a brewing nature, model engineering and steam boating being two that come quickly to mind.

Introduction

In western Canada beer making and beer drinking is carried out with a special gusto. Even cooking with beer is the joy of both local connoisseurs and humble home chefs. Beer is the thirst quencher of active people: those who work hard, play hard and, yes, even love hard. Here in the northwest, one of the last places on planet Earth to be discovered and populated by European settlers, a frothy mug of fresh sparkling beer took on a whole new significance in this new land. Beer was a tonic for the body and spirit—a reward for seemingly endless hours of dangerous, hard work. Miners, loggers, fishermen, farmers, and the construction workers of the new towns and railroads sought out their favorite brews at the end of the day.

Commercial brewing was an effort in pioneering entrepreneurialism. Recipes from the Old Country were adapted to appeal the Canadian mosaic of beer tastes. Conservative liquor licensing laws were always an obstacle to wider distribution and increased profits, and the financing of brewery operations was an adventure fraught with cutthroat business deals and ever-changing partnerships. But as new breweries became established and thrived, the golden liquid poured into kegs and bottles became a source of pride to the brewmasters of the West. Beer labels would display the family name or the town where the beer was brewed, thus Victoria Brewing and Fritz Sick's House of Lethbridge.

Rapid advances in technology, especially after World War II, were applied to the beer making industry initiating the sequence of increased capacity, brewery expansions, and mergers. But among the facts in this book of corporate ownership is the story of the process of brewing and the skilled and dedicated workers who took pride in their trades and their membership in a very important commercial community.

CHAPTER ONE

B.C.'s Pioneer Brewers

British Columbia's brewing history can trace its origin back to 1858 and the time of Governor James Douglas, when thousands of gold hungry people rushed into the wilds of New Caledonia to claim their Eldorado.

This influx meant New Caledonia had a law and order problem never before experienced in Canada. James Douglas, recently Crown-appointed governor of the new Colony of Vancouver Island, quickly decreed all miners and prospectors had to pay twenty-one shillings (one guinea) a month (approximately $5–$6 back then) for a mining license and file a monthly report of the gold they found with the gold commissioner he swiftly appointed.

While difficult to apply, this licensing held promise of some success, even if just to pay the wages of those appointed to enforce it. But Prime Minister Gladstone and the British House of Commons questioned just whose interest this Hudson's Bay Company (HBC) governor was really serving. They ordered Sir Edward Bulwer Lytton, Secretary for the Colonies, to send a magistrate there to administer the Queen's law and to carry to Douglas a proclamation decreeing the mainland territory be self-administered as the Colony of British Columbia, with Douglas appointed to carry out the duties of its first governor. Thus, effectively severing him from the HBC and their interests.

The man Lytton selected to carry these dispatches and maintain law and order in this vast wilderness of rushing rivers and towering mountains was Matthew Baillie Begbie. Judge Begbie quickly earned the title of "The Hanging Judge" among those tempted to find an easier way to the rivers' gold than through the labor of sluice and rocker. His most famous quote thundered at a mob of angry wild miners still echoes through the halls of Canadian justice to this day: "In this land the Queen's law shall rule, and British Justice shall prevail."

Both Begbie and Governor Douglas viewed public drinking as a destroyer of man's vitality and integrity, and the success of the mining license requirement, caused them to propose a similar licensing system for the manufacturing and sale of spirits. Governor Douglas had effectively dried up the Hudson's Bay Company through strict rules for consumption of spirits, and by appointing only those who would follow them. He hoped the requirements of this new law would ensure a like condition throughout his vast domain west of the Rockies and south of the fifty-ninth parallel. Essentially, his law required that "Spirits would only be licensed for public consumption where food and bed was also offered," and that, "brewers of spirits could not sell their product to other then licensed premises."

While it has remained basically thus ever since, this unique policy was soon followed by other provinces as the temperance movement became more vocal, and a lucrative source of revenue was realized by appearing to have the temperance interest at heart. When the attorney general later took licensing and policing out of the sheriff's office, and created a Liquor Control Board (LCB), he effectively placed the government in the role of wholesaler and not only collected all the liquor taxes due, but pocketed the middleman's fat mark-up in the bargain.

Roughly 37¢ of every dollar spent on the sales of spirits goes through LCB to government coffers, another 28¢ goes to the provincial taxman to be split with the federal government, and approximately 35¢ goes back to the brewer to pay wages, transportation, supplies and realize a return on the investor's capital. Plus, every dollar spent at LCB's cash registers today costs the buyer a sales tax which goes in the province's coffers, and a goods and service tax that the federal governments pockets.

With 35¢ worth of spirits costing the consumer a staggering $1.14, Sir James Douglas had unknowingly tapped a source of wealth far greater then all the beaver and mink pelts his company had taken out of this country for the previous 200 years, plus all the gold taken out by the Argonauts! Who ever said booze was the road to poverty and ruin?

While a report from San Francisco in early 1858 states that brewing equipment was being shipped aboard the schooner *Pago* for Victoria, it was later that same year that a William Steinborger, recently arriving from California, relocated this brewing interest from the

The Victoria Brewery, circa 1898.   *Photo: British Columbia Archives C-76185*

Swan Lake area outside the township limits to Government Street within the quickly growing gold port. The Phoenix Brewery thus became the first licensed brewer in the Colony of Vancouver Island, though two years later it was sold to F. W. Laumeister and R. Gowen, who renamed it the Victoria Brewing Company.

Bill Steinborger started another brewery in 1861, out on Head Street near the Esquimalt army barracks, again naming it Phoenix Brewing, which has caused certain historians some confusion. Victoria Brewing was sold to Goertz and Heinman in 1864, and resold again in 1868 to Joseph Loewen and Louis Erb. Erb's son Emil, during this same period, was brew master at Steinborger's Phoenix Brewery, so it surprised no one when in 1892 Victoria Brewing took over the assets of Phoenix Brewing.

Building a new brewery at Discovery and Government Streets, Loewen and Erb incorporated it as the Victoria-Phoenix Brewery and sold their previous holdings. Albion Iron Works (formerly Captain William Spratt's ship and machinery repair yard) built the iron gates that guarded this pioneer brewery main entrance.

In 1895 John Tait (or Tate) built a brewery out on Esquimalt Road, where his son Fred brewed Silver Spring Old English Ale and a fine stout. In 1907 this business was sold to a former employee of the Victoria-Phoenix Brewery, Harry Mayard, and his associates John Day and Philip Crombie who renamed it Silver Spring Brewery. Their brew master was Adolph Brachat, who had been brewer with

11

The Westminster Brewery in 1899. The owner Nels Nelson and his son Lawrie are in the center; the house to the right of the brewery is the owner's home.

Photo: Vic Brachat Collection

Anheuser Busch in St. Louis, and whose father was a master brewer in Switzerland.

Silver Spring Brewery acquired the old Fairall Brewery site in 1908 and built a modern new brewery in west Victoria, donating their former site for a playground to students of Victoria West Public School. In 1910, the year Adolph Brachat's son Victor was born (Vic would become longtime brew master at New Westminster's Lucky Lager-Labatt's Brewery in later years, and assist with this story), Silver Spring offered its first lager beer. By 1928, Silver Spring Brewery was amalgamated with the Victoria-Phoenix Brewery under the Coast Brewery's corporate flag; this giant step will be documented further in this story.

While two of these breweries already mentioned could boast of having the first and second brewing license issued in the colony of British Columbia, license number three (1862) was issued to a brewing venture on the Fraser River at what was then the capital city of this gold colony. This was the City Brewing Company owned by Picht and Hay at Carnarvan and Eighth Streets in New Westminster. Over the next twenty years it had several owners until purchased by Mr. A. Gibson, who changed its name to Westminster Brewery Ltd. The brewery was later bought by Nels Nelson and renamed Nelson's Westminster Brewery.

Nels Nelson, born in Denmark in 1863, left school at fourteen to follow the sea. By 1881 he was sailing as able seaman on a German full-rigged ship that rounded the Horn and arrived later in that year at the bustling seaport of Victoria. British Columbia appeared to offer more opportunity to him than a seaman's lot, so Nels skipped ashore and went to work for Louis Erbe at the Victoria Brewing Company for the next four years. Becoming accomplished in the art of brewing, he moved up island to John Mahrer's Nanaimo Bottling Company, where he became knowledgeable of this new packaging medium.

While fired clay jugs, tuns and bottles have a long history as containers for wines, oils and other still fluids, beer, a slightly pressurized effervescent refreshment, had traditionally been offered in wooden kegs or barrels. During this period, the West Coast brewers began to offer beers in bottles, both pint- and quart-sized, in either glazed clay or glass, cast in chip molds (stone bottles with wire latched stopper, such as ginger beer was offered in, might also have had their origin at this time). Most bottles were sealed with a cork, some had a glass stopper, and others had a glass ball built into the neck of the bottle that acted like a check valve, allowing beer to enter but not exit until the carbon dioxide pressure was vented. The metal type, crimped-edge

The Red Cross Brewery in 1898.   *Photo: Larry Rintoul Collection*

crown, so familiar today to seal a bottle of beer, was still many years in the future.

Nels Nelson may have acquainted the Red Cross Brewery in Vancouver with John Mahrer's new packaging media. For soon after his visit there, J. A. Rekab began to offer beer in bottles. In late fall of 1886 Nels arrived at the river port of New Westminster to become brew master for Andy Gibson at the old City Brewery, and here again bottle beer made its debut shortly after his arrival. Ten years later he bought out Andy Gibson's interest and renamed the business Nelson's Westminster Brewery.

In 1898, Nels Nelson purchased property out on Brunette Street and after relocating the equipment there from the Carnarvan Street brewery, the old City Brewing Company buildings were torn down and the property sold. While this new location gave more room for future expansion and a good supply of water from the Brunette River, it was a fire of prodigious proportions that caused Nels Nelson to up stakes and move. Few people today are aware that most of the pioneer city of New Westminster, that extending west from Mary Street to Eighth Street and south of Royal Avenue to Front Street and the river docks, were destroyed or damaged by this fire. The exceptions were a couple of stone buildings slightly singed, and the wooden buildings of Nel's brewery badly charred, but still intact.

Unlike Vancouver's disastrous fire, which sprung up on a peaceful Sunday morn, New Westminster's fire ballooned into a fierce conflagration on a late Saturday afternoon while the city bustled with people and horse-drawn wagons.

September 10, 1898, was a hot day that drew many into the cool bar rooms along Front Street, by early afternoon a fresh breeze sprang up on the river giving relief to others who had sought shade under the trees. How the fire actually started is not known. Perhaps a careless smoker or a spark from a steamboat's funnel or a locomotive's belching stack, but quite suddenly the 200-ton pile of baled hay on Brackman Kerr's dock was a roaring inferno, which ignited the top works of the small river steamer *Edgar* tied up alongside, driving away her watchman crew.

When her mooring lines burnt away, the river's current nudged the vessel downstream where she collided with the larger sternwheeler *Gladys*; pausing there a moment, she set that unfortunate vessel and her dock afire. Then held against the river's north shore by the fresh afternoon breeze, the *Edgar*, turning end for end under the influence of the river current, proceeded down the line of docks like a flaming fire torch, setting all she bumped against on fire till she became wedged in between the massive bulk of the large side-wheeler *Bon Accord* and the shore, just west of the Eighth Street jetty.

This line of fire, more than eight blocks long and stoked by the freshening wind, began to roar and crackle as it found fresh fuel to feast on inland of the waterfront structures. Over street after street, the furious tongues of flames jumped, until sixty-four blocks of prime downtown businesses were going up in smoke and flames. Fire fighting was in its infancy during those days, and though the city boasted a modern Ronald steam pumper, it was barely saved when the fire station itself went up in flames.

But Nels Nelson, with every penny he owned in the brewery, had his small weekend crew lay out fire hoses and couple them up to the beer pumps and flood the exteriors of his buildings with brewery water. It was this quick action and shear good fortune that kept his brewery from burning to the ground.

Deciding to move farther away from the commercial center of the city, he relocated his equipment eastward of the cemetery on the west bank of the Brunette River. Two years after establishing this brewery he was able to buy up the defunct Jameson Brewery next door, and he built a new cellar block there while reorganizing his business as the Westminster Brewery Ltd.

The new brewery Nels Nelson built was a three-story wooden structure housing an ice plant, steam plant and the first carbon dioxide collection and counter pressure system installed in the province. This modern brewery even boasted a telephone, number seventy-five, in those long ago pioneer days of the magic wire. After 1928, when Nels Nelson sold out his control of this brewery to the Coast Breweries holding company headed by Robert Fiddes, he built a lovely home up on the corner of 2nd Street and Queens Avenue, in which to enjoy a well-earned retirement.

In 1941 this brewery was renamed Lucky Lager Breweries, and in 1958 it became John Labatt's westernmost brewery. Thus, Labatt's Lucky Lager Brewing Co., had its origin in brewing license number three issued in 1862, when this British Columbian river capital was a scattering of tents, shacks and log cabins strung out

Outside the New Westminster Brewery in 1901. The man in the black shirt is J. Munday the chief engineer and the boy on the wagon is Lawrie Nelson; others are not identified. *Photo: Vic Bracht Collection*

along the river bank where the sternwheelers unloaded their passengers and freight. This brewery provided the chance for Molson's to expand from its staid eastern dominion, out into the Wild West beyond the Lake Country.

Today, Vancouver's one and only brewery serving British Columbia and the western United States, can also trace its origin back to Nanaimo's coal town origin. While we'll look briefly at some of the other breweries built throughout the province over the years, the Nanaimo story will now be told because it not only predates by a couple years that of New Westminster's, but also events there have a direct relationship on those that took place in Vancouver, through the intervening years.

While the *Beaver* back in 1851 had carried Joseph MacKay and a few HBC men to sample the coal at "Naymo" on Winthuysen Inlet, which Chief Che-wech-i-kan (Coal Tyee) had brought to Governor Douglas' notice, it was more than two years later before the *Princess Royal* landed twenty-seven coal miners and their families to make it a real coal mining town. Yet, it wasn't until 1858 that the Colony of Vancouver Island issued a retail license to the HBC, as operators of the Nanaimo Coal Company, to dispense spirituous liquors. This cost the HBC $72 each quarter year, and any infractions of the new liquor laws could bring penalties of three months in jail or fines up to $250.

In 1863, the Vancouver Coal Company having bought out the HBC's mining interests transferred this number four license to A. G. Horn and T. E. Peck.

These gentlemen, together with Messrs. Stone, Jerome, Webb and Sabiston who respectively owned the Old Flagg Inn, the French Hotel and the Nanaimo Hotel, built the Millstream Brewery in 1864. This enterprise went under the name of Nightingale & Butler and prospered poorly. Nanaimo was still officially known as Colvilletown (after HBC Governor Colville) until 1874 when it was duly incorporated as the village of Nanaimo. However, by this time the Millstream Brewery had vanished into history, so a new venture was launched and Dick Nightingale was hired to build the Salt Spring Brewery.

Though of stone and brick construction with a supply of water from the Nanaimo Sawmill's flume, and capable of producing 600 gallons of beer a week, it too suffered a quick demise—so quick, that no name was ever registered for their brew. You could say; it was the first "no-name" brew in B.C. John Mahrer, returning from four years in the Cariboo gold fields started a bakery in the newly incorporated town. Then in 1877, he built the Nanaimo Soda Water Factory and large bottling works, down on Mill Street at the site of the old Salt Spring Brewery Works.

In 1890, the Nanaimo Brewing Company was launched there, earning a net profit of 20 percent during its first three years of operation. John Mahrer was its first brew master, and with his share of the profits John bought the Nanaimo Opera House and the Newcastle Hotel and then ventured into the wholesale liquor business. His Nanaimo Brewery also bought out the Red Lion Brewery, before merging with the Union Brewing Company, and this is the company we will follow to Vancouver.

The Union Brewing Company was established in January of 1891, and a contract led Harold McAdie to build a brick building on Dunsmuir Street (named after James Dunsmuir of Nanaimo's coal fame). The brewery had a 900-gallon copper kettle that weighed just over a ton and a refrigeration system that could cool more than 2,000 gallons of wort/beer a day. It went into production in October of that year and in 1892 it merged, as noted above, with John Mahrer's Nanaimo Brewery. A news release of May 1, 1893, declared the directors were John Perry, J. Hough and C. Martin. The B.C. directory listed John Pawson as president, Marshall E. Bray as treasurer, Fred S. Whiteside as secretary and Henry E. Reifel as managing brewer.

The Reifel story, like the Sick story we'll hear about in a later chapter, proved difficult to follow. Both were German emigrants arriving here through the United States, neither wrote many notes of their adventures in getting here or their business dealings through those tumultuous years. However, there is an interesting parallel between their stories, and it may explain the strained relationship between these two brewers when they met in later life, after each had carved out a respected niche in our economy.

Henry E. Reifel arrived in Nanaimo in 1888 after fleeing war torn Alsace Lorraine a few years earlier. Mrs. Norma Reifel, wife of George H. Reifel, Henry's grandson, possesses the family crest, which probably was in fact their family seal or frank. The family had for many generations been the legal keepers of official deeds, sort of the local Notary Public, in the town of Zeiskam where such historic things as water rights and property deeds were zealously guarded.

It would appear, Henry like many young European sons immigrating to the new world, was enticed west by the lure of the siren's promise, for he soon arrived in San Francisco. He began his career learning to brew German lager beer at the Chicago Brewing Company, but the noisy large seaport was not to his liking, and soon after completing his training moved north to the river town of Portland, where he was employed as a brewer for a short time. But as he recalled to his family years later, it too was not to his liking so he sought opportunity farther north.

The Northern Pacific railway had built a line into Tacoma, the former Hudson's Bay's Fort Nisqually, and this lumber town was booming. There is some suggestion that Henry worked in the brewery business for a short time in the Puget Sound area. As this was about the time Fritz Sick arrived in Tacoma, there is some likelihood they may have crossed trails there, for early brewing people with their supply problems got to know each other quickly, and German brewers who have difficulty with the English language, more so.

But Henry did not tarry there long, and what caused his next step remains a family mystery. Like a bird flying home to its nest, Henry arrived in Nanaimo and entered John Mahrer's bottling works where he was treated like a long-lost son. The speed with which events now transcribe almost defies description. Within a year of his arrival in

The Union Brewery.   *Photo: British Columbia Archives C-76185*

Canada, the Nanaimo Brewery was ready to offer a lager beer to their customers, and was the first to offer it in both pint and quart glass bottles.

Two years of profitable sales later, this successful brewery was bought up by a cartel of local investors, with John Mahrer and Henry Reifel retained to operate it. Then after buying out the idle Red Lion Brewery at Mill Creek, it amalgamated with the newly built Union Brewing Company. John Mahrer retired to donate his time to community affairs after this. And Henry Reifel, now a modest shareholder, became the brewing manager.

This brewery triad resolved itself into the Union Brewing

Company of Nanaimo, and soon after it acquired the large property holdings of the Franklyn estate, which included a lovely home. Henry now felt well enough established to seek a wife, and to invite his younger brother Conrad to come to Canada and join him at the brewery. The lady to whom Henry got engaged was herself a rather remarkable person.

Daughter of William Brown, she was the first white female to be born in the roaring gold town of Barkerville. They proved a fine match. In 1893 Anne Elizabeth Brown and Henry E. Reifel were wed, and soon after moved into the old Franklyn house to raise a family. George C. was first to arrive, followed by his sister Florence Anne, then a younger brother, Harry E., in 1896.

Conrad Reifel arrived from Europe in 1898, and took employment at the brewery as a cellar man, gradually working his way up to brew master over the next dozen or so years. While not possessing Henry's keen business ambitions, Conrad soon followed his brother's example and married a good local gal. The redoubtable Bessie Barnes bore him two sons, Edward in 1910 and Henry in 1920, and reigned as dowager caretaker of Franklyn House until it was torn down in 1950.

Union Brewing had acquired the old Franklyn homestead, an architectural landmark out on Dunsmuir Street, when it purchased the five-acre estate from Mayor Bate, for brewery expansion. This beautiful home, built by Captain W. H. Franklyn, became the residence of the brewing manager.

After the Temperance Act shut down the brewing business and Union Brewery's equipment was dismantled, the empty building was later used as a beer delivery center for Vancouver Island. Conrad managed this up to the time of his death in 1933, and then his son, Edward Reifel, took over managership of the Pacific Brewing Agency. Franklyn House, still his mother's home, was purchased by the City of Nanaimo in 1941, though Bessie Reifel lived there for another ten years before moving to Machleary Street. The city then, much to the consternation of those who valued the historic artifacts of Nanaimo's past, tore it down to make way for commercial expansion. However, some of its bricks were saved to make the Pioneer Rock Cairn below the Bastion, that now commemorates the landing there of Nanaimo's mining pioneers in 1854, so in fact a bit of this heritage building has been preserved.

Henry Reifel, sensing opportunity to expand in the beer business, began laying the groundwork that would realize this goal. He sent his eldest son George to Milwaukee in 1907 to train as a brew master, and after his arrival back in Nanaimo, events began to move quickly. Amalgamating with Peter Dilman's Cumberland Brewery and brewing Union Brewing Company (UBC) beers there to satisfy his ever-growing number of customers on the island, Henry made several visits to Vancouver to discuss with Doering and Williams a possible merger or amalgamation to realize brewing his UBC beers on the mainland.

This would cause some misunderstanding within the beer-drinking student fraternity of the newly created University of British Columbia on Point Grey a few years later, which blithely believed this beer had been named for them and became Henry's most faithful supporters.

Henry's success had not gone unnoticed, and investors wanted in, but the shareholders of Union Breweries resisted such inroads, even turning down a $2 million takeover offer from Anheuser Busch. But they did finally accept a $3 million deal from an English syndicate, which ensured them amalgamation with the Vancouver Brewery and the Canadian Malting and Brewing Company. This successful piece of business was marred by the loss of Henry's friend and mentor, John Mahrer. On the last day of September that year, this native of Prague, Austria (pre- World War I), died at the age of 65, after serving many years on the city council and as president of the Nanaimo Hospital Board.

Buoyed up by the brewing merger, Henry arranged for Conrad to manage the Union Brewery, while he moved his family to a lovely home across the street from the new brewery. Joined by his son George C. Reifel, Vancouver Breweries Ltd. offered numerous brews to satisfy the palate of the most critical connoisseur, listing the lager and ales of both Union Brewery and Cumberland's Pilsner Brewery, as well as Red Cross and the D&M's famous labels.

It was here that the Temperance Act would find them when Canada went dry during World War I and the brewery business came tumbling down. The success with which the Reifels survived this calamity and even managed to increase their family worth, will be discussed further along in our story, after we have looked at the pioneer brewers of Vancouver.

In Vancouver before the turn of the century the brewery story becomes a little more muddied, for with both the terminus of rail and shipping and a huge waterfront covered in sprawling sawmills, there were many thirsty men who could afford a drink. And many brewers endeavored to accommodate their needs. From the beginning, Sewell Moody's water-powered sawmill (1866) on the north shore of Burrard Inlet, and Captain Edward Stamp's steam-powered sawmill (1872) at Hastings on the south shore, cut down the huge trees which grew right down to the water's edges, leaving a legacy of equally huge stumps and tangled piles of slash for the settlers who followed them to clear away and cultivate the soils. A trail of sorts meandered westward from Stamp's mill, where squatter shacks and a few log floats occupied the high water line, to peter out at the outfall of Howe Creek (east of the Marine Building today). Deadman's Island harbored a small whale-processing slip and Coal Harbour, still frowned over by giant cedar trees, boasted an Indian village on the Stanley Park shore (opposite the present site of the Bayshore Hotel). Farther west this waterway shoaled and narrowed into a boat passage (Lost Lagoon) separating what is now Stanley Park into an island before finally terminating a couple hundred sandy feet from Second Beach on English Bay.

Moody and Stamp, providing food and accommodation as well as employment at their mill sites, could enforce a religiously stern tee-totaling proviso under these wilderness conditions. The accepted alternative for a man with a thirst was a short boat ride to New Brighton and a long wagon ride or a hike over the Douglas Road to New Westminster to partake of the bright lights and foaming suds of this river city's more liberal amenities.

Captain Jack Deighton, deciding it was more profitable to carry beer to the thirsty than to carry the thirsty to the beer, shipped over several barrels of beer from the New Westminster Brewery and landed them on the beach west of Hastings Mill. Placing a fresh-sawn plank across the barrels he opened shop on Water Street, at what is now the north foot of Carrall Street.

When many of Moody's employees returning aboard Pioneer's fifty-seven-foot steam tugboat/ferry *Leonora* were found to be too drunk to carry out their job, and Captain Stamp's men fell off the jury-rigged bridge thrown across the waterway that bordered the western boundary of his mill, the irate mill owners lodged a concentrated protest to the government about this law-breaking squatter. Located outside the mill's timber lease jurisdiction, they had to await the colony's duly appointed sheriff from Victoria (New Westminster had lost its role of capital city in 1868) to have the captain charged and evicted.

But, by the time the law did arrive, Jack Deighton alerted by friends privy to the pending action, hastily constructed a rough building of sorts to provide bed and food for those who dared partake. Applying for a settler's lease he thus complied fully with Douglas' law and was duly granted a dispensing license as well. Before this speedily built structure had grown into the more respectable Globe Saloon, a shanty town of shacks, cabins and tents had sprouted up around it. Thus, this area became laconically known as Gassy Jack's Town (later shortened to Gastown) because the lessee's owner Captain Gassy Jack Deighton, was such a talkative old mariner.

While the Colony of Vancouver Island had amalgamated with the Colony of British Columbia in 1866, and as noted above the seat of government was moved to the recently incorporated city of Victoria, it wasn't until 1874 and the promise of a railway sea to sea, that British Columbia joined John A. Macdonald's Confederation of Canada to become the westernmost province of the dominion. The construction of a Royal Navy dockyard at Esquimalt, the acquiring of right-of-way for the island's E&N railway and surveys for the mainland's Canadian Pacific Railway promised to stimulate both industry and growth within the province.

In 1879, Jack Deighton gathered a group of responsible Burrard Inlet residents together to draw up and register a plan for the Township of Granville. Laying out Water Street parallel to and facing the inlet's foreshore, with Cordova and Hasting Streets parallel to it and southward of his Globe Hotel, the citizens agreed to provide three roads running north and south to divide the town site into manageable portions. Carrall Street starting at Gassy Jack's emporium became the eastern boundary, Abbott Street divided the plot down the middle and Cambie Streets became its western boundary.

A short time after this, and well outside the western edge of the township where the influential and wealthy had begun to build more substantial homes, Jan A. Rekab built a brewery, believed to be the first steam-powered brewery in this area, and one of his share holders was none other than our infamous Gassy Jack. This brewery was situated on the west bank of a stream of brownish water (the Three Greenhorns had a cabin nearby), which proved none harmful to either Rekab's boiler, which evaporated hundreds of pounds of it an hour, or to his patrons who consumed many barrels of beer brewed from it.

This stream drained a gloomy, marshy lake surrounded by massive cedar trees (now Robson's Square), which were towered over by tall (150–300-foot) fir trees through which now Granville, Seymour and Richards Streets run. The gorge cut by this stream ran northward toward Burrard Street (Christ Church Cathedral was later located on its west bank) to empty into Burrard Inlet just east of where the Marine Building stands today. It was the stone outcrop that stretched westward (now the site of the LRT [former CPR] tunnel), that became the brewery's cooling cellars when John Williams cut caves into them a few years later.

The incorporation of the city of Vancouver, the great fire that almost immediately burnt it down and the final arrival of the railway's first transcontinental train the following year had all faded into history by the time Williams and Barker bought this brewery in 1888. Renaming it the Red Cross Brewery, they built it into a very modern installation which soon boasted electric power and motors, employed a couple dozen men and produced in excess of fifty barrels of beer a day. Originally located on Seaton Street (name since abandoned) it was relocated slightly eastward into the small present-day triangle west of Burrard Street and flanked north and south by Pender and Hastings Streets.

They offered Red Cross Lager Beer in a dark green quart-sized bottle embossed with the legend "RED CROSS BREWERY—not to be resold," and fitted with a porcelain stopper. Later, merging with Doering and Marstrand at the Vancouver Brewery up at 263 East 7th Street, they continued to brew and bottle their line of beers.

While there was a slight lag in the economy on completion of the railway's massive construction, the building of the CPR's Hotel Vancouver way out in the woods (now the corner of Georgia and Granville St.), and an extension of the city's limits east of Main Street and south of False Creek into the Mount Pleasant/Fairview district, opened up a surge of home building that caused a bridge to be built across False Creek, joining Main Street up with the newly constructed Westminster Road (now Kingsway).

Realizing such plans were afoot, Charles Doering had built a small brewery (7th Ave. and Scotia St. today) upon what would become known as Brewery Creek. This was a waterwheel-powered brewery with the source of the tumbling creek's water, a large marshy lake in the Mount Pleasant area south of Twelfth Avenue and east of Main Street. There is purported another brewery built on this stream, in the area of Twelfth and Main Street, called the San Francisco Brewery, but no records were found to substantiate this.

Charles Doering hailed from Saxony, and after immigrating to the United States as a young man, arrived up in Canada in the late 1870s to work as brewer at both Victoria breweries under Louis and Emil Erb. In 1882 after visiting the City Brewery (Red Cross) in Granville, he bought the property in Mount Pleasant and began building the Vancouver Brewery. In 1892, Otto Marstrand, who had learned his brewing trade in Copenhagen, joined him.

Renamed the Doering & Marstrand Brewing Co., the brewery was rebuilt into a four-story structure housing the most modern machinery of its day, and its staff of twenty-five husky young men produced more than 1,000 barrels of Alexandra lager and English ales a month. At the turn of the century, they amalgamated with the Red Cross Brewery, after which Otto Marstrand returned to Denmark.

This business was then renamed Vancouver Brewery and bottled Red Cross and the old D&M lagers, porter and ales with John Williams and Charles Doering as partners. Ten years later, as noted previously, Henry E. Reifel took over this brewery when Chas Doering sold out his interest to the British consortium and retired.

During that quarter century, numerous small breweries had emerged to offer beer to the thirsty in this busy port. In addition to the Red Cross and D&M Breweries, there was the Cedar Cottage Brewery owned by John Benson out toward Westminster Road and Knight Street. The Royal Brewery was situated on Powell Street (near to where Fritz Sick later opened his Capilano Brewery), and the Columbia Brewing Company was down in Cedar Cove where the Princeton Hotel is now located at the north foot of Victoria Drive. Over near Chilco Street in the West End, on the shores of what is now called Lost Lagoon, was Frederick Fouhert's Stanley Park Brewery.

Several events heralded in the prosperity of these early brewers, such as the Union Steamship Line to the Antipodes, which transshipped lamb and mutton via the CPR for the eastern markets and Europe through Vancouver. The advent of the ignoble tin can provided the stim-

The Stanley Park Brewery in 1897. In the foreground is the bridge across Coal Harbour to Stanley Park. *Photo: Vancouver Archives P.115, N.41*

ulus to drive the salmon industry into a multimillion-dollar export item. And the invention of the steam logging donkey engine allowed hitherto untouched, inaccessible stands of giant timber to be dragged down to the salt chuck and towed to the city's sawmills. But no event stimulated the economy and caused such great demand on the city's services as that heralded by the arrival of the Alaskan steamer *Portland* at the Puget Sound port of Seattle in the early summer of 1897.

With the Argonauts arriving from the distant tributaries of the Yukon River, after a winter frozen in the white stillness of the far north, came stories of alluvial gold so plentiful you could scoop it up with a saucepan, and nuggets so large you could bite them with your teeth. These wild stories became gospel truth when the Seattle Times newspaper used two-inch type to bugle to the world, "Ton of gold unloaded today by first ship out of Alaska."

The Klondike gold rush was born at that moment. Within hours, hastily outfitted gold seekers were demanding transportation to Alaska. Through the winter of 1897–98, steamships of every description pushed northward against fog, snow and Willie Waws (local, sudden storms of snow and wind that exceed 100 miles per hour), to provide them service, while unscrupulously increasing the charges for doing so as desperation for transportation overcame prudence for safety. Never was the world to become so crazed for gold, as during those last two years of the nineteenth century.

For the tens of thousands who sailed to Skagway or Nome, almost an equal number clawed their way through the brush and muskeg of northern British Columbia and Alberta to reach the fabled riches of the Yukon. How many perished in the frozen wilderness will never be known, but Inspector Daniel Steele (for whom Fort Steele was named) of the Northwest (name changed a few years later to Royal Canadian) Mounted Police quickly provided patrols over the Canadian part of their journey to ensure they were properly outfitted and duly accounted for.

The courageous feats of his policemen, in traveling hundreds of miles on snowshoes or dogsled to succor the needy and quell the unlawful, has been immortalized in such adventurous stories as *King of the Royal Mounted*. Stories of the Klondike's gold and the men who sought it, are well documented in the literary works of Pierre Berton's *Klondike*, Jack London's *Call of the North* and Robert Service's *Ballads of the Sourdough*. Berton was born there, London sailed there and Service arrived there as a bank clerk when Dawson City had twelve saloons, a dozen outfitters and gold merchants, eight houses of ill repute and no church.

The gold rush brought wealth into the southern B.C. ports, encouraging brewers to build breweries here. Before this event, actually in early 1897, Doering and Marstrand had advertised their beers at $1.50 per dozen quart bottles, 75¢ per dozen pints delivered. Just over a year later beer sold in Vancouver for 15¢ a pint or two-bits a quart, and far north in the Yukon where an egg or fist-sized potato fetched a dollar, beer in pints demanded a similar price, while a lovely big quart if procurable at all, commanded two bucks on the barrel head.

Short supply created higher prices, and the upsurge in both the mercantile trade and industry provided the funds to bid it ever higher. Foreshore, where sawmills were not busily cutting up lumber for the Yukon, were pre-empted by boat builders who laid down ways upon which to build ships to carry it north. Even the foreshore around False Creek was a bustling hive of activity, and east of Westminster Road where False Creek shoaled into a slough that stretched almost to Clark Drive, several schooners and a steamer were built near the outfall of Brewery Creek.

The waterfront and the merchandising area along Hastings, Powell and Water Streets were a madhouse of gold-hungry men seeking supplies and transportation. Captain Irving's Canadian Pacific Navigation Company not only put every ship on this run, but also built several sternwheeler river steamers to go into the Yukon River trade. Their grand two-funneled passenger steamer *Islander* came to her demise in this trade, just as CP Rail was buying out the company. Southbound from Skagway on a dark night in late 1901, she struck an iceberg and sank within sixteen minutes. Although fully loaded, most got off into her boats. But her captain, Hamilton R. Foote, sixteen crewmen and twenty-six passengers did not. Supposedly carrying a large cargo of gold, the salvage of her hulk in 1934 revealed little, if any, remained.

Two years after the loss of the *Islander*, Jim Hill financed a bridge across the Fraser River and pushed his Great Northern Railroad toward Vancouver. Re-routing his rail line north from Blaine along the more placid shoreline of Georgia Straits, it passed through present-day summer retreats like White Rock and Crescent Beach, before springing over the shallows of Boundary Bay on a trestle, to skirt the western slope of Scott Hill before doubling back up the Fraser River.

The bridge over the fast-flowing Fraser River was highly welcomed by the people of New Westminster, for it carried both vehicles and pedestrians traffic across on its upper deck, providing them with a road link to the states. From New Westminster the rail line climbed up the east bank of the Brunette River before skirting the north shore of Burnaby Lake to enter a deep cut that brought it out on False Creek at Clark Drive.

Here, pilings were driven into the shallow waters of False Creek to carry a temporary spur. And as the steam shovels dug the deep cut that today passes under Commercial Drive and Broadway, the gondola cars they loaded were shunted out on this trestle and dumped, slowly filling in the upper end of False Creek. According to my father-in-law Captain Greenhalgh, sweepings from the city's streets of sawdust and horse manure were also dumped into this basin from the Main Street end, where the Ivanhoe Hotel built on pilings offered moorage to small boats.

Skirting along the south shore of False Creek, the Great Northern Railway crossed Westminster Road (Main Street) one block south of Terminal Ave. Swinging northward over trestles carried on concrete piers west of Westminster Road, they landed their passengers and freight at the south end of Columbia Street. (Even today, a sign on the

The Columbia Brewery at Cedar Cove in 1892. *Photo: Vancouver Archives P.115, N.41*

side of the old Mandarin Gardens building on Pender Street is still visible, bearing the legend "To G.N. Trains" with an arrow pointing southward along Columbia Street.)

Sir Richard McBride was undoubtedly one of British Columbia's outstanding politicians. As Minister of Mines and Railways, he encouraged both Jim Hill's Great Northern Railway and William Mackenzie and Donald Mann's westward-creeping Canadian Northern Railway to supply the province with needed rail services. Later when premier, he supported the Grand Trunk Pacific's thrust west to the newly surveyed port of Prince Rupert, and McCulloch's dream of a terrifying rail link through the Coquihalla River canyons, requiring eighteen tunnels and seventeen bridges to realize.

Before his government tumbled to defeat in 1915 he had sponsored thirteen new railways in this province, the Kettle Valley Line supplying them coal from Merritt and Coalmount areas and the Pacific Great Eastern Railway destined to connect North Vancouver with the wheat, oil and gas of the Prince George Peace River area. He had girthed the West Coast for war by mounting guns on its seaward promenades and had purchased two Seattle-built submarines for the infant Canadian Navy before stepping down.

With more than 10,000 steamships (1907 *Pilot's Guide*) on the coast and most of those using this port, Vancouver was growing into a very prosperous city that shipped out lumber, ore and canned salmon in ever-increasing amounts and imported such highly prized

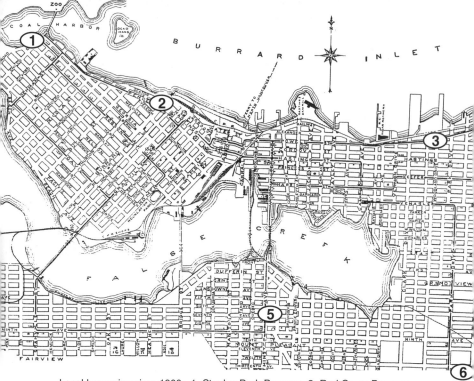

Local breweries circa 1900: 1. Stanley Park Brewery 2. Red Cross Brewery
3. Royal Brewery 4. Columbia Brewery 5. Doering & Marstrand (Vancouver)
Brewery. 6. Cedar Cottage Brewery.

commodities as spice, tea and silk from the Orient, bananas and
pineapples from Hawaii, mutton and lamb from New Zealand, and
sugar from Australia and the Fiji Islands. By this time, according to
the city directory of those years, the breweries had resolved themselves into a more compact number, even though several new companies had been formed.

John Williams, as noted earlier, closed up his brewery near the
future Marine Building to brew his Red Cross beer at the Mount
Pleasant brewery. The Royal Brewery joined forces with the Stanley
Park Brewery and moved their equipment to 725 Chilco Street, while
Mister Benson converted his other brewery at Cedar Cottage into his
residence. This left just the Columbia Brewery, where the Princeton
Hotel now stands, and a newcomer Seattle Brewing and Malting,
agents for Pacific Bottling Works at the foot of Gore, who bottled
Rainier Beer. By 1911, the Stanley Park Brewery, Columbia Brewery
and the City Brewery had all closed their doors.

CHAPTER TWO

One Great War to the Next

The closing of a number of Vancouver breweries reflected the dark economical events that were forthcoming, but nothing could have foretold the tragic events that now blazed into prominence.

The first horror story began around midnight of April 12, 1912, and could be said to signal the beginning of a great recession across Canada. It staggered those constructing the Grand Trunk Railway toward the newly built western port of Prince Rupert, and it shocked with disbelief people in every walk of life around the world. Cape Race, on the extreme southeast point of Newfoundland listened in consternation to the spark gap signal from a Marconi transmitter. The message spelt out, chilled their blood: "CQD-SOS from MGY. We have struck iceberg—sinking fast—come to our assistance. Position lat. 41°46'N, 50°14'W, MGY – TITANIC."

There were 2,206 people facing the prospect of abandoning the unsinkable four-funneled liner as it settled ever lower into the frigid dark Atlantic, about to plunge two miles to the bottom below. Some did it nobly, others at least calmly and some panicked, their minds deranged by the fear of the freezing unknown. But some, aware there was no place to go, no escape, helped the old and frail, the mothers with young children, then stepped quietly back to meet their maker with as much dignity as they could muster. Such a man was President Hays of the Grand Trunk Pacific Railway, returning successfully from England, with funds to complete his railway to Prince Rupert.

During the years immediately following this disaster, there were further reductions in brewing. By 1915 only B.C. Breweries at 12th and Yew, agents for both Vancouver Brewing and Canada Brewing and Malting, plus the Westminster Brewing Company at 214 Brunette Street in Sapperton were noted in the city directory as still active. The reason behind this consolidation was economic; from 1912 onward the country was slipping ever deeper into depression.

Overproduction, five whaling companies, one Canadian and four American, produced in excess of 150,000 tons of whale products; over speculation, a dozen railways were being built in B.C. alone; and a tighter foreign investment dollar was plunging local payrolls to desperate levels. People sold their holdings at devaluated prices to stay alive, and this sent more merchants and banks to the wall. Big investment companies such as the British Empire Trust Co. declared bankruptcy and this created untold misery for those whose retirement dollars had been lost.

Shipping lines like Union Steam cut their sailings by half; people wrapped themselves in gloom as their incomes disappeared. Then, in the summer of 1914, a shot rang out in a far away principality, and the "Guns of August" spoke with a voice heard round the world. The Great War, "the war to end all wars," had begun.

Shocked, Canada froze to a stand still. Only Richard McBride, Premier of B.C., seized the gauntlet and acted with dispatch. He ordered guns mounted and manned on the seacoast headlands, he bought and sailed two big submarines in under these same guns to protect shipping. The fear of a surprise attack by sea raiders, and the rumored report the German cruiser *Emden* was steaming for our shores, caused the Grand Trunk's two new three-funneled liners to be hastily fitted with naval guns and converted to light cruisers to patrol the West Coast.

Prime Minister Borden's slow response to the West Coast's vulnerable position as Germany's China Squadron under Admiral von Spee was reported steaming across the north Pacific, created near panic reactions from some, and noble gestures from others. Entire towns volunteered their men folk for service in the forces. Militia, reservist and retired regulars lined up for kits and arms; few had uniforms and less had orders.

When the federal government finally acted, they brought in the War Measures Act, which not only authorized troop and arms movement, but controlled and distributed all the food and material produced in Canada. Alcohol became a rationed restricted commodity, beer became its favored substitute, until the Women's Christian Temperance Union (WCTU) successfully lobbied the government to keep Canadians sober on the war production front.

The Ontario Temperance Act (OTA) became official July 1, 1916, and B.C. followed suit on August 14, 1917. Prime Minister Robert Borden, not pleased with the tardiness of other provinces to enact temperance legislation, moved an order-in-council through the house in the spring of 1918, which shut down the entire Canadian alcohol industry. Both distillery and brewing businesses plummeted to rock bottom. Some hung out for sale signs within the year; others found ways to stay alive until prohibition was repealed. By 1919 only B.C. Breweries was listed in the city directory.

The following year, on January 1, Borden's order-in-council expired, and the distilleries began to fill their vats again. Then just twenty days later on January 20, 1920, the Eighteenth Amendment was passed in the United States Congress prohibiting the manufacture and sale of alcohol in America. To put teeth into this decree, the Volstead Act made it a federal offence to import or transport alcohol in the United States, and though federal agents were empowered to police this act, few American took the Volstead Act seriously because the penalties it imposed were easily affordable.

This turn of events provided an opportunity for certain Canadians to profitably supply their southern neighbors' needs. Harry and Sam Bronfman snowballed their activity in this trade into the Seagram Empire; Harry Hatch bought out Gooderham's and later Hiram Walkers to create his empire. Thus, the era of the whiskey barons was ushered in.

From here on through the rumrunning days, the story gets more exciting, and certainly more confusing. It must also be mentioned that with the exception of the twenty-one-month closure of alcohol production (and our American friends never allowed us to get desperately thirsty) Canada's Temperance Movement only stopped the sale and public consumption of alcohol, not its manufacture. Thus both breweries and distillers could manufacture alcohol products, but only for export outside Canada.

The American's Eighteenth Amendment and the Volstead Act prohibited alcohol production, transportation and sale. Thus, whiskey smuggled into Canada across the U.S. border or trans-shipped via nontemperance Quebec connections had previous to January 20, 1920, created modest returns for modest endeavors. After the flow of alcohol across the border was reversed, many aggressive Canadians became very, very wealthy in the process.

The legality of this flow was the B-13 export license, which allowed unbroken shipments of Canadian liquor to be sent to legitimate brokerage firms in foreign countries such as Mexico, Newfoundland and Cuba. What happened to it after that was not a government concern. But, what became a great concern, and at times an embarrassment, to the officials who both administered the act and politically benefited from its revenue, were the local smugglers who surreptitiously obtained shipments of liquor through a B-13 export license, then broke this into small lots and landed this contraband on American shores. Nowhere was this more prevalent than around the Great Lakes area.

On the West Coast during those earlier years, smuggling and rumrunning were almost insignificant compared to our eastern cousin's endeavors, though the Reifels would change this status as the Roaring Twenties gave way to the desperateness of the Great Depression.

Vancouver's United Distilleries Ltd. (Whitelaw, Norgan, Kien, McLennan and Bell) out at the south foot of Shaughnessy Street supplied only a modest flow of export liquor, while Braid's Distillery in New Westminster supplying the pharmaceutical trade with uncut, pure alcohol had few, if any, such connections. Thus, when Borden's order-in-council shut them down for those twenty months, the former almost faltered, while the latter went into receivership. As liquor supplies diminished in the U.S., imported liquors arriving in bond at Vancouver were spirited via fish boat or tin lizzie into waiting hands across the border, simply by bribing those whose duty it was to keep it out.

Smuggling or rumrunning as it was to become known, while considered a profitable and slightly daring game, was not considered a criminal act. United Distilleries (UDL) quickly restarted to cash in on this unexpected bonanza, but the Braid Street distillery had to await a new owner before joining this profitable excitement.

Vancouver Breweries also rose to the occasion of offering this lucrative market their fine beers, and how they did so will soon be told. But Henry Reifel and his sons also were proficient in distilling and soon bought up the idle New Westminster distillery to become a major player with Harry Hatch and the Bronfman brothers, siphoning millions of American dollars into Canada's economy.

No one really took the risk as serious; money trading flourished,

The Reifel family: left to right, George H., George C., and Henry E. This picture was taken in 1939 at George C.'s palatial home on Southwest Marine Drive.

and American speakeasies ran night and day on Canadian suds and booze. Only when Canada tightened its export licensing and the American Coast Guard service policed contraband shipments more stringently, did Canadians begin to view it as dangerous.

Elliott Ness commissioned by the U.S. Treasury Board to stop the flow of booze dollars going out of the country, focused world attention on the criminal aspect of this lucrative trade through his raids of warehouses, transportation systems and finally speak-easy outlets. Though this caused little inconvenience to Al Capone and the officials in his pay, it did cause many Canadians to back away from any connection with this criminal element, and the twelve mile off-shore limit became the demarcation line for those who remained as suppliers. F.D.R., determined to eradicate this ulcer, inadvertently gave impetus to Canada becoming a world leader in the whiskey trade when his Twenty-Second Amendment abolished prohibition, and Americans finding their own distilleries bare, lined up to buy Canadian booze at American liquor stores.

How Henry Reifel gained control of Vancouver Breweries, parleyed Union Brewery equipment into Japan's first brewery, then used these funds to buy a distillery and become a leading player in the local rumrunning enterprise, is still much a mystery. But from George H. Reifel's account of these events, this much is known: Henry Reifel had sent his youngest son Harry down to Hentkes Brewery School in the States to train as a brew master before the Ontario Temperance Act became law. When the United States entered the war in 1917, Harry put aside his brewing books to join the American Air Force as a combat pilot.

B.C.'s enactment of a temperance law in August, 1917, effectively shut down most breweries in this province, and this must have given Henry the opportunity to buy up controlling interest in B.C. Breweries at a reduced dollar value. He then began to produce near beers (1 percent alcohol) and bottle Felix Dry Ginger Ale, thus paying the rent and possibly a bit against his indebtedness for the brewery. With this in place, he and George sailed on the Empress of Japan to Yokohama where they met with some Japanese businessmen who had expressed an interest in producing a beer for regional sales.

Due to language differences, lengthy discussion often bogged down through difficult interpretation. Henry returned home, leaving George to plow through these, and began organizing the various parts of the old Union Brewery for overseas shipment when the deal was finalized. George sealed the deal when he assured the concerned investors that the original highly costly plan to import Canadian Malt could be almost eliminated by brewing a light beer from Japanese-grown rice. It was something we at Burrard Street would experiment with forty years later to make Sick's Select Beer.

The Japanese brewery built by George C. Reifel in 1921. The whitecellar block on the left was complete in the mid-1930s.   *Photo: N. Reifel*

By the time George got the contracts signed, Henry had the parts and pieces en route, and George stayed in Japan to oversee the building of the new brewery. Over the years this highly successful brewery has grown considerably, yet even in its infancy, it was a very impressive concrete structure, at least by Japanese standards. For George's young wife, their two-year tenure living in a paper house and dining on raw fish must have been very trying, but for George the reward seemed worthy of the deed. After training the Japanese in beer making, the Reifel partnership was sold for Japanese Yen and George rushed back home where Henry had another deal cooking quietly on the back burner waiting on the funds.

Harry had returned from the States, where he had spent a couple years after the war flying surplus warplanes with the barnstormers. He had made many contacts there and knew a few of the fliers who often made early morning flights from an American farmer's field to another on the Canadian side with a cargo of booze. When prohibition reversed this trend, he pondered how the family might get involved. Henry had the idea, and on George's return from Japan the Reifel Trinity was born.

In those days near beers (under 1 percent alcohol) were created by brewing and fermenting full-strength beers, then diluting it down to acceptable levels with chilled distilled water or by distilling off much of the alcohol, bottling the low-alcohol brew as a near beer and selling the distilled alcohol to the pharmaceutical houses. Henry had a plan to take this secret inventory of white lightening and use it for start up of the Braid Street distillery closed by Robert Borden's order-in-council. Thus, as Norma Reifel informed me, it was a simple step from brewing beer to making spirits, and her father-in-law George C. Reifel and his dad were experts in both.

The Braid Distillery became the B.C. Distillery for just pennies on the dollar and was soon busy making liquor for both local and foreign markets. The government lifted the two-year aging requirement to get them started and by 1923 the distillery made its first big overseas shipment.

After installing the *Prince Rupert* and *Prince George* back in the coast service, Grand Trunk Pacific sold off their older ships. Thus, the thousand-ton steamer *Prince Albert* joined the rumrunners transporting booze to Mexico. Until then, rumrunning had been a sporadic affair, mostly with imported bonded booze spirited by very suspect methods in small parcels of contraband, which crossed the U.S. border in farm wagons, tin lizzies or improvised fish packers. When competing rumrunners began to annihilate each other with more efficiency then the federal authorities paid to carry out the same function, it was time to put this very Canadian profit-making enterprise on a more businesslike footing. The Reifels were one of those Canadian families who came forward to do so.

The Braid Distillery, built on the west side of the Brunette River and east of Westminster Brewery, had been touted back in 1912 as the most modern in Canada. The site for its construction had actually been cleared in 1903, and it had distilled its first gallon of whiskey in 1905 for the pharmaceutical trade. By the time Teddy Roosevelt was pushing the Panama Canal towards completion in 1914, this small distillery powered by a seventy-five-horsepower mill engine and two Dutch oven R. T. boilers, was fermenting 600 bushels of rye wheat a day and held in charred oak barrels more than 5,200 gallons of prime whiskey. Naturally, little of this remained by 1922.

But liquor could be shipped legally in bond using the B-13 export license to such far away places as Ensenada, Mexico, or the tax free port of Papeete in Tahiti. From there they could be reshipped offshore of the United States, where American rumrunners took all the risk of getting them to the speak-easy market. Thus, most people could honestly swear they did not know what happened to this Canadian booze. This little bit of tomfoolery blossomed into a giant wholesale business through the coming years, supplying the hundreds of rumrunners who surreptitiously crept out beyond the U.S. twelve-mile limit in high speed boats, to load their contraband cargo from mother ships, evading the U.S. Coast Guard patrol's to rendezvous with truckers on the shore.

Reifels eased into the export trade of booze cautiously, filling the holds of the *Prince Albert* and sending her south to Mexico, where they quickly realized that both the shipment of their product to the rumrunners and the relaying of money and booze orders back to Canada had to be under their control to function profitably. They created a duly registered company, Pacific Forwarding, to carry out this function with an office and warehouse, both here and in Ensenada, Mexico.

Thus, the Reifels acquired a vested interest in such ships as the *Malahat*, *Quadra* and *Vigilant*, while building up a fleet of smaller boats of their own to compliment this interest. Harry became the salesman, contacting booze distributors in the States and arranging shipments and payment through a legitimate business front in California. George was the brewer and distiller, even supervising the loading of their boats, while Henry looked after the political and Canadian organizational aspect. Their own vessel was the 500-ton former German U-boat tender *Erma David*, renamed *Principio*.

On one occasion, perhaps not the same one my father-in-law Captain Fred Greenhalgh recalled from his days on the small oil tanker *Armonco*, the *Malahat* got into difficulties and the *Principio* had to sail 2,000 miles down the coast to tow her back to Canada for repairs. This meant her cargo had to be offloaded or jettisoned before they could re-enter Canadian waters.

Vancouver Brewery, pre-WWII, shipping bottled beer in wooden barrels.

Ruth Greene in her book *Personality Ship of British Columbia* interviewed many of the former rumrunners and the people who organized and ran the trade from this port. The five-masted schooners, *Malahat* under command of Captain Vosper, and the *City of Alberni* (ex *Vigilant*, which in her WWII role as a lumber schooner had me as an able-bodied seaman for a short time), were both in this offshore trade, as was the former government steamer *Quadra*, which Captain Walbran commanded during her more legal endeavors as a patrol vessel guarding our coast from the landing of contraband.

The man credited with organizing and managing much of this lucrative trade was Captain Charles Hudson, a former highly decorated Royal Canadian Naval veteran, who had commanded several armed Q-boats during WWI. His official title was Marine Superintendent of Consolidated Exporters, whose offices and warehouse on Hamilton Street handled thousands of cases of booze a month. Capt. Hudson had started rumrunning with Archie McGillis, who had placed the *Etta Mac* and *Trucilla* (two 112-foot, ex U.S. subchasers) in this trade, and operated under the guise of the Canadian Mexican Shipping Company from a small office in Coal Harbour at Bidwell and Georgia Streets.

Both Consolidated Exporters (United Distillery) and Pacific Forwarding (Reifel's B.C. Distillery) were to successfully operate out of Tahiti for many years, before joining forces with their eastern counterparts. The lucrative shipping of booze across the Great Lakes and waterways that contained the international boundary between Canada and United States, became a war zone in the early 1930s, during which time the rumrunners were losing the battle to the much-increased militancy of both the U.S. Coast Guard and the Canadian Provincial Police. The Bronfman and Hatch organizations (Seagrams and Hiram Walker) seeking a safer route for their booze, entered into agreement with the two successful West Coast transshippers, to funnel their products through BCDL and UDL's Ensenada/Papeete connections.

Possibly the acquiring of the Pioneer Distillery at Amhurstberg, south of Windsor in Ontario by Henry, had brought the Reifel's modest western enterprise to these two big-time eastern players' attention. Renamed Franco Pacific Trading Company Ltd. (UDL in Marpole) and Societe des Entrepots Generaux du Sud (Reifel's BCDL), each put up qualifying stocks of liquor with Hatch and Bronfman to start the business and signed a promissory agreement to supply further stock as required.

Capitalized at seven and a half million French francs, it gave each partner about 30 percent of the share. It was a forty-page agreement that spelt out every detail of the business. None of these principles could claim ignorance of its intent, nor need they; it was all quite legal and very rewarding. Though they realized an annual return in excess of a million and half dollars, which could buy many an honest man, it could not last very long. By 1933, repeal of the Volstead Act was being strongly advocated.

While history may modestly claim only a few Canadian vessels and a few hundred Canadians operated in this shipping business,

Vancouver Breweries, racking 25-gallon wooden barrels. *Photo: Larry Rintoul collection*

many a local family's fortunes were created during this period. Back in 1922, while British Columbia was still dry and Alberta was offering government vended beer in quart bottles via a mail order business that caused many in B.C. to become their best customers, two new brewers registered their business in the Vancouver directory. Rainier Brewing at 718 Granville Street, (Henrich's) Canadian Rainier Brewery was located in Kamloops, west of the Overlander Bridge, and Silver Springs Brewing at 850 Hastings Street, agency only. (Their brewery built by John Tait in 1908, was out on Esquimalt Rd. in Victoria.)

In 1924, encouraged by the results of the two prairie provinces becoming their own vendor, British Columbia legislated a liquor act that required the creation of the Liquor Control Board to administer it. Beer was stocked in bottles only, but by 1928 this encouraged two more brewers to offer their trade, Empire Brewing at 509 Richards Street and Vancouver Malt and Sake Brewers (which Fritz Sick later bought), at 2235 Triumph Street.

During these same years, Henry Reifel donated the site on west Georgia Street for Vancouver's original art gallery, and George C. Reifel bought the large holding on Westham Island that today bears his name as a waterfowl sanctuary. His son George H. Reifel farmed this area during WWII, producing more than one-third of Canada's sugar beet crop.

Of those halcyon days, my father-in-law Captain Fred Greenhalgh recalled a few instances about the rumrunners that may throw light on this otherwise little known trade. While stories have since been told of some highly doubtful but adventurous tales, other stories quite factually deny it being other than a risky business (like the *Beryle G.* murders) that paid extremely well to the successful.

Seldom is it pointed out that the one criteria of successful smuggling is that few knew about it and the fewer the better. Thus, it is understandable that only recorded personal reminiscences highlight this exciting far-off moment on our coast.

Naturally, liquor cargoes that moved through regular shipping points, were disguised as legitimate freight. Those ships that loaded undisguised liquor cargoes at obscure, out-of-the way docks looked like, and acted like, regular vessel in the freight trade. The difference between them and other ships was not easily seen to the casual eye. Larger fuel tanks and more powerful engines were not obvious. Hulls stripped to bare essentials to include double floors and false holds were concealed to exclude even the most critical eye. These vessels departed or shifted to loading berths in the dead of night, or in the muffled gloom of a snowstorm or the ghostly curtain of fog. Thus, few saw them leave, fewer still knew where they were going, and damn few ever saw them arrive. Captain Greenhalgh's first story relates to that period during the Roaring Twenties when the trade seemed more adventurous and less sinister than during the Hungry Thirties.

He was mate of the small oil tanker *Armonco*, on charter to Shell Oil Company of Canada, when orders were received to fill their tanks with marine gas and load on deck 700 barrels of diesel oil. In precarious trim, with barrels stacked up as high as the wheelhouse, they carefully shifted over to their rendezvous with a dozen or so former fishing vessels. No explanation was offered; the gas was pumped into each vessel's tanks as she came alongside, the barrels of diesel oil unloaded into their small hold until the decks were almost awash.

To ensure tight stowage below decks, the tough crew manning

Vancouver Brewery, shipping quart bottles of beer in boxes and slack barrels.

Photo: Larry Rintoul collection

the boats would even lay on their backs to kick and push the 500-pound barrels up against the deck heads. While working unstinting-ly against the clock to load and clear away to sea, they appeared a jolly enough bunch, happy for the work and anticipating a fat pay check for their effort, yet none could or would divulge the reason behind their effort. And the tanker's crew knew better than to ask the more silent somber guys who oversaw the operation.

It was later that Fred found out the cause behind their midnight delivery. The schooner *Malahat*, loaded with high-priced spirits, much locally distilled and some imported from the land of the heather, was being dogged by the American Coast Guard off San Francisco. Every time she found a fog bank and slipped away with her silent sails, the cutter would relocate her when it lifted, and begin a deadly circling just a few miles off, while the huge schooner tried to hold a safe position outside their jurisdiction by burning up precious fuel to run her old Bolinder engines. Under this harassment she managed to make only a few deliveries to the high-speed rumrunners who raced out from shore each night and was in danger of running out of fuel before her liquor cargo was off loaded, thus preventing her to enter port and fill them.

Those small old fish packers Fred lowered barrels of oil into were gasoline engine powered and no longer insurable for the fishing trade. Canadian Fishing Company had offered them to Archie McGillis at a price worthy only of a one-way voyage. Thus, they were to be sunk after their ocean voyage to the *Malahat*, their crews taking up duty on the 240-foot, 1,500-ton sailing ship, which allowed those so relieved on the mother ship to return to Tahiti for a well-earned rest in the sun, or ship back to the coast to visit their families.

Another instance of Fred's recall had more sinister overtones and happened when the mafia's gangland slayings became more commonplace. Crossing the Straits of Georgia with a long tow of logs for Fraser Mills, the fogbound *Gleeful* was hauling down against a strong flood tide. Feeling her way in toward the North Arm Jetty, they heard the sound of powerful motors and the cascading of a large bow wave coming toward them from within the dark gray fogbank ahead. Turning on their bright carbon arc searchlight to illuminate themselves and the angle their long tow had taken across the shoal channel astern of them, they flashed it onto the onrushing boat to alert them of this danger.

Into view came a small speedboat almost hidden behind its huge bow wave. As it approached, her size grew swiftly, until the crew on the *Gleeful* realized it was longer and larger then their own eighty-foot tug; yet not one indication was given she intended to slow down. Her engines roared ever louder and her bow wave threatened to swamp the tug as she closed to within a few feet and swept by. What Fred Greenhalgh recalled most vividly was the people who silently populated her decks.

"A half dozen or more guys lined her rail, all staring silently across at us. God, they were the toughest, meanest looking fellows I'd ever seen," he grunted, reliving that long ago moment. "Probably shoot you, if you said a word. They all wore heavy dark long over-coats and black bowler hats, and each had a hand under his coat as though holding a rifle or machine gun. The boat was so loaded her stern was nearly under water. They disappeared into the fog, but we could hear the roar of their engines as they hauled around the end of our tow, heading south to the border till their sound muted away and all was silent again."

While the brewers themselves are reported to have resorted to some shady practices to ship beer beyond the border, such as stowing it in either ends of a box car and plugging the whole center section where the doors slid open with hundreds of bundles of cedar shingles that would discourage other than the most dedicated border guard to check beyond. Many more stories have been told about the ingenuity of the smugglers to disguise American-bound contraband, such as the tow of logs booms, which actually concealed a large shipment of bottled booze.

In this case, they slung sacks of bottles from thin ropes below the booms of logs. In those days many booms of Canadian logs were towed down to Bellingham, Everett and Tacoma, so they were seldom given a second glance. If they arrived undetected at the backwater log storage yard, the sacks could be easily retrieved. If this was considered hazardous, the smugglers could arrange to drop the sacks off when crossing a convenient shoal area, with a buoy line suitably weighted with rock salt that would melt away in a few hours, and allow the buoy to float to the surface for retrieval.

Back in 1928, things had never looked better for this province. This was the year of B.C.'s golden jubilee of confederation, and Premier John Oliver declared his government would end it with a modest surplus. Four million dollars was allocated to upgrading the roads (some of this was budgeted for the new Burrard Street Bridge crossing False Creek). He put through legislation (first in Canada) to provide longtime B.C. residents of over sixty-five years of age with a monthly old age pension check. Not much, but it was a beginning.

Vancouver city, a world leader in vehicular fire protection, belatedly recognized its marine obligation and launched the fireboat *J. H. Carlisle*, and work was commenced on what was touted to be the tallest building in Vancouver. The rock that had housed the Red Cross Brewery's cellars was blasted away to place the deep foundations for the Marine Building at Burrard and Hastings Streets. Then in the first months of 1929, confident the upsurge in the economy would continue, the city absorbed the municipalities of Point Grey and South Vancouver into its metropolis.

With more than 200,000 citizens now stoking the furnaces of

Vancouver Breweries' last team of Clydesdales "on parade."

Photo: Larry Rintoul collection

industry and home alike with sawmill waste or Nanaimo coal, a continuous pall of grubby smoke lay over the harbor and buildings of Vancouver. It turned white washing on the clothesline gray, stained windows and buildings black, but people reveling in the prosperity such industry brought, ignored the inconvenience.

In October, 1929, the prosperity bubble burst. The 210 million board feet of lumber cut for export rotted on the docks or in the sawmill's yards or out in the woods where it had been felled, no one needed it. Canned salmon plugged the warehouses and cannery's closed their doors. About 17 million bushels of grain froze in elevators and boxcars, while city people starved in the bread lines that began to form outside the welfare offices.

Instead of one-quarter million taxpayers funding the city's coffers, the jobless ranks jumped to over a hundred thousand, and many had to let their homes go for delinquent taxes. The city tottered on the edge of bankruptcy. Civil riots and protest parades were commonplace, so was the militant means of the police in subduing them.

While hard times may cause a man to slate his thirst with beer instead of whiskey, few in those terrible times found even that possible. The breweries finding their LCB sales falling so drastically, had to curtail or suspend production, and this drove some almost into receivership. The Reifels, buoyed up by their sale of spirits, charitably offered these breweries a conditional loan to safeguard their investment, but exacted an agreement not to market beer within Vancouver Brewery's established area, in return.

Thus, by the time Fritz Sick arrived out on the coast in 1933, and with repeal of America's prohibition appearing imminent, the principles of Vancouver Malting and Sake Company were quite happy to sell their investment and recover twenty-five cents on the dollar. Twenty-five cents would buy five loafs of bread or quarts of milk, two and half pounds of hamburger or three schooners of beer at the recently opened hotel beer parlors. In purchasing power at least, these shareholders were much better off than when they entered the brewery business.

While it was the Reifels who contested Fritz's legal right to brew and sell beer in B.C. (addressed in the following chapter), it was the astute businessman Bob Fiddes who suggested they should challenge Sick's exclusive domains on the prairies and build a brewery there. After Fritz Sick had won his right to brew and sell beer in B.C., it was this same Robert Fiddes, head of Coast Breweries Limited who invited Fritz to join their association, and moved that he be offered a generous 21 percent portion of the Vancouver beer sales.

Up to then Vancouver Breweries had enjoyed a whopping 48 percent of all B.C. sales, with Victoria-Phoenix realizing 16 percent, Silver Springs and Rainier 12.5 percent each and Westminster a modest 11 percent. Each agreed to assist only hotel's that handled their beers on tap, thus reduce any embarrassing public notice of patronage. During the austerities of WWII, they even created the Pacific Brewers Delivery system, which shared the cost of truck operation by pooling their allotment of fuel and tires, earning public applause for their war effort.

In September of 1945, Henry E. Reifel, age seventy-five, died of pneumonia in Vancouver, and with his passing away his son

George C. Reifel also decided to retire. The end of an era had passed into history. After selling their large inventory of spirits to the Bronfmans, Seagrams took over their distillery on Braid Street, while the newly incorporated Western Canada Breweries funded by Rothmans of Pall Mall, took over their 12th Street Brewery and under took a $2.5 million reconstruction program.

George's son, George Henry Reifel, who actually enjoyed being a farmer (wartime sugar beet fame) more than the brewing executive he'd been trained for, moved to Calgary in 1946 to build and operate the Alberta Distillers. His father had been approached by Frank MacMahon to undertake this project, but declined due to health and suggested his son should go in his stead. Frank MacMahon was the well-known Vancouver businessman who created the Trans Mountain Pipeline Company to bring Alberta natural gas out to the coast, through an overland pipeline whose difficult construction costs had deterred many less courageous investors.

Vancouver up to this time had a very limited gas system in place, and this was supplied from a coal-gas distillation plant at the foot of Union Street. Coke created as a byproduct of this process had a ready market as fuel for the blacksmiths and foundries, as well as for heating homes fitted out with proper furnaces to burn it. Alberta's oil fields, which prewar had produced a modest portion of Canada's petroleum need, was accelerated in the postwar era by a more aggressive drilling program that would prove up many more oil fields.

Over the years, the natural gas given off by these wells became almost an unwanted commodity, until Frank MacMahon proposed piping it out to the Pacific Coast where it quickly replaced the more noxious wood and coal fuels, thus gifting us a cleaner atmosphere to breath and a safer place in which to live. Albertans showed their appreciation to Frank MacMahon's enterprise, by offering him an exclusive distilling license, which George H. Reifel turned into the profitable Alberta Distillery.

The success of Alberta Distillery was a feather in George's hat, but his young wife Norma also was due some accolades, for she gave him two sons before they returned to the coast in 1953. George in 1950 and Randy in 1952. After settling into their home on Marguerite Street in southwest Vancouver, they had two more children, Barney in 1956 and Tracy in 1960. But George Henry felt more at ease on a tractor plowing the land, than sitting behind a desk as the executive of

Alberta Distillers in a Vancouver skyscraper, so in 1962 they sold their home in town and moved their family onto Westham Island.

In the late 1970s, George Henry Reifel gifted to the people of Canada all of this property placing it under the Canadian Wildlife Services, and they designated the foreshore as the George C. Reifel Migratory Bird Sanctuary. Five years before his death, George and Norma moved into their retirement home on Point Roberts, and here a few of the Reifel's memorabilia are treasured by this lovely prairie girl who is the family matriarch of this now almost-forgotten brewing dynasty.

CHAPTER THREE

Sick's Capilano Brewery

The brewery at 1550 Burrard Street nestled serenely behind the majestic rising sweep of the Burrard Street Bridge's southern approaches, its tall grains handling tower was capped by a multicolored neon sign that encoded the latest weather forecast. A large, revolving neon number 6, the official logo of Sick's Breweries Ltd., topped it and was highly visible throughout the Vancouver area surrounding False Creek.

Neat lawns of green grass bordered by beds of colorful flowers were tucked around the western and southern boundaries of the massive cellar blocks and the one-story administrative office building, as well as around a smaller employee's building, that sat in an island of green at the rear of the large complex. These lawns, flowers and the clumps of slender white birch that dotted much of these areas were curbed by white cement and the remaining expanse of yard was black topped for service trucks and parking.

A low, cement-railed fence separated the western lawns from the sidewalk along Burrard Street. A high wire fence topped with barbwire enclosed the other three boundaries of the brewery site, and a manned gatehouse guarded the main entrance driveway leading off First Avenue east of the Seaforth Armouries parade ground.

From the B.C. Electric's rail line coming off the Kitsilano trestle, a spur line entered the brewery property behind the gatehouse to run west along the north side of the boiler and engine room to terminate under a train shed at the base of the grains handling tower. In this covered area the malt, adjuncts, hops and other supplies were unloaded. Except for a small, black-topped area north of the spur line and east of the bottle shop's shipping bays, the remaining brewery property was graveled providing convenient storage for items salvaged from the Powell Street brewery, such as the old eighty-barrel copper kettle, the vertical round pasteurizer and the antique bottle washer.

During those long ago, more leisurely brewing days, the cooker and kettle vents pulsated out copious clouds of steamy vapors, heavy with the smell of hot grains or the sharp pungent odor of hops. At certain times, the smell of yeasty beer mixed with carbon dioxide gas might waft by from a cellar vent, and at other times the rather fragrant smell of fresh beer might also be carried out into the yard from the bottle shop. The noises that bespoke all this activity were the hum of fans and pumps, punctuated by the metallic clank of metal kegs being washed and readied for filling, and the steady muted chorus like clinking of bottles passing through the fillers, labelers and drop packers on the bottling line.

It purred with a gentle life, one that probably never will be enjoyed again, and housed mysterious processes officiated over by white-gowned seniors whose meticulous attention to detail ensured perfection in every drop. It offered a good living to those who were chosen to work there, and a modest pension to those beginning to come of age to select retirement.

This was the brewery that Emil Sick envisioned as the epitome of modern brewing, and he commissioned well-known American brewery engineer Don McRoberts to build it for him. It became a show place for both visitors and local citizen, and a source of pride to all who worked for Emil Sick. Polished and sparkling clean at all times, most visitors marveling at its grandeur likened it to the standards only expected to be found in sterile hospitals, posh fancy hotels or regal government offices. Yet within just a few years, though the brewery would grow ever larger, few people would recall anything about the man who created it, and many more would not even know his name. Our story will try to bridge the gap created by time.

Emil Sick was the eldest son of the master brewer Fritz Sick, the founder of the House of Lethbridge. Fritz's is a story stuffed with the ingredients of legends—the fervent dream of most immigrants who landed on these shores and strove to establish for themselves and their families a better and more meaningful way of life. Born near Freiburg in Germany during 1859, the son of a brewer, Fritz apprenticed to the trade of making wooden kegs and barrels. At age twenty-four he sailed to America seeking employment and opportunity.

Landing in New York in 1883 he bought passage on the train to Cincinnati, Ohio. His worldly wealth at this moment comprised a few special tools of his trade and a suitcase of modest belongings, plus a five-dollar bill in his pocket. From these meager beginnings he amassed a family fortune in the brewing industry, which became the corner post to build the huge international brewing empire realized by his son Emil.

Most accounts of those early days as Fritz Sick migrated westward, say he worked in various breweries, even learning to make lager beer at Boco, California, before arriving five years later at Tacoma, Washington. This was the period of the great industrial revolution that sprang up after the terrible civil war had taxed the resources of the country to the limit. Andrew Carnegie was creating a fortune in the new steel trade; his giant Bessemer furnaces were spewing out steel for plowshares and locomotives, and John D. Rockefeller was corralling the oil refining business upon which his huge Standard Oil Company would rise.

In the process, Colt's pioneer methods of assembly line production of his famous "peace maker" six-shooters had been copied by industrial manufacturers of everything from clothing to machine tools. All demanded huge supplies of coal and iron, cotton, oil, minerals and timber. A great spate of ship and railway building was undertaken to carry the raw materials to the central states, where many of these industries were located, and to transport their finished products to eastern and western markets.

All this activity created a ready market for a thirst-quenching beer, and many enterprising brewers quickly built small local breweries near these industries to satisfy this need. A competent barrel maker who was also knowledgeable of the brewing craft would have found ready employment anywhere west or north of the Ohio River.

Tacoma, a pioneer lumber port on lower Puget Sound, grew up near the site of Fort Nisqually, the Hudson's Bay Company's trading center on the West Coast. It had become the terminus of the Northern Pacific Railway when Fritz Sick arrived there. In fact, fifty years before Fritz arrived there, the HBC had supplemented their fur shipments back to England with huge deals of hand-hewed prime timber felled by their woodsmen on the site where Tacoma grew. In the same year Fritz arrived at Tacoma, Olympia became the capital of this new state of the Union, and Northern Pacific Railroad initiated a steamer service from the port of Tacoma to the Orient, with the scheduled sailing of the *Phra Nang*.

The brash young timber port of Seattle founded around Yesler's

Fritz Sick, master brewer, in 1928.   *Photo: City of Lethbridge Archives P19901005161*

steam-powered sawmill on Elliot Bay in 1853 strove to become the most important seaport on Puget Sound, but had to await Jim Hill's Great Northern Railway and the Klondike gold rush, still a few years ahead, to earn the title of Gateway to Alaska and the Orient.

Fritz Sick took employment with Huths Brewery as a brewer in 1889, and within a year he married his childhood sweetheart Louise Frank. They were blessed with five children over the next ten years, Louise, Emil, Fred, Helene, and Leo the baby, who arrived in 1900 as the family finally arrived at Lethbridge. Emil George Sick, whose story we will follow later, was born in 1894 at Tacoma, a year before the family began its migration eastward.

Fritz, then in his thirty-sixth year and with little prospects for advancement at the Pacific Coast Brewing Company (Huths) as the lumber industry began to wan under the influence of a worldwide recession, had little to show for his investment in a small local vinegar factory and felt it was time to strike out on his own as a brewer. He moved his tiny family inland to Spokane, where the arrival of the Great Northern Railway was changing this wilderness farm community into a bustling hub of commerce, which bespoke a possible market for a good quality beer.

It was here, before he could establish himself as an independent brewer, that Robert Smith, creating a brewery in the mining town of Trail just north of the International Boundary on the Columbia River in central British Columbia, offered him a brewer's position. With a large force of thirsty miners busy digging out coal, gold and other minerals and several small smelters in the planning stage, Smith claimed it a likely place to seek their fortune. When coupled with the fact that the area between Trail and Spokane abounded in rich fertile farm areas capable of growing the hops and barley vital to a brewery's needs, Fritz's quickly agreed to join him.

But probably the main reason for their northern adventure into the wilderness, were the plans announced by the two major railroads that served the West Coast. The Great Northern Railway, which ran west from Chicago to arrive at Everett via Steven's Pass, and the CPR running northerly out of Calgary through Kicking Horse and Rogers Pass to arrive at Vancouver via the Fraser Canyon both promised to run branch lines into this prime fertile area, hither-to ignored in their race for the quickest and most affordable route to secure the Orient trade.

Without going into all the events that created such a fierce competition between these two giant railroads, it is sufficient to note that the wiry, fierce, one-eyed promoter Jim Hill had guided the engineer William Van Horne into the Canadian railway business to ensure his own American rail link east would carry the Canadian Pacific's traffic around the Great Lakes. Van Horne was wooed by Donald Smith and George Stevens, and beguiled by John A. Macdonald, to forge the costly link through the Cambrian Shield and realize an all-Canadian route, sea to sea. Ironically, the Canadian-born American

The brewery in Fort Steele. *Photo: British Columbia Archives C-52082*

railway magnate James Jerome Hill never forgave the American-born Canadian master railroad builder William Cornelius Van Horne. Their railway wars became classic Canadian history.

Though Hill, Smith and Stevens had been the powerful three-some that John A. Macdonald had entrusted to build his Canadian Pacific Railway, Hill had venomously denounced them and William Van Horne after his own plan was discarded. Hill then commenced building his Great Northern railway westward from Chicago, poking up branch lines into Canada at every opportunity to siphon away dollars from the CPR, while he raced Van Horne for the Pacific coast and the great Orient trade he hoped to capture. Ignored by Van Horne's more northerly route into British Columbia, the mining interests in that great rich underbelly of British Columbia known as the Boundary Country approached Jim Hill for a rail link north from Spokane to carry their products to market.

Swiftly sending out surveyors and grading crews north of the border to comply, the move belatedly alerted William Van Horne of his oversight of this potential business, and he quickly offered branch lines south from Golden and Revelstoke. Thus, six years after spanning the continent, and almost twenty years after being promised a railroad into British Columbia's original gold rush area, the Boundary Country was about to realize not one, but two, first-class rail links to the outside world. Undoubtedly, Smith felt this information would assure him sufficient investment funds to complete his brewery, and he sent Fritz Sick north with all the equipment to set it up.

The small brewery they created at Trail was short lived. The mining boom fizzled and Jim Hill rerouted his northern extension westward of the rugged Cascades to Grand Forks where their smelter had become operational. Van Horne, with an eye to the silver mines in the Selkirks, drove his Revelstoke line to Galena and down the Arrow lakes, thus delaying arrival at Trail for several years to come. The Golden extension bogged down in the Rocky Mountain Trench, but was expected to pass through Fort Steele on its way to the mining areas around Yak, before heading west along the border. Unfortunately, Smith ran out of funds to sustain the brewing business until these prospects were realized, and he declared bankruptcy.

Fritz Sick accepted the brewery's equipment as payment for lost salary and investment; joining forces with Fred Kaiser a former saloonkeeper in Trail, he made plans to relocate the tiny brewery. In 1897 Louise and Fritz packed up their possessions and moving eastward through British Columbia and arrived on the outskirts of Fort Steele where they leased a brewery type building erected by Albert Mutz. Here Fritz brewed his Black Ace lager beer and sold it in barrels, kegs and bottles. Advertising this fact in the local newspaper *The Prospector* in June of 1898, they listed their telephone number as #1, and the capacity of the two and half storied brewery as forty to seventy barrels per day with six men on the payroll.

Fred Kaiser decided to open a saloon nearby and a Chas Williams joined Fritz in 1899, but the railway's decision to bypass Fort Steele and run into the huge new lead mine at Kimberly caused Williams to look there for his Eldorado. Thus, Albert Mutz was forced to join Fritz Sick as operator of this brewery just to help pay the rent, so to speak. They invited Albert's brother-in-law to join them and with his funds built a proper bottling works and began manufacturing soft drinks and ginger beer.

It proved an unhappy relationship for Fritz, as Albert Mutz and

The first brew by Fritz Sick at Lethbridge.

Photo: City of Lethbridge Archives #P19901005054

his brother-in-law often out voted him on principles he felt strongly about. Their rather high-handed offer to buy him out for $10,000 if he didn't like the way the brewery was run, came just when he had arrived at the decision he had made a mistake coming to British Columbia. Clutching their money before they could reconsider, and loading his family and their possessions into a wagon, he turned the mule team's head east and crossed the great divide into Alberta, not

Fritz Sick and family on the front porch of their new home, 1905. Emil is standing by his father's right shoulder. *Photo: City of Lethbridge Archives #P19760224046*

stopping for more than a rest until they reached the small prairie town of Lethbridge.

Here he found all the things he required to create a great beer, barley, water and coal. Lethbridge was just coming of age when Fritz arrived there; the prairies abounded in crops of lush grains and reasonable roads to interconnect the farms to the shipping elevators. A first-class railway linked the town with Calgary or south with Montana, and an open-pit coalmine operated by the railway gave the town a valuable payroll. The farmers and miners were thirsting for a good cool beer and had money to afford it. The railway had even sunk a deep well to provide irrigation water to the area, and this was pure and clean—ideal for beer making.

This was the strangeness of Fritz Sick's story. How did he know that just within the year a well of pure water had been drilled, where several other earlier breweries had failed because of tainted surface water supplies? How did he know that a large open-pit coalmine and a rail link with Calgary had just been realized? But, he must have known. Just as he must have known that some of the best brewing grains were being harvested from the rolling prairies south and east of Lethbridge, which recently had mushroomed up into a town of

The Lethbridge Brewing and Malting Co.

Photo: City of Lethbridge Archives #P1990010005038.GP

more than 2,000 people, comprised of coal miners, railway employees, retail and wholesale staff, as well as the original farmers.

Interestingly enough, there were already people in the area with the name of Sick who had come from the area around Duluth, Minnesota. However, there is no record of Fritz's family and the local Sicks being related. In fact there are people who have stated for a certainty that they were not related at all. But is it possible that the Sicks who had migrated there from Duluth were responsible for Fritz's knowledge of the area?

Leasing water rights on the Alberta Railway and Irrigation Company's Artesian well in 1901 and purchasing a parcel of land on the west side of town adjacent to the rail way, Fritz began building his own brewery. The plan was his own; he'd spent years acquiring his skills and knew just what he needed. He hired a carpenter versed in building heavily timbered sheds that would house his cooking vessels, vats and cellar tanks. The entire operation was confined in the one wooden building, with a stable for the mules at the rear. He even erected a lean-to cooperage off this building, where he fashioned all

The bottle shop at the Lethbridge Brewing and Malting Co.

Photo: City of Lethbridge Archives #P19901005052.GP

The slack barrel shop at Lethbridge Brewery, 1912. The bottled beer was shipped in the barrels.

Photo: City of Lethbridge Archives #P19901005051-GP

his wooden kegs and tanks using the very same tools he had brought with him from Germany. There was nothing grand about this small beginning, except the tremendous effort Fritz put into realizing it. Never had Louise seen him work so hard and long, and knew instinctively that this time he would succeed.

He stated to his wife and family as they watched the rough pioneer structure take shape, that here it would be "quality first," and he never deviated from this standard. He called his small business Sick's Alberta Brewery and his first brew was Alberta Pride. It proved so acceptable to the European miners, settlers and farmers in the area, that he sold more than 3,000 barrels in his first year of operation. At forty-two years of age, Fritz Sick was in his prime, and brewing at Lethbridge demanded all the talent and energy those years had amassed.

Speaking later of those same years, Fritz observed, "I had one helper in the brewery and another who worked outside driving the mule team and delivering beer to my customers. I was my own brewer, my own maltster, my own salesman and my own office force, even my own cooper."

Once the brewery building was realized, and while the first brew was aging, work was begun on a house for the Sick family. Located across from the brewery, on Second Avenue south, its shingle cottage roof covered a three-bedroom, clapboard-sided dwelling with a large front porch. It was the first real home Louise had enjoyed since coming to America.

During the summer of 1903 a brick malting building was erected. And in 1904 at the Lethbridge Springtime Fair, the brewery's mule team pulled a wild hop garland wagon laden with barrels of Alberta Pride to the fairgrounds. Leading this gift of bubbling spirits was ten-year-old Emil on his new pony Frank. The year 1905 saw the creation of a new brick brew house beside the cellar block, and the brewery incorporated as the Lethbridge Brewing and Malting Company.

These were the years when Canada was enticing immigrants to till the fertile soils of the prairies, and the Irish potato famine and a depression in Europe gave them added incentive to take up the offer of a section of land (640 acres) for little more than their signature. The CPR, anxious to create more profitable freight and passenger business for their rail line that spanned hundreds of miles of uninhabited land, put on settler trains of second-class coaches and cars at special reduced fares for homesteaders who took up the government's offer. Hundreds of new people flooded out onto the prairies, and most appreciated a refreshing beer after a hard job of work. With beer offered at only a nickel a schooner, many found a coin or two to enjoy Fritz's brew.

By 1913 with production reaching more than 20,000 barrels a year and supply still falling behind demand, Fritz initiated a major expansion of the brewery that brought production up to 40,000 barrels a year, allowing him to ship beer out to nearby towns. The new three-storied cellar block boasted a refrigeration system capable of turning the hot prairie summers into winter within its insulated walls.

By this time Fritz had build a number of company homes beside the brewery for his employees. Deciding his own family needed more area to grow up in, he bought a small farm on the outskirts of Lethbridge.

Fritz Sick insisted his sons should all know the family's business. His three-part philosophy was that: "one should always know one's job; one must always be a worker; and, finally, a lazy boy will never be heard from—he's beaten from the start." Thus, Emil Sick spent much of his time, when not at school, working at the brewery. From his father he learned the brewery skills, when not carrying out the more mundane chores usually allocated to those of youthful age or simple talent.

At age nineteen, having completed his formal schooling at Lethbridge, Emil elected to study law and get a legal degree. His father sent him to Tacoma, the city of his birth, to study at Stanton University. While he was away, Canada went to war, and then eighteen months later, on July 1, 1916, Alberta and Lethbridge went "dry."

Unwilling to allow his large new brewery to fallow in idleness while his fellow Canadians suffered the temperance pangs of prohibition, Fritz and Louise weathered out the war years and the beer drought by renting out the cold storage buildings to the wholesale green grocery trade, bottling soft drinks for the temperance crowd, and brewing an acceptable near beer for those who longed for a tangy hop-flavored refreshment.

The wartime production of goods increased the prosperity in almost every area of Canada, and the scarcity of men to take care of this, enticed many women to enter the world of commerce, manufacturing and agriculture. The absence of alcohol in the worker's tummy kept most on the straight and narrow, and the rationing and restrictions in the market place, caused bank savings and bond purchasing to increase accordingly.

When the veterans returned home, they found a country burgeoned with a surplus of almost everything and little likelihood of employment until the surplus had been sold. They also found that many of those who had stepped in so patriotically to carry on their work while they went overseas to fight in the terrible trenches of Europe were not of a mind to give up those jobs to a returning vet. Then a terrible flu epidemic swept the land, killing those with fatted wallet as surely as those who were blamed for bringing it home from the war.

In the United States, the Eighteenth Amendment and the Volstead Act of 1920 closed down the breweries, wineries and distilleries, throwing thousands more out of work. Civil revolt became commonplace in Canada when government repatriation was not forth coming to the destitute soldier sons of this great nation.

Emil Sick, marrying Kathleen MacPhee in 1919, had become a father of a baby daughter before the flu sweeping through Lethbridge killed the husband of his sister, Helen Ferguson. Emil consoled and looked after his frail sister and her infant son. Later, when she too passed away, he adopted her son as one of his own.

Specializing in corporate law, he associated himself with J. Cyril Malone, K. C., of Regina who had established ties with law firms both in the east and those closer to local governments in Edmonton and Calgary. By 1922 the scars of the great war were beginning to heal, rebuilding in Europe was revising export trade and in both the United States and overseas, investment dollars were itching to grow. The era of the Roaring Twenties was about to unfold.

Aware of this upward trend and versed in the American philosophy of marginal buying, and the pyramid building of paper assets, Emil discussed with his father the opportunities that could exist if Canada moderated its position on alcohol consumption. Fritz Sick, a staid master brewer with more than a quarter of a century's success at going it alone, and a conservative man who firmly believed in cash on the barrelhead investments was not always in accord with his son's more speculative thoughts. Most fathers are not—but many will eventually accede to a strong offspring's urging, if not wholeheartedly, at least sufficiently to prove the offspring right or wrong.

International brewer Emil George Sick, Fritz's son.

Photo: City of Lethbridge Archives #P19901008029

But after years of prohibition's lean income, the Sick coffers were basically without any investment dollars to take advantage of any opportunity, so Fritz appointed Emil general manager of the brewery, while he carried out a watchful role as president of the family business. The United State's more stringent restrictions decreed by the Volstead Act, forbade both the manufacture and sale of alcohol, while in Canada the Temperance Act only forbade the sale of spirits. This would work to certain Canadian's advantage during the years ahead, as breweries and distilleries fell into ruin in the United States.

With Lethbridge Brewery operating as already noted, Emil's argument was that they should capitalize on this fact by being prepared to buy up those breweries around Lethbridge who had not been able to diversify into different brewing activities. His knowledge of corporate building and acquisition was premised on another philosophy—buy into a depressed market, invest only sufficient to gain control and then utilize the expertise of the principals to bring the business back to a viable position.

With his father's cautious consent, Emil approached the pioneer investment firm of Hanson Bros. in Montreal to arrange forms of financing for possible takeover of other breweries. Lt. Col. E. G. Hanson's services in putting together the various companies required to realize this investment plan over the next six years, proved invaluable to the Sicks. Emil firmly believed, and the fact was proven out with a swiftness that caught everyone off guard, that few brewery stockholders watching their investment dollars slowly become worthless over the eight years of nonproductivity would refuse an offer that could assure their investment dollars would again become valuable. In fact, Emil and Fritz Sick were to be lauded as saviors, not opportunist, when Canada rescinded the temperance act in 1924 and Emil's plan was put to the test.

Alberta and then Saskatchewan were first in western Canada to allow beer to be sold for public consumption. But the provinces stipulated it had to be sold in quart bottles, and they created government liquor stores to dispense it. Lethbridge Brewery was the first to brew beer and fill the government shelves, and thus established a large share of this new beer market. This also put them in a position to expand sales of their production into other areas, where former breweries were not as ready to seize the opportunity.

By March of 1924, and undoubtedly with great trepidation in Fritz's heart, they acquired the Prince Albert Brewery and got it into production bottling Bohemian Lager beer, while carrying out an ongoing rebuilding that would realize a valuable sister brewery to Lethbridge. R. J. Chiswick moved up from the Lethbridge brewery to manage this first Sicks' brewery in Saskatchewan.

This successful maneuver accomplished, and before Fritz could even sigh with relief, Emil brought to the boardroom table at Lethbridge a plan to acquire the old Regina Brewery in southern Saskatchewan. This capital city brewery was located in the great Canadian wheat belt, and though originally built in 1907, it had been closed for many years. Hard water had always proven a problem in this area, so Emil proposed they install a water softener and filtration plant and a new bottling line.

In June of 1924, Sick's name went up over this old faded brick brewery, and they began brewing and bottling a beer which was to become synonymous with the Sicks. Old Style pilsner beer was born here, as was its famous label commemorating the House of Lethbridge, with its Canadian scene of Indians, tepees, crows, farm road and steaming locomotive. Sent up from Lethbridge to manage this new business was Bill Hutton.

Two years later, in December of 1926, the House of Lethbridge completed its grasp on the prairie beer market by acquiring the Edmonton Brewery. Built in 1903 by W. H. Sheppard and controlled for many of those years by the Ker family of Victoria, B.C., Emil Sick enticed Robbie Ker to become a director in their enterprise and William Sheppard to remain as manager of the brewery.

Edmonton Export and Rex Pilsner became two of the successful beers produced in this capital brewery, and for less than a year after this coup Fritz's son appeared satisfied with the reach of his claw marks on the business tree of Canada. But, Emil sensed he was racing the clock in a world seemingly gone mad in a gorging frenzy of speculative promotions, and was quietly putting together a plan to combine the Sick empire under one holding company suitably financed to weather almost any storm.

In 1927 Emil moved to Calgary, and left the Lethbridge brewery in the capable hands of J. A. Blair, husband of his sister Louise, while he created the new company to control all four breweries. Under the guidance of Col. Hanson, Emil incorporated a $5-million holding company called Associated Breweries of Canada, with headquarters in Calgary. In appreciation for Col. Hanson's continued guidance, the Sicks offered him a directorship on the newly formed board and appointed him their eastern representative.

Fritz gratefully took over as chairman, and Emil sat on his right as secretary of the board. It was now Emil's turn to sigh with relief as he had parleyed his father's lifetime worth into a multimillion-dollar company controlling four large, modern breweries supplying most of the beer within two prairie provinces. He could afford to smile with satisfaction at the solid slate of table officers who represented the hundreds of small shareholders who had shown confidence in his plan. Their company was solvent, no debt had been left unpaid, and he could foresee a handsome dividend payment being offered.

How fortunate his timing had been was realized less than a year later during the fall of 1929 when the speculative investment bubble burst. Often referred to as Black Friday, it was followed by a failing economy in Europe that saw the German currency become almost useless, and frenzied stock and bond selling in America caused all stock values to plunge and companies to fail. The consequences were far reaching; many speculative ventures crashed pulling down with them the fortunes of men in all walks of life. This in turn, caused many to sell stock in other more stable businesses, just to shore up their family's holdings. This was certainly true of many families holding stock in idle American breweries.

With much of Canada's grain harvest of 1928 still sitting in elevators unsold when the stock market crash echoed across our thinly populated lands, the 1929 crop was left to rot in the farmer's silos or unharvested on his fields. Lumber, paper, pulp, minerals and canned salmon also lay unsold in huge stockpiles. Erecting high tariff fences to protect its own failing economy, the United States effectively negated any opportunity for sales of these Canadian products south of the border. To make matters even worse, extreme weather conditions began to erode the soils, turning farms into dust bowls. Construction and manufacturing ground to a halt, and a nation of unemployed began to migrate back and forth across the land seeking solace and a square meal.

While all this must have been viewed by the Sicks and their investors with great trepidation as their $5-million company shrunk to less than half its value, it still proved one of the good investments during that difficult time. The breweries continued to produce a certain amount of beer, and this allowed them to employ most of their people on a reduced scale of pay by sharing out the hours of work. This, while thousands of others went without.

The reason behind this was two fold, first lower wages and lower supply costs allowed the brewery to offer it beer at lower prices. While capital value of its holdings had devalued and the earnings of both its shareholders and labor force had been reduced in dollars, their purchasing power really had not changed substantially. A postage stamp cost only 3 cents (1 cent for a postcard), a loaf of bread 4 or 5 cents; milk was three quarts for a quarter and top grade beef for under a dime per pound. Twenty-five cents an hour for even just a thirty-two-hour work week could feed and house a family of four in marginal comfort; for fifty cents an hour or $4 a day, a man and his family could live like princes.

The second condition that continued to keep the brewery viable was that even though dividends shrunk and work hours and work rates were reduced, a thirsty man often could find a nickel for a beer. A man usually equates his tastes to suit his means—when income exceeds the bare essentials, his taste can be influenced by his ability to afford. Imported Scotch and foreign wines are often signs of a man's affordability, not his needs. All of us, when we have such an opportunity, must make our own judgment call as to what we wish to afford. But whenever a thirsty man's income allows him to buy just one drink, he'll usually buy a beer and reverently claim it the "nectar of the Gods."

Fritz Sick had crossed over the threshold of his seventieth birthday as these events unfolded. He had spent most of those years working long hard hours to husband his earnings so that he could buy another board, a nail or a piece of equipment with cash on the barrel head. He had built a successful brewery through this philosophy. Under Emil's prompting and persuasive arguments, he had spent the past ten years acquiring three more breweries and finally creating a $5-million holding company to manage them by using other people's credit. They had squeaked through this adventure just ahead of the crash. And though he, like all those around him, was appalled at their devaluated assets, he could sigh with relief that at least they were still solvent and in business.

In 1932, when Emil returned from a visit to his old *alma mater* in Tacoma and began discussing the possibilities that might exist to enter the American brewing market as talk of rescinding the Volstead Act became more widespread, Fritz Sick pondered the wisdom of gambling on such a chancy possibility during a worldwide depressed economy. Emil's argument that a depressed market offered a golden opportunity to invest at pennies on the dollar provoked interest in many of the major shareholders. After a great deal of discussion, the directors voted to carry out an experimental thrust that would test out brewing opportunities in the U.S.

While Emil quickly took the train down to Montana to check out two idle breweries, his mother and father took the train to Vancouver for an extended vacation. Fritz Sick was beginning to feel his years weighing upon him and thought the milder climate on the coast would be beneficial to his health. With Emil down in Great Falls and Missoula, Fritz and Louise stayed out on the coast and enjoyed one of Vancouver's best summers on record. The sun-sparkled waters of English Bay, the warm, scented beauty of lush gardens and shaded streets and path were like a balm to their weary souls. Certain this was the place to spend their retirement, they found real estate agents only too happy to show them many of the posh homes in the Shaughnessy area that were begging for a cash sale. Mister Sick, the wealthy beer baron from the prairies, did not go wanting for a choice. Fritz and Louise finally selected a lovely big home out on Marguerite Street, south of 49th Avenue, whose large gardens and shaded oaks seemed to invited retirement. Returning to their Lethbridge farm to pack up their belongings, they moved out to Canada's West Coast Riviera.

Meanwhile, satisfied with his first American investments, Emil Sick entered the Seattle brewing scene in late 1933, by acquiring the Bayview Brewing Company at 3100 Airport Way, and moved his family down from Calgary to live in Seattle. When the Volstead Act was rescinded this plant began to brew and market Rheinlander Beer. And in early 1934, Emil joined forces with his longtime friend Harry Goetz and bought out the small Martin Brewery in Spokane. Renaming it Goetz Breweries, its successful acceptance soon created the need to increase their capacity and caused them to buy up the older and larger Spokane Brewing and Malting Company.

This brewery had been incorporated long before WWI from the merging of Galland-Burke, New York and the Henco Breweries, with each brewery making its own brew. During prohibition, the Burke-Galland Brewery kept the plant running, producing a near beer, much as Fritz Sick had done at Lethbridge before Canada rescinded its temperance act. Thus, little was required to brew beer after repeal was enacted, but Emil Sick decided on an ongoing modernization program that would place it in the forefront of most western breweries.

All of this was undertaken during the most difficult years of the Great Depression. Five years of hard times had depleted most people's savings, and most government bodies were running deficit budgets trying to assist the needy. Franklin Delano Roosevelt had entered the White House with his New Deal, lending low-interest money to encourage businesses to restart production and providing make-work programs for the unemployed. The repeal of prohibition got the country buying legal booze again, and many breweries and distilleries quickly struggled to supply it. Emil Sick, hoping to beat out most of the possible competition in the northwest, cast around for more breweries to buy out.

Meanwhile, Fritz and Louise Sick, settling in at their new home in Vancouver, were learning to lead the life of the retired gentry. Two of their new acquaintances, living a few blocks away on Southwest Marine Drive, were the sons of Henry Reifel, acknowledged Czar of booze in British Columbia. Collectively, the Reifels owned Vancouver Breweries at 12th and Vine, B.C. Distilleries out on Braid Street in New Westminster and Pioneer Distilleries in Ontario. While Henry Reifel enjoyed a patriarchal role similar to that now enjoyed by Fritz Sick, his sons George, the brewer, and Harry, the salesman, were at their pinnacle of business success. As noted in the previous chapter, their financial fingers reached far out in the community, commanding respect from all who wished to profit with them.

While other brewers had not fared well in Vancouver during the temperance years of enforced idleness, the industrious Reifels had parleyed their interest from the old Union Brewery of Nanaimo into controlling interest in both the 12th Street Brewery and the Braid Street Distillery. Then entering the export booze business through offshore distributors, they acquired the Ontario distillery and joined forces with the Bronfman family (Seagrams) and Harry Hatch (Hiram Walker), in a cartel that controlled the flow of alcohol from Canada to our thirsty cousins in the U.S.A.

Within a year of arriving on the coast, Fritz Sick became restless with his idle retirement role and yearned for the happy times of his youth when he ran a small, simple brewery where leisurely brewing fostered quality and personal satisfaction. Such a place would be ideal for him to pass on his talents and skills to new hands wanting to learn and would offer employment to those needing a pay check during these trying times. Possibly he discussed this with George or Harry Reifel, for by some rare chance he learned of just such a place.

There was a boarded-up small brewery in east Vancouver that hadn't turned a wheel in years, yet it had held onto its brewing license and maintained its corporate identity. The Vancouver Malt and Sake Brewing Company was located at 2235 Triumph Street, not far from Pandora Park. The area had grown heavily residential during the intervening years with lovely large homes and shaded streets.

Fritz did not think the old buildings worthy of repair or brewing suitable to the area. His inquiries uncovered another defunct business up for sale that had the stoutly timbered construction a brewery required, which was located in an industrial area.

This was a former vinegar plant at 1400 Powell Street near Woodland Drive. Impulsively he bought both in 1932 and made plans to shift the brewing equipment down to Powell Street and then sell the property on Triumph Street. Elated with his plans, he went back to Lethbridge and enticed some of his former lead hands to join him in creating a brewery on the West Coast. His nephew, Karl Mueller was one of these, and here again we have a intriguing coincidence—Karl's aunt, Emma Mueller, niece of Fred B. Hose, owner of the Stanley Park Brewery, had been herself brew master of the Royal Brewing Company, which absorbed the tiny Stanley Park Brewery on the south shore of Lost Lagoon.

Fritz soon realized a problem that had not been hinted at by the vendors of the Vancouver Malt and Sake Brewing Company nor by his new friends, the Reifels, who were quite knowledgeable of its possible constraints to brew and market beer; for it was they who had made it a condition of earlier funding to VMSB Co. Beer sales in B.C. had become keenly controlled after the Pacific Brewers Association created each brewery's quota of distribution, and the Pacific Brewers Association had been the brainchild of a very astute businessman named Robert Fiddes.

The Henrick brewing family of California, wanting to keep their Rainier Beer label active through prohibition in the states, decided to brew beer with it in Canada. Building the Rainier Brewery in Kamloops at the south end of the Overlander Bridge, they managed to secure a modest toehold in that local market. As hope of repeal faded in the states, the Henricks lost interest in this marginal endeavor and were quite eager to rid themselves of it when a group of local investors, headed by Bob Fiddes, made them a reasonable offer.

Realizing the potential for Rainier sales in the lower mainland area, Robert Fiddes approached New Westminster Brewery to brew and bottle his beer. This proved so popular with this area's large population that he was able to convince his group to close the Kamloops brewery and buy up Nels Nelson's brewery to brew both labels of beer. After lengthy discussions with the two Victoria breweries, which were also feeling the threat of Henry Reifel's powerful organization, they agreed to merge themselves into an equally commanding identity. In 1928, with Robert Fiddes elected chairman, they registered themselves as Coast Breweries Ltd.

Black Friday and the depression years that followed convinced both companies it was better to parcel out the reduced beer dollars peacefully than waste them fighting for a market that shrank daily. Forming the Pacific Brewing Association to administer and voice their desires, Henry Reifel and his sons accepted 48 percent of the market. The remaining 52 percent was divided between Westminster/Rainier and Victoria-Silver Springs breweries. A gentle, concerned businessman, Bob guided this organization into greatness that supplied all involved with handsome fortunes, his own share being valued just over a million and half dollars.

Though Bob Fiddes strongly supported Henry Reifel's fight to keep Fritz Sick out of local brewing, even suggesting they should invade Sick's private domains and brew beer on the Prairies, he was the first to invite Fritz to join the Pacific Brewers organization, and thereby enjoy a generous portion of their market shares, after he won his right in 1934 to brew and market beer in B.C. To appreciate the arena in which Fritz's fought his battle, we should consider the legal sword that had just then become available for him to do so.

In 1931, on the bequest of Canada, the British Parliament passed an act called the Statute of Westminster, which provided that only the British Parliament could amend the British North American Act. (The BNA Act gave Canada's parliament authority to legislate for the whole of Canada and each province legislative power to govern within the boundaries of the province.) As law is territorial, this meant that any province of Canada could decide the legality of any private agreement, assumed or otherwise, within that province.

Private law is divided between the law of property and the law of obligation. The latter is the law that defines the ways in which one person may be bound to another person, either by agreement or operation of law, to do or forbear from doing something, as related to a contract or bill of sale. Private law, and certainly the law of obligation, originates from the ancient trading laws known as the Byzantine Laws, which were practiced by both the Isle of Rhodes and the Isle of Ole'ron in their mercantile trade, and thus predate all laws created in the last one to two thousand years.

This interpretation is quite liberal, but the consequences in Fritz

Sick's Capilano Brewing Company in 1945.

Photo: W. Weisner Collection

Sick's case were quite far reaching. It would appear that Vancouver Malt and Sake brewing company had solicited funds from the Vancouver Brewing Company back when the brewery was forming in 1928 with the intent to supply the rumrunning trade. To secure these funds, the principals of Vancouver Malt and Sake signed an agreement that they would not sell their brew of beer within the area supplied by Vancouver Brewing Company—quite a normal precaution where goodwill constitutes a marketable commodity. This was not the first time Fritz had heard of such a restraint; indeed, it was commonly used within business transactions. What caused him to bristle up with indignation was that neither his search of liens and encumbrances nor his bill of sale gave any indication such a restraint was implied. Second, he felt he had been beguiled into this trap by the Reifels, who were the principles of Vancouver Breweries holding power over this agreement. This turn of events got even more outrageous when he approached his neighbors with an offer to buy out their agreement at a generous return on their investment.

George H. Reifel, son of George C. and grandson of Henry E. Reifel, chuckled when he related to me the gist of his father's reply to Fritz Sick's offer. "We owned most of the brewing action around here, if old Sick wanted a piece of it, Dad felt he should offer us a piece of his prairie brewing action in turn. Fair is fair, you know!"

Fritz Sick stomped away from that meeting, angry at being put

The Capilano Brewery on Powell Street.   *Photo: Vancouver Public Library VPL#15734*

into a compromised position by the Reifels. His pride and his faith had been greatly shocked; stubbornly he refused to consider such a proposition, threatening to fight such a dastardly thing through the courts of the land until he won. While this standoff was very noble, few believed he could win an annulment of the long-standing agreement, certainly not Reifel's lawyers when advised of Fritz Sick's intentions.

Emil Sick was busy down in the States putting together the brewing empire he would soon realize there, and Fritz was determined to overcome his problem by himself. He hired a law firm in Vancouver to take the matter into the local courts, confident the reasonableness of the law would not obligate him to the limiting conditions agreed to by the former principals of Vancouver Malting and Sake Company. So sure of this was he that he had his nephew Karl Mueller hire help to install the equipment at Powell Street and begin brewing sake until he got his beer license.

When the local court handed down a decision that supported the Reifels, Fritz Sick had the matter placed on the provincial court's calendar and put his crew to work bottling the Japanese rice wine. When the provincial court rendered a decision in favor of the Reifels, Fritz Sick ordered his lawyers to take it to the Supreme Court of Canada. A surprised visit by Emil to see his mother and father provided an opportunity for Fritz to seek his son's consul. Emil's law training came to the fore and, unsure of what might happen through the Supreme Court, he began to prepare a plea to the High Court of England, which makes the final decisions on any intent of the Canadian Charter.

Emil was busy at this time securing the holdings of the old Seattle Brewing and Malting Company, which would involve a $2-million merger with the old Georgetown Brewery and the rights to the historic trade name Rainier throughout Washington, Idaho and Alaska. Promising to advise his father more fully on his high court application should the Supreme Court findings go against him, Emil traveled back to Lethbridge to report to the directors, before returning to Seattle.

Rainier beer dates back to 1878 when the Henrich family of San Francisco built the Bayview Brewery on the site now occupied by Rainier Brewery. In 1893 they built the Georgetown Brewery, then the sixth largest brewery in the world and the largest industrial complex in the State of Washington. Prohibition closed it down and it did not brew again till Emil Sick bought it in 1935. The following year Emil built a huge new bottling plant there before going on to other acquisitions, but back to the Sicks legal battle in Vancouver.

After losing his case in the Supreme Court of Canada, Emil's plan to take his father's plea to England bore more satisfying results. The High Court agreed with Fritz Sick, he was not bound to honor any contract or promise made or implied by the former owners of the small brewery he had bought, because he had neither agreed to it nor had his bill of sale made it a condition of the contract.

In early spring of 1934, he had Capilano Brewing Co. Ltd. printed on the glass of the front door of the office on Powell Street, and began to brew Ace Lager beer, the same old Black Ace lager he had so successfully brewed and marketed at Fort Steele when he first arrived in British Columbia before the turn of the century. Next he brewed an ale beer, calling it V.C. Ale (for Vancouver Capilano). Finally, in 1938 he produced his famous Old Style pilsner beer with the House of Lethbridge label, and he placed a huge sign on the roof of the brewery facing Powell Street proclaiming this fact.

Walter Weisner was one of those hired by Karl Mueller to get the Capilano Brewery ready to run. He helped the carpenters put in the large wooden fermenters, the brew kettle and the cooking vessels. When that was done, Mueller put him to work wrapping insulation on the refrigeration piping and other jobs until they began to brew. Walter Weisner was a well-built, obliging young twenty-four-year-old unemployed and was happy for the work; jobs were extremely scarce to come by back in 1934.

Sicks, always noted for paying top wages offered Walter fifty cents an hour at a time when four dollars a day was considered top tradesman's pay for machinists, fitters and engineers. By 1935, Local 300 of the Brewery Workers Union had negotiated a contract for them that assured a base rate of $28.50 for a forty-eight-hour work week. Walter had never had it so good, and he proved that by staying with the brewery for over forty years.

"I think over the years I've had almost every job in the brewery—brewing, bottling, racking, even driving truck for awhile," Walter noted modestly, looking back over his eighty plus years to

Outside the Capilano Brewing Company in 1938. Walter Weisner is on the far left.
Photo: W. Weisner Collection

those of his youth. "We began brewing April one, 1934, and had beer ready for market by June 30. But a problem with Reifels delayed shipping any of it till July first. Forty years later in 1974, after ten years as foreman, I retired."

Walter held up a picture of Fritz Sick from the Lethbridge days. "He looked older than this when I first met him. You know he fired me," Walter chuckled, "Not once, but twice in the same day. And for doing the same thing!

"Mister Mueller had me separate the different colored bottles before putting them through the bottle washer. He wanted the cases filled with either all green, white or brown bottles. Mister Sick came through the brewery one day and spotted me lifting all the green and white bottles off the line and putting them in boxes on the floor. He told me to dump them all on the conveyor regardless of color. Not realizing who he was, I just kept working and suggested he should see Mister Mueller who had given me my orders.

"He fired me right on the spot, said I was wasting time, and he couldn't afford time wasters. Mister Mueller came by shortly after that, and I told him about the old guy who had just fired me. He told me not to worry, that I had just met Fritz Sick who owned the brewery and to go back to work separating bottles, while he went and had a word with his uncle.

"I guess he didn't get a chance to talk with Mister Sick, and the old man doubled back on his trail before going home just to check if I was still there, because only brown bottles were coming out the other end and being filled." Walter chortled, as he concluded his tale. "Fritz Sick stormed up to me and roared, 'I fired you once for doing that, now I'm going to fire you again. Get out of my bottle shop!' I went to see Mister Mueller and he just shook his head ruefully, then led me over to the beer filter room where he put me to work making up the pulp filter pad. I never had a run in with the old man again, and I don't think he recognized me whenever he visited the brewery after that.

"To my knowledge we never did run mixed colors, but the separating was done less obviously. We ran both quarts and pints and had to hand label the quart bottles. We put out around 2,500 dozen bottles a day, yet I don't believe there were more than two dozen employees all told." Walter continued, "Ferguson was manager, I believe he was related to the Sicks. We had some difficulties while he was in charge, 'Pushing beer out too close to the kettle.'"

Questioned, Walter explained. "Too fast on fermenting, too short in ruhing (aging), what used to be called 'green beer.' Made a few people sick. Fritz Sick put Robert Blair in charge and everything improved.

"You know, we use to hand paddle the old fifty-barrel brew kettle. It was a long-handled Sitka spruce paddle. And because I was tough and strong, I often got the job. Before we closed down Powell Street we were brewing 66,000 barrels a year. I understand Burrard Street brewery was built with the profit earned at Powell Street. Emil Sick didn't have to borrow a penny so I'm told, and I believe Burrard Street brewery cost over $3 million—pretty good for a small brewery we built out of an old vinegar works, eh?"

During the period Walter recalled, and while Fritz Sick was establishing himself as a master brewer in Vancouver, his son Emil, after consolidating his brewing holdings in the States, was endearing himself to Seattle sports people by bringing them into prominence as a baseball capital. It was to prove a very rewarding experience, not only to Emil who added to this first effort with many more contributions into other community projects, but for the Sick's brewing industry, which quickly acquired many staunch supporters of its products.

This adoration stemmed from the many philanthropic gestures made by Emil on behalf of his brewery.

In 1937 he took over a rundown baseball club, built it a lovely new stadium, and brought the pennant home to Seattle four years in a row. Sick's Seattle Stadium was officially opened June 15, 1938, and his Seattle Rainiers baseball team enjoyed record attendance at all their games.

In that same year, Emil Sick purchased the Apex Brewing Company on Airport Way and enlarged its storage and cellaring capacity. In 1939, he bought out the Horluck Brewing Company on Westlake Avenue and renamed it Century Brewing—the home of Brew 66. Seattle's leading newspaper, *The Times*, devoted a front-page editorial written by the publisher C. B. Blethen to Emil Sick, in which he lauded the philanthropic contributions of this rising giant in the U.S. brewing industry. Since then many other publications, including *Look* and *Time* magazines did feature articles on Emil Sick's public service.

Emil Sick convinced his father that public sports promotion and support were good business investments and that sports people staunchly and faithfully reflected their approval of this support with their purchasing dollar. Together they sponsored Vancouver's entry into the Western International Baseball League, by creating the Vancouver Capilano Baseball Club under the management of R. P. (Bob) Brown. Capilano Brewery then built a large baseball stadium to the east of the south end of Granville Bridge, about the area of 6th Ave. and Helmlock, and this became Capilano Stadium, the club's home field. With this accomplished, Louise and Fritz sold their Vancouver home and moved back to Tacoma, where their married life had begun, and Fritz restricted his activities to those of President of the Board.

In the spring of 1939 the King and Queen of England thrilled Vancouverites with a royal visit, and on September 1st, Hitler ordered his German forces into Poland and we went to war to preserve freedom. In a swift nightmare of aggressive invasions, the Nazi forces swept over much of Europe and into North Africa.

Many of the strong young men who worked at Capilano Brewery during the time it had grown into local prominence, appalled at the terrible scourge sweeping over Europe, quickly traded their work clothes for Army khaki, Navy black or Air Force blue. They rushed to England to defend her shores. The Brewery donated a field ambulance to the Red Cross, while the Vancouver Capilano and the Seattle Rainier baseball clubs raised money to help care for the thousands of bombed-out British children who had been evacuated out of harms way.

In 1941 Hitler marched into Russia, creating a blood bath that had no equal in history and this encouraged Japan to sign a tri-pact agreement with the Nazis and Fascist to compliment her own plan of attack on the rich oil reserves of Indo-China and the Philippines. Sending a huge amphibious attack force southwest into the South China Seas to carry this out, she spirited her large aircraft carriers eastward with orders to blowup the American's Pacific Fleet at Pearl Harbor, thus negating the U.S.A. from retaliating until much of the Near East was safely under the flag of the Rising Sun.

On Sunday, December 7, 1941, before a bungled diplomatic communiqué could be presented to the American State Department, and in what was nothing less than a Sabbath morning sneak attack, the Japanese bombed the American naval base in Pearl Harbor. The terrible carnage in American lives and the destruction of much of

Sick's Capilano Brewery baseball team, 1938.   *Photo: W. Weisner Collection*

their capital warships roused the indignant fury of this formerly neutral but mighty nation into a giant fighting Argonaut, who vowed nothing less than unconditional surrender would ever be accepted.

Becoming president of the Seattle Chamber of Commerce during that first year of the war and heading up many fundraising efforts to ensure "Victory on our Terms," Emil Sick carried out a massive sale of War Bonds within his many breweries and even managed to acquire another brewery in the process.

Salem Brewery in Oregon was built in 1866 by Samuel Adolph; Emil rebuilt it to produce Brew 66, and this Sick brewery was the first to incorporate the number 6 in its logo. That same year another first was reached, Sicks Brewery Enterprises, Inc. invested $5 million to create a hop farm in the Yakima Valley, in the state of Washington. This 200-acre operation was such a success it was considered a model of its kind in North America, and averaged a dozen bales per acre (200 lbs/bale).

In 1944 Fritz Sick, feeling the weight of his eighty-five years, decided to retire from the brewing scene. Accepting a position of honorary chairman in the great company he had given birth to, he

Brewery site looking north across the bridge approach. Bottle shop basement forms are in place, June, 1951. *Photo: Sicks/Molsons*

was content to rest on those laurels while Emil Sick, succeeding him as Chairman of the Board of Sick Breweries Ltd., managed both the Canadian and the American enterprises of the Sick's empire. In 1945 as the war came to an end, so did the long fruitful life of Fritz Sick conclude. His children and grandchildren gathered around their mother and grandmother to see him put to rest, then assisted during the trying moments of putting this pioneer brewer's affairs in order, before returning to their various functions within the huge family business.

Capilano Brewery had functioned well through the trying years of wartime shortages, rationing of beer and spirits by government liquor stores, and the restrictive hours of beer parlors (opening at 11 a.m. until 5 p.m., and again from 7 to 10 p.m.) had allowed the brewery to maintain its stock of supply and share it out equally. With the lifting of rationing after the war, the beer business took an upward swing, which though leveling off once in a while, has continued more or less up to this present moment.

This increased demand, began to tax the Powell Street brewery shortly after the slump in wartime construction had been replaced by postwar construction to house the returning veterans. Many of these returning veterans found valued work at the brewery, as scheduling of brewing and packaging became a round-the-clock operation.

With civil engineer M. E. Bell supervising the planning and construction of a $2-million expansion at Rainier Brewery (located next to the present day Interstate 5 Highway and overlooking Boeing's Field), Emil Sick appointed Lt. Col. N. C. K. Wills (related to the Reifel family by his marriage to Henry's daughter Florence Ann and a veteran of both world wars with twenty years of brewing experience behind him) to manage the bustling, straining little brewery on Powell Street.

After Rainier's expansion was completed in 1950, it became obvious to all that Capilano Brewery could not fulfill its full potential from the site it was on. Don McRoberts was appointed engineer to locate a new site and design a new brewery that could fulfill these expectation for the next twenty years.

The Seaforth Armouries at 1st Avenue and Burrard Street had acquired a large piece of property during the war to house and train

Burrard Street brewery in October, 1951. Cellar block A in foreground and bottle shop roofing is being laid. *Photo: Sicks/Molsons*

Installing the 12,000-gallon beer tanks in cellar block A, April, 1952.

Photo: Sicks/Molsons

their hundreds of new "hostility only" soldiers. After the war, as their command shrunk back to peacetime proportions, this property became redundant to their needs and was offered for sale through the War Assets Corporation.

Though more than a dozen sawmills still actively cut lumber in False Creek and much light industry surrounded the foreshore of this waterway east of Granville Island, many heavy industries had already begun to move to the outskirts of the Greater Vancouver area, away from the crowded downtown core. Few appeared interested in this large piece of choice land stretching west and south of the B.C. Electric car barns to excite the bidding.

Sick Brewery's bid bought the whole thing, even though their proposed brewery with capabilities of production four fold that of Powell Street, required only the large area north of the Sea Forth Armoury. In a move that surprised many, Emil Sick approved the selling of the portion of this property east of the main entrance driveway in from 1st Avenue. Years later when the brewery decided to buy it back again, it cost many times over what Emil realized from it. It was probably one of the few real mistakes Emil Sick ever made.

The brewery was a masterpiece of design, few who came either to work or to see it could fault it, many admired it and all who were

The brewery in October, 1952. The employees' building is in foreground and the boiler room, grain towers and train shed are west of it. Note the old paint shack in right foreground. *Photo: Sicks/Molsons*

fortunate to work there were inordinately proud of it. I count myself in with the latter. During the three years it took to build, the small Capilano Brewery on Powell Street strived by stint and might to maintain production while increasing its market share to justify the dollars it was providing to build the new and larger brewery on Burrard Street. Surprisingly, it generated almost all the capital required to build its replacement facility. Not one penny was borrowed to meet the $3 million-plus cost of the project.

Don McRoberts was a Seattle-based engineer and consultant with several other large engineering works in progress below the border, thus Sick Breweries Ltd. felt it prudent to ensure their best interests by having some of their own people on the project. They appointed T. H. (Tom) English, who had served as accountant, controller and executive secretary of the Powell Street brewery through the years, as manager of this new brewery. They hired A. G. (Art) Pugh as chief engineer of services to assist Don McRoberts as project engineer, and appointed Grant Waddell who had served at both the Regina and the Powell Street breweries as its brew master.

These three highly skilled and knowing men ensured the new Sicks' (6) Capilano Brewery was a success in all ways. Not an easily reached accomplishment, but one that is a credit to their diligence, tenacity and unstinting energies.

CHAPTER FOUR

Making a Brew

During those more placid first few years at the new Capilano Brewery, three brews a day, two or three days a week were all the marketplace required. Everyone, with the exception of the shift engineer and the plant watchman, would enjoy themselves at home from Friday evening until Monday morning. Seldom, if ever, did even a brewery truck turn its wheels. A quiet reverence seem to cloak the brewery buildings during those hours, with just the watchman clocking his rounds through its mysterious gloom, and the duty engineer stoking his boilers and oiling his engines in the brightly lit steam plant.

While improvements in both procedures and processes have changed greatly through the years, the basic process still remains much the same. Naturally brewed is still the hallmark of Molson's beers, as it was back in those days of the Sicks. Wholesome natural materials such as malted barley, adjuncts of corn or rice, hops for flavoring and brewer's yeast for fermenting are all that are necessary to make a good brew—aging makes it a great beer.

Before following through a typical day of brewing at this establishment, one should be acquainted with the various areas of the brewery as they were almost fifty years ago. The brew house, containing the large 200-barrel copper kettle on the ground floor and a lautre tun to drain off the wort from the malt, plus the mash and cereal cookers tiered above it on the open mezzanine level, occupied most of the area in this imposing building. Only the brewing offices and quality control lab shared part of its top floor. Large front windows faced the setting sun as it dipped daily into the vast expanse of the Strait of Georgia, beyond the merging traffic of Cornwall Street. To the north (right of the brew house), where the combined traffic ascended the approach to the Burrard Street Bridge, was the packaging center comprising a bottle shop, and a shipping and receiving department. To the south (left of

The Sick's new Capilano Brewery, 1953.

Photo: A. G. Pugh collection

the brew house) were three massive concrete stories of refrigerated beer storage—fermenting, aging and finishing.

To the east (directly behind the brew house) was the grains handling tower, comprising five tall cement silos, with grain handling conveyors below and milling and distribution equipment located above them. On the roof of this prominent structure was the steel logo tower with its neon-lit, coded weather sign, above which rotated the large illuminated number 6, the trademark of the Sick brewing empire. An adjoining single-storied building, spread out behind the cellar block and grains handling tower, housed the keg handling department, beer filter room and the power plant. The single-storied administrating office building sat southward of the former, while an equally low building housing employees facilities plus a 12,000-volt transformer vault sat eastward of the latter, across a driveway built over a 20,000-gallon fuel oil tank.

The brewing week actually commenced late Sunday evening/ early Monday morning, when the engineer cracked steam into the brew house and bottle shop pipes and began to heat the brewing tanks, pasteurizer and bottle washer. Gerhard Schulz, a stocky, con-

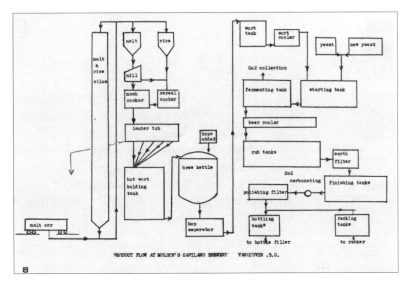

The product flow at the Capilano Brewery in the 1960s.   *Photo: Fred Kirby*

genial middle-aged man, arrived between 1:30 and 2:00 a.m. to begin the brewing. Dropping off the last interurban train in from Steveston, he had arrived in the brew house to start 200 barrels of Old Style lager along its carefully orchestrated forty-eight-day trip to the keg room and bottle shop. His arrival at the brewery was normally announced by the clatter and banging of lids as he began transferring the previously milled and weighed malt into the cookers.

Within the hour he had cranked open the large floor-mounted brass valves and steam was flowing into the cooker jackets. There were two steam-jacketed stainless steel cookers, both fitted with revolving paddles to keep the thin slurry from settling on the steam-heated plates. The smaller one was called a cereal cooker; into this the flour (about the fineness of cream of wheat cereal) from the milled barley was simmered, while in the larger cooker (referred to by the brewers as a mash tun) the cracked malted barley husks (shell) and the hard ends from the milling process were precooked.

Ideally, the milling process would crush just the shell of the kernel of barley, and the powdery contents of the kernel would be shaken out and put to simmer in the cereal cooker. The purpose of malting is to condition a kernel's husk so it could be cracked or crushed to allow the powdery pulp to fall out without itself falling apart. Thus, it

The mill room in the tower. The malt elevator is to the right of the Buhler mill and the weight hopper is overhead, 1954. *Photo: Sicks/Molsons*

could perform two important jobs—supply the necessary starch for conversion to sugar from the pulp, and then provide a suitable filter bed on the floor of the lautre tun (holding tub) through which to leech off this sugar water (referred to by the brewers as wort).

In days of yore, malting barley was just another of the many processes undertaken by a good brewer to supply a renowned, or at least a distinctive, local tankard of good cheer. Today, large breweries, as well as hobby brewers, rely on commercial malsters to create this important ingredient in either small batches of thick rich syrup or in large rail car lots of bulk graded kernels of barley. As brewmaster Tom Buckley deals with both malted barley and hops further along, it will only be noted here that when a grain of barley has been encouraged to the peak of its germination cycle in a warm moist environment, it is roasted thereby slightly caramelizing the kernel's husk to increase its friability (easily crumbled or pulverized).

The malt (brewery term for barley) mill's rollers were set to just crack the husk of the average-sized kernel of malted barley passing through them. This might range from a tight 1/32-inch to 1/8-inch gap between the rolls. There were at least two, though usually three, sets of rollers; between each set of rollers are fine screens to allow any powder or flour to sift out of the malt and be gathered in hoppers for weighing, as the barley comes in various sizes. Small grains might be only lightly crushed if at all, large grains grossly over crushed, and only the average size properly crunched if the rolls were not gapped to prevent this. With three sets of rolls, the first set squeezes the large kernels, reduced in size by much loss of their starch body, they pass through the second set where most grains of malt are crushed, thus reduced even more they pass through the third set of rolls which are set to squeeze the smallest grains of barley.

The hard ends of the malted husks, the over-crushed barley shells and the smaller kernels hardly crushed at all that are retained by the separator screens were dumped into the mash tun (German equivalent of tub, i.e., large cooking vessel). Their cooking and agitation was a bit more boisterous than the more sedate simmering of the starchy creamy cereal cooker. When ready for conversion, the cereal cooker is pumped over into the mash tun and allowed to simmer. A color titration test using a drop of weak alkaline solution in a small sample of wort, results in stronger and stronger hues of blue as the simmering progresses until the brewer is satisfied most of the starch had been converted into sweet wort.

While the mash and cereal cookers were coming up to conversion temperature, which took about eighty minutes more or less, Gerhard found time to hoist and mill malt ready for his second brew. Once the wort tests proved acceptable, this steaming thick soup was pumped into the large, flat-bottomed lautre tun. The overly sweet liquid quickly filters through the various sections of the lautre tun's perforated bottom, and flowing through a dozen or so pipes and valves, entered the long testing grant to run down into the brew kettle below.

Hot treated water, known as sparging liquor, is sprayed from a revolving pipe above a driven, heavy rotating arm employing adjustable bronze blades that sweep through the thickening mash bed of husks within the lautre tun, allowing the sparging liquor to flush out every last morsel of sugar and carry it down to the grant. Monitoring each steaming tap of the grant, Gerhard quickly shut off any that indicated excess of sparging liquor to wort. The sweeping blades quickly thicken up any thin areas with more malt husks, and when tests indicate the filter bed is performing properly, the test drip is opened to a full drain-off.

When the lower steam coil of the kettle was covered, steam was admitted to begin the boiling process, which caused a hot misty vapor to rise from the kettle stack on the roof. This is called lautering and it took up to an hour. While it was in progress, Gerhard found time to rinse out the cookers and charge them with brewing water and malt for the next brew.

The crackle and banging of condensate in the steam coils was replaced by a quieter pulsating throb of energy as the steam trans-

The mezzanine level with lautre tun in the foreground and the cereal and mash cookers in the background, 1954. *Photo: Sicks/Molsons*

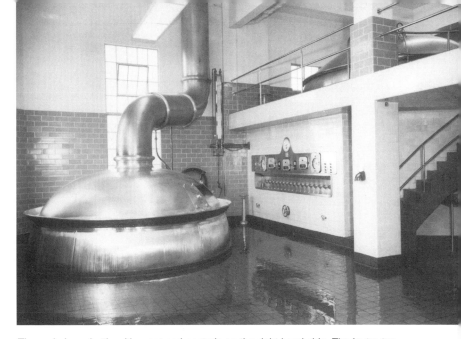

The main brew kettle with grant and controls on the right-hand side. The lautre tun, visible in the upper right, is on the mezzanine level, 1954. *Photo: Sicks/Molsons*

ferred its latent heat to the quietly rolling wort. During this rather sedate moment in the 200-barrel kettle operation, Gerhard began heating the mash and cereal cookers for the second brew. Between 5:00 and 5:30 a.m., while the kettle was at a modest boil, the hops were added, then steam was turned onto the boil rings and a central ebullition of a much more violent type took place, and this was maintained until the specific gravity of the wort reached 11.5 or higher.

This period was the most dramatic in the brewing process and was signaled to all who viewed the brewery from afar by the huge plumes of sweet-smelling steamy vapors that discharged from the kettles' tall vent into the morning air. It was also the most dangerous of the whole process. Like a pot of boiling rice or candy, excellence of cooking requires a heavy rolling boil, and this requires diligent attention to keep it within the cooking vessel. The engineer did not venture far from his roaring boilers during this time. And Gerhard, on the kettle floor where any error in the process could cause a boil over of frightening proportions, hovered near his throbbing charge and its vital control valve.

The grand finale was complete when a dipperful of this hot wort floated the hydrometer at the proper specific gravity reading, and a

The control panel in the boiler room, 1954.

glassful of the slightly amber liquid displayed the proper number of slender protein chains. Kettle knockout, the emptying of the brew, usually took place about 6:00 a.m., which normally created brewing cycles of four hours duration. Andy Yonkers, the head kettle man, and clean-up man Johnny Wittenberg arrived about this time to assist Gerhard in dumping and washing out the lauter tun for the next load of mash.

The spent grains (as the mash is then referred to) was swept off the lauter tun plates and down through the dump valve by hanging a

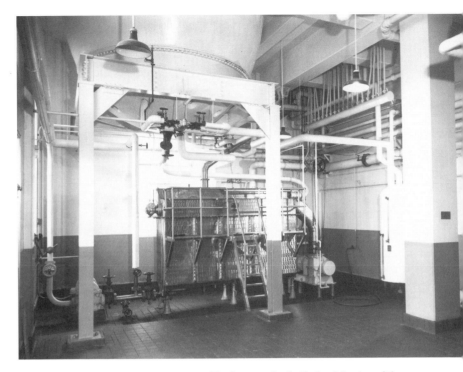

The main floor of the brew house, 1954. The bottom of a kettle is at the top of the picture with the hop jack under it. The hammer mill is on the right-hand end and the hot wort pump is on the left-hand end.   *Photo: Sicks/Molsons*

flat board over the rake blades and lowering the rotating arm into the mash until all the plates were swept clear. These grains dropped down into a small hopper in the train shed area, where the mash truck backed under to fill its dump box. When Gerhard decided the boiling wort in the kettle was ready for knockout, Andy Yonkers leaving Johnny to finish preparing the lautre tun ready for the next mash over, took his station up on the hop jack under the kettle.

The kettle knockout valve is the most important valve in the brew house. Located above Andy's head, it protruded down from the large, round, insulated bottom of the copper kettle like a teat from the udder of a great cow. It held back more than 5,000 gallons of scolding hot wort—the basic ingredient of 80,000 ten-ounce glasses of cherished suds.

Gradually opening this rising stem valve, Andy Yonkers allowed the wort to flow through a slightly graded perforated pipe, where the hot liquid dropped down into the hop jack's large stainless steel tank. Within this pipe, a motor-driven auger conveyed hops and any other solids left behind to a hammer mill where it was reduced to a flush-able pulp and washed into the industrial sewer. A large beer pump below the hop jack tank pushed the wort up to the top of the four-storied cellar block adjoining the south side of the brew house. Cooled and filtered, it would flow sedately into starter tanks in the upper cellar where brewer's yeast would be added to begin the fermenting cycle that would finally create Sick's very popular Old Style beer.

This was a brewing secret that dates back to at least the era of the monastery-brewed ales and beers, where gravity supplied the movement of grains and beer through the whole brewing process. Built into the slope of a hill or mountain, the grains, hops and brewing water were delivered to the top level of the brewery. Each process, such as milling, cooking, lautering and boiling, carried out as the wort descended level by level, until it reached the cool area provided by caves and caverns dug within the hill or mountain to control fermentation and age the brew. Descending on through the cool caverns, fermenting, aging and finishing were all carried out before the finished beer of those years was racked into wooden barrels or hogsheads for the convenience of the thirsty patrons in the nearby town.

It was a very leisurely process for the beer, but a very strenuous one for the brewers where manual labor, and many hours of it, was required to produce a viable product.

In our scenario, the hot wort collected in the hop jack tank below the kettle on the ground floor was then pumped up four stories to the hot wort tank located in a penthouse above the cellar block. Over the next four to six weeks it would be fermented and clarified, finished and polished in 12,000-gallon, glass-lined steel tanks to stabilize the beer with its distinct flavor and bouquet.

Les Banks, arriving about the same time as Andy and Johnny, readied the most interesting phase of the beer-making process—the converting of hot wort into cold beer. Rinsing out the 12,000-gallon, glass-lined horizontal starter tank, he connected it to centrifuges through long, white, sterilized rubber hose. More of the same rubber hose connected up the hot wort tank pump to the plate cooler, ready for Gerhard's first brew.

With attempered chilled brine and cold city water turned on the two stage plate cooler, the centrifuges were brought up to full speed

The wort cooling room with the plate cooler in the foreground and white centrifuges to the left, 1954. *Photo: Sicks/Molsons*

before Les started the hot wort pump to begin cooling and filtering of the wort. To reduce the load of solids on the centrifuges, the inlet suction within the hot wort tank stood several inches higher than the bottom of the vessel; thus creating a weir that excluded a remarkable amount of this troublesome trube (brewer's term for the slurry of hops, milling/cooking malt parts carried over in the wort).

And right here in Les Bank's department was the first of many money-saving ideas found in Emil Sick's brewery. The 200+°F hot wort rushing through the first section of the plate cooler heated the city's cold water (40–50°F) to 160+°F and this valuable hot water was stored in two large, insulated tanks located in the same penthouse as the hot wort tank, ready to serve the brewery's needs. This was a very important fuel dollar saving, often referred to by the engineers as a heat balance. The attemperated brine (cold brine that has had its 28°F temperature raised slightly by contact with the warmer return brine

The fermenting cellar in block A. The facing door is for the yeast room. Note the carbon dioxide collection hoses on the columns. The 12,000-gallon glass-lined steel fermenting tanks are in the foreground, 1954. *Photo: Sicks/Molsons*

through a tube and shell heat exchanger) chilled the final section of the plate cooler to maintain a wort discharge to centrifuges and starter tank of 58–62°F—the optimum temperature for fermentation.

Discharged from the plate cooler, the wort enters the spinning centrifuges to have its carry-over of fine trube material cast out before dropping down to the top floor of the cellar block, where a glass-lined starter tank awaited it in the fermenting cellar. Flooding in through the bottom-filling valve of this tank, brewer's yeast (to

Three ammonia compressors in the engine room. Carbon dioxide compressors are in the background, 1954. *Photo: Sicks/Molsons*

induce fermentation) was injected into the stream of wort by a special lob-pump. (From this point on the product is never allowed to cascade). Yeast, the jealously guarded brewer's gold, becomes his greatest difficulty to eradicate before offering a refreshing drink to the market place. Yeast spores are so tiny and multiply so quickly at ambient temperatures that even a coagulant introduced before filtering fails to remove all yeast spores so bottled beer is pasteurized. Racked beer must be kept chilled to prevent spore growth.

Within twelve to twenty-fours hours, as the yeast began to work and much of the remaining solids had settled out, the contents were carefully transferred to fermenting tanks. Here brine coils maintained optimum fermenting temperatures of 58°F while the carbon dioxide gas, a by-product of this conversion of sugars into alcohol, was collected for use in the counter-pressure and carbonating processes.

About a week later, the fermentation cycle was chilled to a halt, as the brew acquired that delicate balance of body (malt sugars) and alcohol content, that gave it the distinct flavor enjoyed by all Old Style advocates. Here again, a standpipe had been fitted into the fer-

The quality control lab, looking out onto Burrard Street. *Photo: Sicks/Molsons*

menter's bottom opening to act as a weir during removal of the beer (no longer referred to as wort), and retain as much yeast and trube particles as possible. Shifted down one floor to the ruh cellar, where air temperature was maintained at 34–36°F, the beer is properly aged before final filtration and carbonization.

Once the fermenter transfer is complete, the standpipe is removed and the remaining contents washed over into the yeast culture room to be processed into a useable culture for later use. The fermenter is rinsed clear of its life-threatening carbon dioxide gas, allowing cellar men to safely enter it and scrub the glass-lined interior back into a hygienically clean surface ready for another brew.

Both the usability of the recycled yeast and the cleanliness of the vessels are meticulously checked by the chemist from quality control. Nothing moves beyond here until cleared by quality control. It takes two brews from the kettle (200 barrels equals 5,000 gallons) to fill a 12,000-gallon beer tank to within a twenty-inch headspace. Three weeks later, more or less, the ruh tank contents were led down to the filter room where pulp filters remove many of the yeast spores and fine trube that may have been carried down into these vessels.

Stored in the finishing tanks on the ground floor cellar for one to two weeks, the brew was again passed through the filter media and lightly carbonated before being placed in the racking or bottling tanks ready for packaging. Within approximately forty-five days, the brew Gerhard had boiled in the little scenario above, could have been leaving the brewery on one of many large trucks headed to a favorite pub.

About the same time Les Banks began cooling the wort high up in the penthouse of the cellar block, Karl Smith, Mike Bock, George Whitehead and others far below in the basement of the packaging center, were uncasing returned beer bottles. From here the torn and dirty cartons, which once had proudly bugled forth in brilliant brewery colors their promise of what lay within, were stuffed into a chain-driven press to be bundled up into 200-pound bales destined for the recycler's pulp digester and another role (possibly duroid roofing shingles, for the many subdivisions of new suburbia homes changing the city's appearance on all sides).

The beer filter room in 1954. The fine filter and carbon dioxide injection are on the right and the pulp filters can be seen in the background.   *Photo: Sicks/Molsons*

On the ledges and beams surrounding this machine were collections of strange and wonderful objects. Naturally, not all the oddities that were dumped out of the old cartons during the uncasing of the bottles were on display. Money, jewelry, watches and expensive pens were things to gloat over in private. Ammo in all shapes and sizes, a tiny brass chassis of a home-built electric locomotive along with both mentionable and unmentionable items of attire were found among the empties and cartons. If an old beer carton could talk, what a tale it could tell!

The bottles conveyed over from the uncasing area were stuffed into the slow-rising pockets of the massive bottle washer that dominated both the main floor and basement in the southwest corner of the bottle shop. Scrubbed clean, both internally and externally by whirling brushes, after soaking in vats of strong caustic solutions, the bottles passed through an inspection section where random samples were removed for quality control tests and checks. They had taken about an hour to reach this point, and after being filled would spend another forty to sixty minutes being pasteurized.

Meanwhile, there were other interesting events being carried out in the beer filter room and noisier ones taking place in the keg department. Around this same time each brewing day a dump truck backed under the spent grains hopper at the head of the train shed, and the 5,000 pounds of steaming mash from Gerhard's first brew cascaded into its box, ready to be delivered to the dairy farmers in the Fraser Valley for cattle feed.

This was underway as Charlie Stannard and Walter Weisner entered the keg washhouse and began creating a din rolling empty aluminum kegs and barrels toward the automated keg washer. After auguring out the wooden plug in the side filling hole and ensuring the top bung hole was faced the proper way, it was rolled into the keg washer where it tumbled around until the interior spray nozzles could enter these two openings and washing commenced.

Internally check by Walter Weisner using a light wand and extension mirror through the same two openings, it was directed either over to Charlie Stannard's repitching department for a new coating to its interior surface or, driving in a new cork into the top bung hole, Walter rolled it into the cold damp racking cellar where Max Schmidbauer did the needful at a triple-spout racking machine.

Once filled to the brim with Sick's finest, Max drove a new

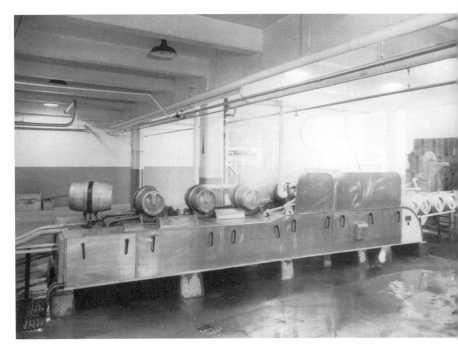

The keg washing department with drill press on right side. Pitching area is in background.

Photo: Sicks/Molsons

wooden plug into the side filling hole of the full keg or barrel (12.5-gallon keg or 25-gallon barrel) with a large mallet kept handy for this job. Then he kicked the keg or barrel down a discharge ramp, where it clattered into others that had preceded it to await a truck to deliver it. Max had been the longtime cooper at the Powell Street brewery where wooden kegs had been historically used since day one. He had taken his training at the Victoria-Silver Springs Brewery under Vic Brackat's father's eagle eye; he was a noted master at his craft as the highly polished oak donation barrel he crafted for the Crippled Children's Hospital could attest.

While Max, Walter and Charlie carried on their noisy pursuits, Paul, Hans and Otto just as industriously, but much more quietly, prepared to filter beer for the finishing tanks on the main floor. Paul Moline pressed out the filter pulp, which had been boiled sterile, into large thick pads and fitted them into the primary beer filter, ready to remove minute particulates of both the cooking and fer-

The racking cellar with beer pump on the left and three-arm racker in middle, 1954.
Photo: Sicks/Molsons

menting processes still present in the beer. Hans Warneken and Otto Neitch, completing the coupling up of a myriad of white beer hoses and copper/brass fittings necessary to polish and carbonate the next day's supply of beer, filled the coagulant injector with a fine powder that would coat any minute spores of yeast still present in the beer, and thus retain their enlarged size from passing through the finishing filter's fine filter media.

Over in the bottle shop, shortly after 7:00 a.m., sparkling clean bottles marching like soldiers on parade along the conveyor swung one at a time onto the many filling pads of the revolving carousel. After one swift ride on the merry-go-round, their glistening interiors aglow with Old Style bliss, a bright metal hat was snapped on their heads in a whirling crowner as they bravely sallied forth in a long red line to enter the terrifying spray filled steamy confines of the pasteurizer.

Back in the brew house the second brew was being pumped over to the lauter tun, while Johnny Wittenberg finished rinsing out the kettle and hop jack. Andy Yonkers stationed at the grant, set the valves for a telltale dribble as the first hot wort reached them. And Gerhard Schultz, putting in the last hours of his shift, completed milling the malt for number three brew and prepared to shift it down to the cereal and mash cookers.

By 7:30, as more brewery workers arrived, George Marshall's and Herb Wilmon's trucks, both on contract to the brewery were backing into the keg shipping dock. Two flat-bed trucks owned by Sicks, which had spent the night backed into the covered cased beer shipping dock, were being carefully loaded. Gordie McLeod, Alex Pashalko Earl Hardy and Bill Jones oversaw a steady stream of one- and two-dozen beer cartons being hand loaded onto these trucks' wide open stake decks, where a heavy tarp would be drawn over the

The bottle shop looking west. Carton gluing unit is in foreground and drop packer and soaker in background with single-deck pasteurizer between the two. Note the formed and stapled cartons conveyed up from the basement. *Photo: Sicks/Molsons*

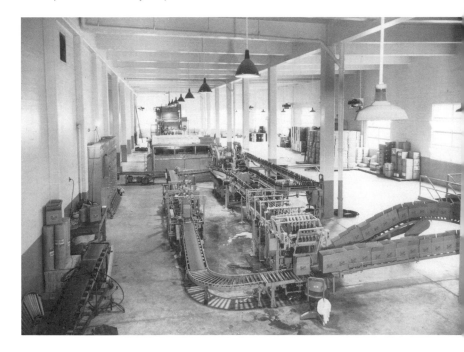

load to protect the cartons of beer from the elements (mostly precipitation around the Lower Mainland), as Casey Van Dyke and Frank Sclotthauer delivered them to the LCB and hotels on their routes.

By 8:00 a.m., as yet another group of brewery workers got suited up and filed in to their work stations, the first of the long thin red line of beer bottles exited the pasteurizer and clink clanged their way into the embrace of the labeling machines. Proudly wearing the House of Lethbridge's decorative seven Indian label around their chest and the distinctive gold "OS" neck band, they formed squads of four abreast and six in line to drop through to the specially divided cartons below. Flaps glued up in the carton sealer (designed and built within the brewery), the beer cartons were loaded up for a truck ride to the nearest LCB or hotel.

Carried on the new day's hop-scented breeze, the muted, sporadic bangs, clatters and hisses from the stirring brewery created a bass chord upon which the bottle shop's melody of clinking bottles accentuated a musical qualities to the ears of brewery manager Tom English as he stepped out of his car. Assured by these indicators that all was well, he paused a moment on the steps of the administration office for a fleeting chat with Grant Waddell, as the brewmaster carrying his morning mail and en route to his own office atop the brew house, slackened his usual brisk steps to make an observation or two.

A new week in the exciting life of the brewery had begun. In the ruh and finishing cellars more large white hoses were shifting beer down through the filter room. Mike Hummel was busy washing out the filter pulp and pressing it into new filter pads and Charlie Stannard, in a noisy crescendo of clattering aluminum kegs, was melting out the pitch lining and spraying in a new protective coating. In the engine room Alf Humphries and Harry Payne were busy changing the carbon deodorizing filters on the carbon dioxide collection system, and Cec Graham was removing and overhauling the contact pads of the first stage compressor's cross-the-line starter switch.

In the lab, its windows gazing down on the busy traffic sweeping by onto Burrard Bridge, quality control chemist Dave Kirayk was checking his yeast cultures. Down in the dusky, cool bottle shop basement, Maurice Turcott was receiving another load of returnable bottles from a Torrey delivery van off-loading in front of the shipping office, while Eddy Gobelle busily overseeing the bottle shop's production, smiled reassuringly as Bob Henry, superintendent of the department, came through on his morning inspection.

By 10:00 a.m. Gerhard had left for Richmond where he would work on his farm for a few hours, and at noon Nick Thun came in to help Andy Yonkers knock out the last brew. Around three in the afternoon the last dusty bottles were put in the soaker and the uncasing crew swept and cleaned up their area before leaving for the day. Less than an hour later the last full bottles were headed into the pasteurizer, and the filler man and bottle inspectors cleaning up their area, prepared to leave for home.

By five in the afternoon, the evening wash up crew in the bottle shop were cleaning the soaker and trucking away the barrels of broken glass, old crowns and pulp of waterlogged labels. The clatter of empty kegs fell silent after the last trucks had unloaded at the washhouse and parked, then the roller doors at both the washhouse and bottling shipping bays were closed for the night.

With the transfer of beer through the cellars and tanks cleaned and ready for the morrow, the cellar men changed their clothes and headed home. Nick Thun hoisted and milled the malt for Gerhard's first brew, before he and the bottle shop cleanup crew drove away an hour later. With the main gate again locked, a soft silence fell over the darkened brewery. Bob Berger, the afternoon shift engineer, and Huey, the night watchman, were alone again—though not quite. From the wooded area across the tracks behind the brewery, the creatures of the wild moved back into the deserted yard to continue their forage for interesting eatables that had been disturbed by the day's activity.

The foregoing little scenario is offered to illustrate the placid conditions that were enjoyed during the early days before this brewery began to stretch and struggle into a giant during the turbulent years ahead. It was not unusual, way back then, to see one or two staff members practicing their golf swing during a lunch hour, or some of the union employees playing a bit of baseball on the spacious green lawns that surrounded the brewery.

Indeed, sports of all sorts were very popular at this new brewery, but baseball was almost a middle name for the Capilano Brewery. Though Sick sponsored several local scrub teams, even an employee's team, the big league team was still the pennant-winning Vancouver Capilanos. The brewery even underwrote the bonds that financed the city's purchase of the newly built Capilano Stadium on

33rd Ave. and approved their renaming it Nat Bailey's Stadium. As will be noted, the community activities of this brewery and its employees were significant. It was the people who made the difference, and their great strength, foresight and fortitude created the successful giant seen today.

CHAPTER FIVE

Joining the Big M

The Sicks were noted for their generous employee benefits and this, coupled with their well above average wage scale, ensured them of diligent thoughtful employees who faithfully mirrored the company's commitment to excellence. Within ninety days of being hired, an employee's family was covered by a medical plan and after a year's service a life insurance policy plus pension plan was offered. They also provided paid vacation holidays at that time, at first just a week, then a week plus a day for each year's service thereafter.

The annual brewery picnic and the children's Christmas concert were highlights still fondly recalled today. Several of the longtime Sick employees were entrusted with organizing the picnic and a month's notice ensured everyone who wanted to attend could arrange to be there. It was usually held near the end of June, when good weather could be expected and before most families had left town for a summer vacation. With the brewery usually shutdown on the day selected, 10:00 a.m. was sailing time and all showed up at Gore Avenue to see what the day had in store.

The foot of Gore Avenue was the hub of historic Vancouver; here Gassy Jack Deighton had landed his first kegs of beer. Captain Edward Stamp built the first steam-powered sawmill. And city wharfs berthed such well-known pioneer steamers as the HBC paddlewheeler SS *Beaver*, the harbor ferry *Leonora*, and the strangest craft of all, the Union (nicknamed the "Sudden Jerk" by those required to ride on her).

The *Harbour Princess* was the ferry to Belcarra Park, and clutching tickets, picnic baskets and kids, the brewery employees threaded their way aboard. An hour later, they struggled just as exuberantly to get unloaded and up to the picnic site. While the men folk got the huge wood-burning stoves going to make coffee and fry hot dogs, the women spread out the tablecloths and set out picnic delights.

Fritz Sick had ensured Lethbridge's first spring picnic fair would be a success by supplying a wagonload of beer, and his son Emil followed his example by ensuring there would be plenty to drink at these picnics. With no concerns about transportation responsibilities, and within a remote shoreside picnic site to enjoy their leisure, almost everyone partook of the Sick's generosity.

Unfortunately, as the company grew bigger and the pace of brewing demanded more from employees, the picnic was discontinued. But, happily the children's Christmas party survived the pressures of growing pains Actually, it improved with age, and like the Brewery Ball (discussed later) it was originally funded jointly by Lucky Lager, Vancouver Brewery and Sicks, under the auspices of Local 300 of the Brewery and Cereal Workers Union.

Through the years from 1959 onwards, the production of beer at Capilano was creeping slowly upward—nothing spectacular, but definitely indicators of greater things to come. The brewery went from nine brews to twelve a week, then up to fifteen. Packaging began to work longer hours, and then added a second shift. They added another arm to the keg filler and sped up the keg washer. Then there was talk of building a new cellar block, and perhaps a new warehouse.

Herb Wilmon bought a new truck with a longer deck to handle the overload, and then created brewery history by building a roof on it. Until then, brewery trucks and wagons had always been open, but the popularity of the new cardboard carton, which marketed bottle beer in a vertical position, was vulnerable to soaking by the rains even when covered by tarps.

The new Social Credit government under W. A. C. Bennett, projecting a holier than thou image toward the sinners of drink, felt justified to tax the breweries liberally. To give them their due, the Minister of Highways managed to put much of this revenue back into road building, and this gave the breweries an opportunity to expand their truck-delivered sales area. Phil Gaglardi's improvement of the Fraser Canyon route to the Cariboo, and his creation of the Hope-Princeton Highway over the old Dewdney Trail to the Boundary country, encouraged trucking companies to put trailer trucks in service from the coast to as far north as Williams Lake and Quesnel and as far east as Trail and Nelson.

With the exception of plant management, the engineer probably enjoyed the greatest overview of the brewery. The engineer certainly had the best opportunity to get this kind of knowledge, and Art Pugh , as chief engineer, encouraged the engineer's motivation along these lines. He took time to provide good examples of engineering and machinist skills to those who valued acquiring such talents, and provided his engineers with information not normally available to others. In the layout of the brewery, the engine room, where Art had his office and kept much of this information, and the boiler room, where the shift engineer had his desk and recorded the details of the day to day operations for these files, was central to all.

Trucks and delivery van drivers usually arrived there first to get direction to other areas or to contact those in charge of various areas to receive or deliver materials. Because all roads led to this area, visitors, people on business calls or those just making general inquiries arrived at the engineer's domain. And because most other exterior routes into the brewery were subject to weather conditions, traffic hazards or remote locations, they were often given the grand tour through this glistening, pulsating and fascinating realm to the brewery elevator, which lifted them up to the inner sanctum of the brewmaster's offices.

Employees lauded the modern plant's capabilities with modest pride, and took keen pleasure in the surprised accolades voiced by the uninitiated as they were guided through. It was an opportunity seldom accorded visitors to other highly complex industrial facilities, for in a small way it did put them at risk and could have created grounds for lawsuits if an accident had happened. Fortunately, during those more liberal times, few visitors would have even considered such a flagrant misuse of goodwill.

Before continuing, there should be some comment on how the above confused traffic pattern actually came into being. When Don McRoberts proposed this piece of property as admirably suited to the Sick breweries needs, he must have been attracted by the majestic sweep of Burrard Street as it rose around the western boundary to climb onto the bridge approaches. He then designed the brewery buildings to compliment it, by sweeping the western foundations and walls around the foot of the embankment, with lawns along the rolling slopes and capping the embankment on Burrard Street with a post and beam concrete fence, just inside a curved row of flowering cherry trees.

He commanded attention of his masterpiece by placing the tall, bastionlike brew house to face the intersection of Cornwall Street, and on top of this he placed the impressive steel weather forecasting tower that supported the brave revolving 6 logo that Emil Sick had decreed should adorn each of his breweries. The models of this new brewery and the number of engineering drawings it required to gain civic approval all accentuated the impressive aspect this structure would offer to the eyes of all, especially those approaching it from the west.

Unfortunately, few people could approach it literally from the west as the busy multilane sweep of Burrard Street got in the way of a proper entrance—a driveway was cast in the curb and sidewalk though never connected to the brewery's parking area. The brewery itself was built with only a pathway to its front door, as was the administration office. (My first attempt to drive into the brewery was quite naturally from Burrard Street, and this found me sweeping by in utter consternation with the heavy traffic onto Burrard Street Bridge, after failing to find any way into this impressive structure. Circling back around by way of the new Granville Street Bridge, eying the brewery below my right shoulder like a flier looking for a landing site, I decided to dive into the cluttered area of 1st Avenue and find the back door. Most first-time people to the brewery, echo my experience and final solution. Thus, they usually pull up near the boiler room to get direction or assistance.)

For the first twenty years at least, nearly all plant personnel, if not most visitors, entered the administration office by the back door, the brew house and cellar block through the power plant, and the packaging and shipping areas by the loading doors, the latter requiring a sharp eye to avoid trucks and tow motors. In some way, the aspect viewed by the uninitiated from the rear of the brewery, was even more impressive than that viewed from the front, and remained so until all the lawns, gardens and silver birch trees had been replaced with black top, buildings or brewery vessels.

While the entry for most people is now directed away toward a new entrance, during those earlier years, large tours of brewery visitors paraded through the engine and boiler rooms, en route to see the large copper kettle or the sterile white chilled cellars. I first met such dignitaries as the owner Emil Sick, George Whitmore president of Sick Breweries, Les Chiswick his vice-president, and Tom Dancer, his general manager, while carrying out my watchful engineering duties in this area where machinery stopped and started on mysterious signal, bells rang, whistles blew, fans hummed and boilers pulsated in hot readiness of the brewer's demands.

While the shift engineer enjoyed a certain privileged position as guide or temporary host to befuddled or lost souls, he also performed an even more important role during the normal working hours as contact person for help or maintenance assistance. Nearly all calls for emergency equipment, ambulance, fire or police arrived by running feet to the shift engineer's desk, as did requests for cab or cartage under less strenuous exertion. The engineer's knowledge of the various service system, and most important of all, the whereabouts of the maintenance engineers or the chief engineer, caused him to be the person most charge hands approached when a problem arose.

During those early years, the engineers provided the only real maintenance in the brewery; thus, after-hours emergency repairs were often carried out by the engineer on shift. Fortunately, the safety features built into the power plant provided some flexibility in the engineer's attendance to its operation, which could provide ten or fifteen minutes quite readily to these needs. The government safety codes, which dictated the responsibility of shift engineers, also provided a reasonable degree of flexibility of his charge.

In Canada, only government certified engineers operate high-pressure steam generating boilers. The Pressure Vessel Act, which governs the construction requirements of all these types of pressure vessels, also decrees the responsibility of their operation to people who have qualified through proven skills and knowledge to be competent. Such competency is qualified through examination of job experience, skills and schooling into grades of competency. The size of the power plant determines the level or grade of competency the engineer in charge must have acquired.

The chief inspector appointed by the government to police the act creates the standard of examination for each grade of engineer and the amount of boiler horsepower each grade may be allowed to take charge of. The plant engineer so designated by this act is deemed the chief engineer of the power plant. He may appoint one or more shift engineers of one grade lower than himself to operate the power plant during those hours of each day when he is absent or involved with other duties. For absences longer than this, the engineer so appointed must first be approved by the chief inspector to carry out the role of chief engineer in the latter's stead.

The Carlings O'Keefe Brewery at Broadway and Boundary; it is now Weston's Bakery.
Credit: Molsons

Where the shift engineer is provided a thoroughly trained firemen or assistant engineer, he may absence himself from the boilers for such time as is considered prudent to carry out other job-related duties. The shift engineer unable to delegate his boiler watching duties can only be absent for that amount of time allowed by maximum evaporation of the boilers within safe limits. With Bailey Meter combustion controls fitted to the brewery's 18,000 pound per hour Babcock & Wilcock boilers, this period was not to exceed fifteen minutes.

During those earlier years, when the workshop with its fifteen-inch Wilson lathe and other power equipment were in one corner of the boiler room and the portable welding equipment was stored just a few feet away in the shipping bay across the tracks, even the shift engineer was expected to do minor repairs, turning or fabricating during quiet periods of his shift. Their skill and these tools also carried out small personal repairs at times for others in the brewery who had neither the talent nor the tools to do so.

During this pre-Molson period, E. P. Taylor's Canadian Breweries took over Vancouver Breweries and announced plans to build a new brewery at Boundary and Broadway to market the O'Keefe label. Labatt's also announced purchase of Lucky Lager Breweries in New Westminster, and their national advertising increased their local sales far out of proportion to those of the Capilano Brewery. For the first time, Capilano had to work hard so as not to get left behind.

In the early spring of 1957, John Lindsay, a congenial big Hoosier from Indiana who had joined the brewery as assistant brewmaster replacing Vic Munroe, plotted with Grant Waddell to offer two novelty beers for St. Patrick's Day. Using a food-grade coloring material, they offered hotel outlets a bright Irish green beer for their taps. Green beer has a very real hazardous overtone both in marketing as well as brewing, as was noted in the third chapter when the Powell Street Brewery offered improperly aged beer to their budding clientele.

Capilano's St. Patrick's Day green beer went over like a lead balloon, and much had to be returned. But dumped? No, never—not while the brewery offered free beer on tap in the lunchroom. Here it was ingested with the same gusto as the regular brew, but the exercise was never repeated again. No brewery wants to be known for its green beer, even if it's just an Irish joke.

The other brew they offered had much more promise and was repeated many springtimes through following years. This was a heavy German bock beer; traditionally brewed for the Easter season, it was made from barley malt—both lightly caramelized malt and black (roasted) barley—which created a much stronger lager beer, well received by Old Style drinkers who sadly lamented the shortness of the Easter season. Folklore has it that bock beer was the spring clean out of the old German beer tanks. And because all the good stuff had settled to the bottom and aged much longer than the others, it was considered the finest brew of the season by certain local drinkers. Victor Brachat, the long-time brewmaster at Labatts, chuckled over this tale and explained that if such a product were ever offered it wouldn't be very palatable and could have a nasty yeast flavor and possibly bacterial contaminations. He stated that every brewery he knew had a policy that the last few inches in each tank were either mixed with the spent grains for cattle feed or were flushed to sewer.

Emil Sick had successfully launched his famous Select rice beer in the U.S., and it was decided that the brewery should offer it here as a new brand. Sacks of rice were shipped into the plant. After considerable experimenting in brewing and fermenting, Al Thompson, the controller and a former flying boat pilot with Coastal Command

A new bottling line with drop packers in foreground and labelers in background, 1963. The overhead conveyor moved full goods from carton sealers. *Photo: Molsons*

who had a broken nose to prove it, was able to announce to an in-plant meeting, that the company had launched the new Select rice beer on the B.C. market. Initially, its reception appeared to justify the aspiration he alluded to at that time. But times do change, and Select became one of its casualties.

The brewery also experimented with a form of in-line pasteurization, in the hope of reducing the time bottles of beer had to remain in the pasteurizer to ensure their freedom from any carryover of yeast spores. E. P. Taylor had built an experimental brewery in the States, which was designed to brew, ferment and also ruh (age) beers within a continuous labyrinth of piping. It was never deemed a success, nor were Capilano's experiments using a stainless steel plate heat exchanger where beer was heated to pasteurizing temperature through contact with live steam. The company also began to ship more beer out of town by boxcar, and built a special conveyor to load cartons directly from the bottling floor by spotting the railcars alongside the boiler room. There had been a few innovations and streamlining of production during the last few years to allow for increased efficiency.

With established sales shares being eroded by Carling's Black

Label and Labatt's Blue, and Capilano's failure to provide an appealing brew to the many new arrivals who were swelling the suburbs of the lower mainland, the company frantically inveigled a former northern bush pilot who had joined George Bell as sales representative, to appear as Mister Old Style in various advertising scenarios. Ben Valerie not only appealed to the style of adventurous beer drinkers through his daring-do newspaper ads, but also went on to greater things on television as the brewery's sales recovery began to hurt the competition.

Remember Ben—his "Perils of Pauline" scenarios, with his handle bar moustache and daredevil grin? He was the gallant, silk-scarved aviator in the open cockpit biplane or the fearless mountie in the frozen north, who always saved the pretty damsel in distress then quaffed a refreshing Old Style beer as his manly reward. Ben's gruff, winning style stemmed the inroads of the multinationals for a while. Even after Molson's began to pay his salary, Ben continued to amuse on nightly TV with his daring-do, his lady-killing charm and his wonderful gusto for an Old Style beer.

Outlandish rumors echoed through the grapevine during late

The new carton-forming machines, 1963. *Photo: Molsons*

The new bottling line with filler and crowner in foreground and bottle washer in back.

Photo: Molsons

1957, claiming the brewery was to be sold to eastern interests. These were more amusing than concerning to most at the brewery. The actual announcement in the spring of 1958 that Molson's was to be the new boss caused more concern than humor to accompany the snort of disbelief that went up. Quite ignorant of this great brewing family of the east, the company provided a copy of *The Barley and the Stream* by Merrill Denison to acquaint workers with "John the Elder," and the 200-year-old Molson saga on the St. Lawrence River.

Only then did workers hear the story about a Mr. Wilson, who was really Mr. Tom Molson incognito, who had visited several breweries while trying to negotiate a deal with Emil Sick. Eddy Morison, who had recently started work in the bottle shop but had worked for a short time in the Montreal brewery of Molson's, asserted that while their brewery had very strict rules of conduct, if you followed those rules you'd have no trouble with the company.

Fortunately, Senator Molson sent out his nephew, Eric Molson, to learn Capilano's quaint ways, and this gave everyone a chance to see and talk with a real live Molson. And this, for most, allowed a much more generous opinion of the new boss.

CHAPTER 6

Molson's Capilano Brewery

Modern Canadian history was written within the era spanned by the Molson family. The company is the oldest surviving private business in Canada, with the exclusion of the Hudson's Bay Company, which enjoyed a Royal Charter. Molson's brewery was established before the North American colony was divided into Upper and Lower Canada.

Its founder, John Molson, arrived in Montreal just a few years after Benjamin Franklin and the U.S. Army of Occupation had vacated this War of Independence acquisition. And he and his sons fought the last battle between the United States of America and this two-language colony during the War of 1812.

The enterprise of the "Honorable" John Molson (the Elder) and his sons, reads like a Horatio Elder list of conquests: Canada's first commercial brewers, they built and operated the first steamships in Canada, created the first private bank and minted the country's first money. They built and operated the first international hotel in Montreal, its first theater, and even supplied its citizens with millions of board feet of cut lumber from their early sawmill. John Molson sponsored Montreal's first general hospital, its first public library and incorporated Canada's first commercial steam railway.

Elected to the Legislative Assembly of Lower Canada, John Molson later served as the founding president of the Bank of Montreal, before being appointed an Honorable Member of the Legislative Council. The Molsons contributions toward creating a strong Canadian economy have been equally contributed to by the long generations of Molsons who followed them. Two of the many excellent books that have written about them, *The Molson Saga* by Shirley E. Woods Jr. and *The Barley and The Stream* by Merrill Denison are recommended reading for those who wish a deeper insight into this truly great Canadian family. Just a brief outline of John Molson and the family company that became the owners of the Capilano Brewery in 1958 will be offered here.

Born in Lincolnshire, England, in 1763, John Molson came under the guardianship of his grandfather in 1772, when his father suddenly passed away. Appointed trustee of the nine-year-old's estate until he came of age (reached his majority), Samuel Elsdale charged his grandson for room and board while he completed his grammar school education. This was payable from a small allowance allotted the lad, and every cent of this meager budget had to be accounted for. Such harsh, austere treatment created little affections between the two, but did force John Molson to become very self-reliant at an early age, and probably this was reflected in the events that follow.

At seventeen, in company with the Pells from Lincolnshire, John Molson sailed for Canada. His sea voyage was a moment of high adventure that lasted eight weeks, required three ships to complete, and saw them almost founder on two occasions. For a rural lad trained for the role of gentleman farmer, the close encounters with danger excited a love of the sea that stayed with him for the rest of his life.

Landing in Montreal in the early summer of 1782, the twelve-foot walls erected during the American War of Independence just six years earlier to protect it from the Yankees, surrounded narrow dirt streets bordered by stone houses with tin roofs. Predominately French speaking, the city's walls housed black-robed priests, red-coated garrison troops, Indians and roughly dressed voyageurs from the fur trade. Most of the merchants were British or Scottish, and its population numbered under 8,000. Many United Empire Loyalist who had fled from the Thirteen Colonies, which had gained their independence from British rule, resided outside its walls while they prepared to migrate into Upper Canada to find new homesteads.

Here was based the North West Company, which each spring sent out fifty or sixty trading canoes into Upper Canada manned by French Canadian voyageurs. Returning each fall loaded to the gunwales with prime pelts, these were shipped along with timber and grain to England. Trade at the moment, especially the fur trade was of little interest to John Molson, but agriculture was. He noted the conditions of soil, the farming practices that prevailed and most important the cost of labor and the lack of good work habits.

That fall, he noted that a former neighbor of his from Lincolnshire had erected a new malting house about a half mile east of the walled town on the St. Lawrence River fronting a broad rapid known as St. Mary's Current. By the end of October this Mr. Lloyd had sold fifty hogsheads (a large wooden cask—about 63 gallons) of ale for £7 local currency per hogshead. Satisfied that brewing could be profitable, John Molson decided to invest in this pioneer venture.

John's optimism was based on the fact that the market for locally brewed beers was practically untouched. While brewing had been tried in New France, they had all failed because the French preferred wines or spirits to the frontier brews made from local grains and hops. But with the arrival of British emigrants, garrison troops and the United Empire Loyalist, this situation had changed rapidly. Because wines and spirits were often enhanced by long sea voyages, they could be imported from Europe, but beers usually suffered badly during these tempest crossings. This meant local brewing was required to reach the consumer in their peak of body and flavor.

The economics of brewing were very favorable in Montreal. Property and buildings could be acquired at nominal expenditure; a good carpenter cost less than a dollar per day and laborers less than fifty cents. Water was free and local barley and hops, though of marginal quality, were inexpensive. Being a slow natural process, brewing equipment was simple and labor minimal. Best of all, few if any taxes or duties were levied on this trade, as all sales were either in cash or trade.

In January of 1783 John Molson risked a small amount of the traveling funds advanced to him by his grandfather, and joined Mr. Lloyd as a partner. They hired John Wait as their brewer, maltster and laborer. Unfortunately, the growing season was a very wet one and the barley crop fared poorly, so Mr. Lloyd had to substitute wheat for brewing needs. This appeared to answer well and encourage John Molson to write his grandfather for an advance on his allowance stating he intended to settle in Canada and go into business. This was putting the cart before the horse, but he was still a minor and he did not want his grandfather to know he had entered the brewing trade.

This money when it came was invested in some lakeside property on Missisquoi Bay, promoted by the then Receiver-General of British North America. However, later in 1783, when the Peace of Paris Treaty redefined the border between the United States of America and Canada, title to this property appeared to be lost, and in June of the following year Thomas Lloyd and John Molson dissolved their partnership. It appeared that Mr. Lloyd owed John Molson more than £150 sterling and also owed John Wait his back wages. By mutual consent, some of Thomas Lloyd's possessions were sold off to pay John Wait's wages, and then the brewery was put up for sale to pay off John Molson.

In October of 1784 when no buyers had come forward, the sheriff slated the auction of the property to January, 1785. This just happened to fall one week after John Molson reached legal age to take possession of both his family's estate and control of a business. Surprisingly, or perhaps not, Thomas Lloyd was bequeathed the four hundred acres at Lake Champlain (the Missisquoi Bay property) soon after John Molson became sole owner of the small log cabin brewery at St. Mary's Current. Satisfied with this arrangement, John Molson sailed for England in June, leaving James Pell to keep an eye on the brewery.

While his visit home was to arrange the affairs of his estate, and this caused him to remain over the winter, it did allow him time to visit a number of breweries and study their operations. Most impressive was the large Whitbread Brewery on Chiswell Street in London, where he saw a large steam engine supplied by James Watt, pumping liquids and grinding malt that did the work of fourteen horses. He also spent considerable time shopping for brewing equipment and, most important of all, he purchased a book on brewing principals by John Richardson. During his return voyage to Canada he studied this manual thoroughly, and on landing at Montreal in June of 1786, immediately rolled up his sleeves and began rebuilding his brewery, which during his long absence had suffered a break-in by river pirates.

Securing residence near the brewery, the warm days of summer were quickly passed installing the equipment he had brought back from England and commencing his first brew. Visiting a number of local farmers, he gave them barley seed purchased in the old country that would be much superior for his brewing needs, and thus ensuring a supply of this vital ingredient for his winter brewing. On July 28, he bought his first eight bushels of fresh barley (about 250 pounds) and began to malt.

This involved soaking the grains in tepid water for about a week to induce germination (sprouting), then drying the grains by light roasting before crushing them sufficiently to crack or break the husk. He removed the malt extract from the husk by steeping it in hot water (brewing liquor) in a large copper mash cooker (tun) to create a very sweet liquid (wort). Draining off the bottom of the tun, he boiled this wort in a copper kettle to drive off excess water and distillates, adding hops to reduce the insipid sweetness and give his ale its characteristic tart flavor.

Cooling the hot wort to about 60°F in river water, he added yeast to commence an enzymatic process (fermentation), which would convert 50 percent of the sugar body into alcohol with heady amounts of carbon dioxide gas as a by-product. This process took him about another week, then the ale was held for several more weeks in a wooden settling or aging tank, before being decanted into wooden kegs or barrels to be offered to his potential customers.

While he had hired Christopher Cook in September to assist him and had enjoyed the help of his future bride Sarah Vaughan during that fall and winter, his production of ale and table beer was only about four hogsheads (about 128 gallons) a week—insufficient to supply all his prospective customers. To improve this output, he ordered from England more brewing equipment, including a seven-hogshead copper kettle.

In 1787 he built a stone malt house eighty feet long by forty wide, and beneath it he dug a cellar lined in stone (these still exist today under the huge modern brewery on Notre Dame Street). He converted the former malt house into a brew house and installed his large new kettle there. Costing over £500, they combined to double his capacity. He was able to malt two weeks earlier than his first year and had over 600 bushels of barley and sufficient hops and wood on hand for the winter's brewing needs.

Sarah modestly crowned this achievement when she presented him with a son in mid-October. This first arrival of the second generation of Molsons in Canada was christened John, a precedent perpetuated faithfully thereafter when John Molson decreed his brewery would always be managed by a Molson named John. In 1788/89 he bought more property on either side of the brewery, increasing his river frontage to almost 200 feet, and this allowed him to diversify.

The storming of the Bastille in Paris that July, and the Revolutionary War which erupted thereafter, restricted vital commodities and alcohol reaching the new world, thus putting greater demands on John Molson's brewery. By 1891 he was a respected businessman of Montreal and was installed by his fellow Masons as Master of the St. Paul's Lodge. In September, Sarah again upstaged his accomplishment by presenting him with his second son, whom they named

Thomas. But the brewery had the last word in upstaging when it produced in excess of 30,000 gallons of ale, beer and spruce beer that season. (Spruce beer was made from the seed found in the cones of various species of spruce trees—a favorite brew of the early pioneer in lieu of the real thing.)

Through this period John Molson carried out a work ethic that gave him great insight into the country's needs, as well as ensured his brewery prospered. It became a tradition that did not go unnoticed by his sons. Each morning at first light, garbed in his heavy brewer's clothes, he stood at the brewery gate as the farmers arrived with their wagons of grain. Judging its quality and agreeing on a price gave him ample opportunity to hear the plight and problems of the farmers. After an early breakfast, he joined his help in processing the barley and producing a brew of beer.

By early afternoon he replaced the work clothes with suitable garments to visit the business houses of the city, where he bartered for needed supplies and received orders for his ales and beer. This made him aware of the needs of both farmers and merchants, which he soon sought to supply. Offering hard currency for their discounted deeds and promissory notes and improving their purchasing position soon led him into the banking business.

During evening hours, dressed in his finest attire, he attended social functions and suppers where he had the opportunity to meet and converse with the titled gentry who managed the community and whose political views would guide the destiny of the country. This gave him an exceptional overview to the vital needs of the country and a good understanding of how his endeavors could be both beneficial to many and sufficiently profitable to sustain. This became the greatness of this rather slight Lincolnshire brewer, who developed such finesse in feeling the pulse of this slowly awakening wilderness.

In December, 1891, the Constitutional Act divided Canada into two governing bodies called Upper and Lower Canada, each with its own lieutenant governor, legislative council and house of assembly. John Molson, like many English merchants in Montreal, feared his needs would be ignored by the predominately French-speaking legislature of Lower Canada. Their concern was justified. The French element, fearing increased trade would threaten their national identity, consistently balked at their proposals and frustrated any English attempt to improve mercantile or economical legislation.

John's third son, William, was born two years after this Act came into effect. And in 1795 the brewery was enlarged by a second large stone building and more equipment from England, which increased it production to more than 50,000 gallons a year. While the countryside abounded in prime timber, little had been exported and even less had been whip sawn into lumber for the local market. James Watt and Napoleon Bonaparte would soon change all that.

Watt's steam engine could be adapted to rock a drag saw back and forth, cutting logs into timber and lumber with metal muscles that never tired. Napoleon, blockading the Baltic, would force Britain to look elsewhere for her marine and fortification lumber needs. In the years that followed, Britain created a timber fleet of 500 ships to lug it across the stormy Atlantic from Canada. Even the wild Ottawa and Richelieu Rivers disgorged vast rafts of logs to satisfy this market. But during those years that preceded Napoleon's blockade, and while Sarah was creating John Molson's family, the only evidence of this potentially prime industry were the small log rafts from the Great Lakes area that floated by the brewery on their way to the sailing ships awaiting them at Quebec City. Loaded with produce from the upper river and lake area, plus the crew and their families under white canvas tents, they avoided the turbulence of St. Mary's Current and thus seldom paused at Montreal.

John Molson, seeing a need for this timber floating literally by his back door, increased his water frontage by another 250 feet and invited some of these rafts to land there. Trading some of his refreshing product, plus needed supplies and hard currency, for their prime logs, he created a sawpit and put men to work cutting the logs into timbers and planks. Trading this lumber to the farmers for barley or hops, or selling them for cash or discounted notes, he thriftily utilized all the sawpit's wood waste to fire his brewery's cookers and kettles. Before the turn of the century, he had sold more than 2,000,000 board feet of hand-cut lumber.

The first six years of the nineteenth century were frustrating ones for the Montreal businessmen as the Legislative Assembly of Lower Canada enacted tariff and taxes, which hindered their endeavors to increase trade. John Molson watching the torturous assent of the river by sailing ship and barge, decided a steam-powered vessel might improve on this costly and time-consuming process.

Possibly the success of Robert Fulton's sternwheel steamer

Clermont on the Hudson River that year powered by engines built by Watt and Boulton, plus his own recall of the work effortlessly performed by James Watt's steam engine at Whitbread's, encouraged John Molson to consider such a radically new and daring mercantile venture. But here his plan differed from Robbie Fulton's—he would have his engines and boilers built locally. It was an act of faith in his fellow countrymen that would surface many times through the coming years and climax when his own foundry built the engines and boilers for the *Royal William*, first steamship to successfully steam the full way across the Atlantic Ocean. There is a certain similarity between James Watt and John Molson: both suffered youthful ill health, both pioneered improvements that took their chosen professions from cottage industry into multimillion-dollar successes, and both used the steam engine to accomplish it.

It has been quipped that James Watt improved the Newcomen atmospheric engine into a powerful double-acting steam engine by putting a lazy boy on the valve lever who improvised through string and wire a way to make the engine itself push and pull the levers, thus causing it to go up and down, allowing the lad to daydream away his working hours.

John Molson had no such boy to help him with his valve gear, and this quickly pointed up a bane in his first creation. The vessel he created for a scheduled service between Quebec City and Montreal was a modest eighty-five feet long, hardly large enough to carry a paying load. Like the HBC's *Beaver* (the first steamship built for the western coast of Canada a quarter century later), her steam engines, boilers and fuel pre-emptied much of the available space within her heavily timbered hull.

A modest common room for the first-class lady passengers and a slightly larger separate room for the gentlemen constituted the creature comforts below decks, while a small hold area forward of the fuel bunkers was allocated for first-class freight and mails. On deck milled the unfortunate, unsheltered steerage passengers, along with common freight and beasts, around which the crew scurried to work the ship. The large side wheels that drove her through the water were really just heavy wooden hubs fitted to her horizontal crankshaft, which radiated out long spars fitted with a broad paddle on their ends.

Christened the *Accommodation*, the hull built in Montreal by David Munn and her engines and boiler at Three Rivers, Quebec, she sailed on her maiden voyage to Quebec City on the 1st of November, 1809. While noted in history as the first steamship built in Canada and lauded by the locals as a marvel of the times, John Molson, busy increasing the size of his brewery and carrying on his business of discounting notes for those requiring immediate cash, did not deem her a success.

Fortunately, though she failed to attract sufficient passengers to pay her operating costs, she did provide safe transport down river to Quebec for his discounted notes and securities that had to be forwarded to London by sailing ship for redemption. She also provided a means to deliver his ale and beers to down river points under less harsh conditions than that offered by horse-drawn cartage of the day.

The Molsons were a close-knit, happy, hard-working family. Like Fritz Sick a hundred years later, John Molson knew that through a common appreciation of a healthy work ethic a family gained harmony and happiness. His son's schooling was composed of equal parts of text book learning and brewery work learning. The quiet hours of evening often found the family conversing around the supper table, where John Sr. explained the ways of the world and his thoughts on gaining a comfortable living from this knowledge.

By 1810 John Jr., who had shown a great ability within the brewery, was now twenty-three years of age. He was placed in charge of making a number of improvements to the tiny *Accommodation*, deemed necessary by his father. These upgrades included installing a larger boiler, making her valve gear more efficient and modifying her paddlewheels to double spokes held by a binder ring, carrying full-width paddles.

This gave John Sr. latitude to pursue the planning and construction of a much larger steamship, and he traveled to New York to discuss these plans with Robert Fulton, the then acknowledged dean of steamboats in the new world. While they did not arrive at an agreement for the design and building of the new steamship to be carried out by Fulton, John Molson did take Fulton's advice to fit her with engines built by Boulton and Watt. Four weeks after returning to Montreal and placing John Jr. in charge of the family's business, John Molson sailed for England. Here he visited James Watt at his Soho Engineering Works in Birmingham, to place an order for two large engines for his new ship *Swiftsure*.

On his return to Canada in the spring of 1811, John Molson

learned of a competitive brewer who was eying the Montreal beer market, and he took swift steps to reduce his competitor's inroads. He bought the final piece of property within the block at St. Mary's Current, ensuring ample area for future brewery expansion. Then he bought several houses within the city walls, which he turned into coffee houses to dispense hospitality and provide a gathering place for the merchants to transact business (similar to how Lloyds of London had started). These ventures complimented his own banking activities, thus strengthening his own influence within the business community.

In the fall of 1811, the keel of his new ship was laid at Logan's Shipyard. While the *Accommodation* had not proved a financial success, she had fulfilled John Molson's declaration that he would provide a vessel that could navigate on the river against wind and current. The *Swiftsure* was believed the largest steamship built anywhere in the world at that time, and with a length of just 140 feet and a hull width of a mere fourteen feet, she displaced more than 400 tons. Her paddle boxes were over six feet in depth, giving the vessel a total beam of twenty-six feet. She was capable of transporting forty-five first-class passengers in cabins and staterooms, and 150 steerage passengers.

In June of 1812 the United States of America, incensed over the Royal Navy's highhanded method of boarding lawful American ships on the high seas and pressing into their service any man of British birth, declared war on Great Britain. President Madison immediately ordered a military thrust under General Hull into Upper Canada.

While many Americans were loath to fight their friends to the north, the raid caused great alarm in Montreal. In September, after being captured by General Brock near Detroit, General Hull was forced to lead his defeated American troops through the streets of Montreal, *en route* to a prisoner-of-war camp in Quebec. Shortly after this war scare, John Molson Sr. and his sons John Jr. and William enlisted in the colonial military forces, leaving Thomas to manage the brewery.

The following year, the large *Swiftsure* became the first steamship in the world to be employed in the conduct of a war. It is believed that William Molson was captain of her on these voyages. The war continued through 1813 with the Americans under General Hampton routed from the area around the Chateauguay River, thirty-five miles below Montreal. Colonel Morrison near Cornwall, later defeated a similar American force under General Wilkinson.

The War of 1812 boasted Montreal's importance and improved her economy so greatly that even the American press exclaimed, "Montrealers should erect a monument to President Madison, for the prosperity he had ensured them." In the spring of 1814 when Napoleon abdicated, Britain was able to send seasoned troops into Upper Canada, and the *Swiftsure* carried many of them up from Quebec City.

The demobilization of volunteer troops allowed the Molson trio to return to the world of commerce, and in September, three months before the signing of the Treaty of Ghent re-established peaceful relations, they launched an even more powerful and grander ship than *Swiftsure*. Christened the *Malsham*, a thirteenth-century spelling of the family name, she was the fastest boat on the river. John Molson Sr. who enjoyed taking command of these ships, placed John Jr. master of the *Swiftsure*, while he took over the *Malsham*.

Both ships proved profitable ventures and Molson's enjoyed a monopoly of the river trade, greatly improving their transportation of brewery products and increasing the scope of their private banking business at each port of call. Pleased with these prospects, in 1815 John Molson bought river property at Quebec City and Montreal to build terminal accommodations for his steamship. John Jr. moved to Quebec City to take charge of the company's three major interests at that end.

John Molson Sr., often referred to by his associates of this period as "John the Elder," supervised the rebuilding of Sir John Johnson's former estate on Montreal Island, into a grand hotel called the Mansion House, planning to compliment it with a long wharf out into the St. Lawrence River for convenience of his steamship passengers. Forewarned of a competitive steamer about to enter this river trade, Molson's commissioned the building of an even larger and grander sidewheel steamer to enhance the services he offered his clientele, and thus discourage competition.

Powered with side-lever engines, which James Watt assured Thomas Molson were at least the equal of those supplied the new 170-foot vessel planning to enter the Montreal river trade, the *Lady Sherbrooke* was launched at Montreal in May of 1817. But the difficulties placed in his way to get approval for construction of the Montreal wharf fronting the Mansion House caused a vexed John Molson Sr. to run for a seat in the assembly. In April of 1816, he was duly elected to the legislative assembly, though ironically this came about just three days after getting final approval to build his long new wharf.

Both John Jr. and Thomas took brides during this period. William, still a bachelor, assisted Thomas managing the brewery and shipping company in Montreal, while John Jr. took his bride to Quebec City. Though all three were dutiful and obedient sons, all felt they should become acknowledged partners of their family's enterprises and finally convinced their fifty-four-year-old father to enter into a formal agreement to that effect. Thus, the company of "John Molson and Sons" was born.

Montreal had grown into a bustling center of commerce, through which most of Upper Canada's imports and exports funneled. Boasting a population in excess of 16,000, its medical needs far outstripped the modest capabilities of the Roman Catholic thirty-bed hospital, which had mushroomed up in the Hotel Dieu. In 1819 John Molson presented a petition to the legislative assembly to create a public hospital with capabilities sufficient to handle both citizen and transient needs. Not surprisingly, the predominating Roman Catholic population defeated this.

Undaunted, John Molson solicited support from other thinkers like himself within the community and, dipping generously into their own pockets, they created the Montreal General Hospital. After two years in a rented brick house that held just twenty-four beds, the cornerstone of the MGH was laid on Dorchester Street that would realize a three-storied building, housing up to eighty patients.

In March, 1821, Molson's elegant hotel that housed the North West Company's "Beaver Club" (all members of this famous club had spent at least a whole year trading out in the wilderness west of the Red River) burned to the ground in a tragic fire that cost the headwaiter his life. With the North West Company merging into the Hudson's Bay Company shortly after this fire, the Beaver Club was never revitalized. But the Mansion House hotel was immediately replaced by an even grander creation that was touted as the most luxurious in Canada. Known as the British American Hotel, it was for some time the residence of Canada's Governor General Lord Dalhousie.

The year 1821 was also noted for a great step forward in the brewery's development. That year the first steam engine was installed to grind the malt and pump water, and Thomas began experimenting with distilling spirits. In late fall he sent several hundred gallons of this "spirits of whiskey" to their London agents, who had no difficulty selling it. Deciding to enter the distilling trade, Thomas moved his family to Kingston, Ontario, where plans to create the huge Rideau Canal would link this lower lake port with Bytown (Ottawa). There he created a prosperous business brewing beers and distilling spirits.

The following year, the St. Lawrence Steamboat Company was formed. Though including such large steamers as the *Quebec* and other competing steamships on the river, Molson's held controlling interest, and the business was commonly referred to as the "Molson Line." Also in 1822, Molson and Sons belatedly invested in the Bank of Montreal, and John Molson Jr. was appointed one of its directors.

In 1825, John Molson, the Elder, created the Theatre Royale on St. Paul Street, where Charles Dickens often gave recitals. The following year he became president of the Bank of Montreal in a maneuver carried out by his son John Jr. While this preceded the formation of the Molson Bank by many years, its tumultuous events are worthy of note in our story.

Canada had suffered a monetary problem most of its formative years. As a colony it used the currency and coin of England, yet often it was without either for trade purposes. Letters of credit, due bonds, script and foreign currency were often offered "in lieu," and these were usually well discounted as hazardous world events threatened their redeemable value. John Molson traded in these latter forms of banking business, and through careful handling he realized a good return on these risky funds while creating a tradition of honest and fair dealing.

The Bank of Montreal was created without benefit of a Royal Charter as a private joint-stock company with capital of £25,000 sterling in 1817. Their principles utterly refused to consider renting office space from John Molson because he had refused to invest in their venture. But Molsons were doing quite well in their own way and saw no reason to invest in such a high-risk venture as a joint-stock company. However, in 1822, when this venture was changed to a less risky investment company awaiting incorporation within Lower Canada as a chartered bank, Molson and Sons decided to purchase a goodly portion of shares.

With the granting of a Royal Charter during the summer, and with John Molson Jr. representing them as shareholders on the board of directors, it certainly appeared they had made a good investment, though nothing could have been farther from the truth. A disastrous run on several well-established banks in England and the defaulting on loans and lines of credit of others during the year devalued many old country family fortunes. The newly chartered Bank of Montreal holding promissory notes for funds borrowed against these family assets had a dire crisis on its hands.

This caused great bickering among the shareholders and the tabling of a nonconfidence vote. Orchestrated in part by John Molson Jr., a new president had to be elected, and this left a vacancy on the board of directors. John the Elder graciously agreed to fill this vacancy,then just as graciously agreed to fill the office of president when the recently elected incumbent stepped down in favor of him. Now sixty-four years of age, John Molson Sr. would guide the Bank of Montreal through the next four years to realize an 800 percent increase in business, while paying the highest dividend ever to its shareholders.

By 1827 John the Elder had stepped down from local politics, but five years later did accept an appointment by Lord Aylmer to the legislative council becoming "The Honorable John Molson" on his sixty-ninth birthday. That same year of 1832, the assembly gave Royal Assent to the incorporation of Canada's first railway. The Champlain and St. Lawrence Railroad would span the fourteen-mile land gap between Laprairie on the south shore of the St. Lawrence River and St. Jean at the head of navigation on the Richelieu River.

Running on wooden rail capped with strips of wrought iron, the tiny 2-2-0 wood-fired locomotive pulled several stagecoaches fitted with flanged wheels, carrying passengers from Molson's steamships on the St. Lawrence to vessels on Lake Champlain, who would deliver them in comfort and safety to New York City. Molson's were a major investor in this venture—John Molson Jr. was president, and his brother William one of the original directors. Unfortunately, its inaugural run on July 21, 1836, was saddened by the failure of its staunchest supporter to attend. The Honorable John Molson had passed away after a severe bout of the flu.

Suffering from fatigue after a stormy fall session of the council, he passed quietly away at his country estate. In a will intended to ensure that a Molson would always control the family brewing business, he had stipulated that the brewery would be bequeathed to his grandson John Molson, son of Thomas Molson. He conditioned this by further stipulating if this could not be realized then the brewery should be bequeathed to his next grandson named John Molson.

The years that followed saw the brewery and distillery at St. Mary's Current change relationship. Political sentiments in Canada were running hot, and Papineau's patriots created rebellious scenes, which called forth the militia and Major John Molson to suppress. Not perhaps too surprisingly, they suffered a mysterious fire at the brewery and, shortly thereafter, another fire at a block of their buildings in Quebec City.

The latter caused a suit to be brought against them by their tenants for loss of chattels; the former saw the distillery rebuilt to production levels far exceeding that of the brewery, as it would continue to do so for the next twenty-five years. John Molson Jr. after his service in the militia was one of twelve Honorable Gentlemen appointed in 1838 by General Sir John Colborne to administer the affairs of Lower Canada during the period of martial law in Montreal.

The enactment in England of the Corn Act of 1843 removed much of the import duties on Canadian wheat, stimulating wheat farming and bringing new prosperity to Canada. The efforts of the English Protestant temperance movement actually enhanced the sales of Molson's spirits, driving their production up over a quarter million gallon a year. This caused William and Thomas to buy up a second distillery, and the spent grain from both were used to fatten livestock, which Molson now began to raise and sell. Gross sales from these enterprises realized well over a million dollars a year.

By 1847, when they became major shareholders in the New City Gas Company, the withdrawal of the Corn Act signaled the beginning of a depression in Canada that saw grain and lumber rotting at shipping points waiting for orders that never came. In 1852 a fire ravished the entire east end of Montreal, gutting the brewery and distillery at St. Mary's Current. Recalling the drastic reduction of spirit sales during the recent depression, Molson's did not rebuild the distillery.

In 1854 William and the "Honorable" John Molson received a license to create Molson's Bank. Private banks were required to always hold one-third their credit in hard currency, and failure to make repayment within ten days could revoke their license. Fortunately, the Molson edict had always ensured solvency, and on several occasions when a run was instigated on this fledgling bank by its big brother, the Bank of Montreal, William Molson had sufficient gold and coins on hand to stave off these demands. Surviving these attempts to discredit it, Molson's Bank received its charter by act of parliament in 1855.

William Molson was also a founding director of the Grand Trunk Railway, and in 1856, its first train from Toronto puffed into Montreal amid cannons roaring, bands playing and people cheering. At the age of seventy-three, during the summer of 1860, the honorable John Molson Jr. succumbed to dropsy (retention of body fluids), an illness that had plagued him much during his final years. Just three years later, his brother Thomas Molson died after suffering a massive stroke, and in 1875 William Molson, president of Molson's Bank, president of the Montreal General Hospital and governor of McGill University passed away in his eighty-second year. His funeral procession was over a half-mile long, and he was interred at the Mount Royal Cemetery.

The brewery at St. Mary's Current, though upstaged for a quarter of a century by Thomas Molson's distillery, proved the undisputable golden horn. It ensured wealth and opportunity to the Molson's off-spring who ventured even farther a field in this country's commerce and defense following their forefather's example. Thus, creating a greater Canada to the betterment of all.

The man we now meet was the epitome of this long lineage of tradition. Senator Hartland Molson, youngest son of Herbert Molson who had been the eldest son of John Thomas Molson, and grandson of Thomas Molson, master brewer and distiller who had been the son of John Molson the Elder. Hartland Molson had been one of those "valiant few" whom Winston Churchill proclaimed saved England during those desperate times of the Battle of Britain when Germany's *Luftwaffe* boastfully alluded to crushing the British people under a continuous rain of bombs.

But the RAF's fighter command, which included Canada's No. 1 Fighter Squadron composed of many young pilots of Hartland's caliber, deemed otherwise. They flew their Hurricanes and Spitfires on round the clock scrambles that saw Hitler's bombers and escort fighters falling to earth in such numbers that the Nazi hordes feared to mount an invasion of this last remaining tiny bastion of freedom.

Afforded the best education Canada had to offer, both Hartland and his brother Tom Molson held commissions with the 27th Field Artillery after graduating from the Royal Military College. Upon the failure of a soy bean/plastic venture in 1933, Hartland, guided by Canada's famous WWI flying ace Billy Bishop, took flying lessons through the Montreal Aeroplane Club. He and his brother Tom then bought Dominion Skyways, a two-plane bushline into northern

Ontario and Quebec. During Hartland's four years as president, they increase their fleet to fifteen aircraft, but still just barely managed to stay out of debt.

In 1938, just a few months before his father's death, Hartland and Tom sold the airline and joined the brewery. Thomas Molson bequeathed his estate to his two daughters and two sons. Hartland received two-sevenths of his estate, his brother got three-sevenths. Both agreed the most capable person to run the family brewery was their cousin Herbert William Molson, who had carried out a role of general manager for more than a quarter of a century. Hartland became Bert's executive assistant.

In September the following year, war was declared with Germany, and the Molson boys were quick to volunteer. John Molson, though a major in the Black Watch, soon transferred over into the Canadian Navy. Tom Molson, after carrying out a ship acquisition for Canada, took up his duty as a gunnery officer, but Hartland applied for commission in the Royal Canadian Air Force.

His flying experience stood him well, and after a winter's training at Camp Borden he arrived in England shortly after the Dunkirk evacuation of Europe. His 115th RCAF Squadron was merged with the Royal Air Force's No. 1 Fighter Squadron, just in time for the Battle of Britain. They became the first Canadians to fight the *Luftwaffe*. Flying the heavily armed Mark 11 Hurricanes, and after two months of almost continuous air battles which discouraged Hitler in launching an island invasion, he found himself under fire from a 109 Messerschmitt, which had locked on his tail.

Shot through the leg and foot, his plane damaged and out of control, he bailed out. Landing in the trees of an English wood side, a patrol of home guard soldiers assisted him to a field station, where after a short stay in a hospital he was shipped back to Canada to convalesce. Promoted to squadron leader of the 118 Fighter Squadron, he became Air Staff Officer of Eastern Command in 1943 and retired in 1945 as group captain.

In 1945, as John, Tom and Hartland rejoined the brewery, Herbert Molson split the company's common shares twenty-five for one and offered 150,000 of these shares to the public at $20 each. This financed an expansion of the brewery and initiated his plan to turn Molson's into a public company. While the first refrigeration system had not been installed at the brewery until 1902 nor the first automatic bottling machine till 1909, this was still considered aggressive management by other brewers like Eugene O'Keefe, Tom Carling, Hugh Labatt and Norman Dawes.

However, when Molson's hung onto their last brewery horse until 1947, and many chuckled at their conservativeness, the events that follow prove Molsons was still very aggressive and hardnosed where business was concerned. Herbert Molson's failure to act swiftly on Norman Dawe's offer to sell controlling interest in National Breweries to Molson's, allowed E. P. Taylor of the Toronto-based Canadian Breweries (which then owned O'Keefe, Brading and Carling breweries) to offer much higher prices for the preferred shares (each carrying four votes). Thus, they gained control of the company and a foothold in the Quebec beer market.

Merged into Canadian Breweries in 1952, and renamed Dawe's Breweries, E. P. Taylor began a beer war with Molson's that aroused the interest of another Ontario brewer. John Labatt in Ontario began advertising their product's French-Canadian ancestry to encourage more sales in Quebec. But by 1953, through the introduction of Molson's Golden Ale and the lightening up of their Export Ale, Molson's reversed the trend of these inroads, while quietly setting the stage to enter E. P. Taylor's and John Labatt's private preserves in Ontario.

Herbert Molson's decision to retire caused some concern about who should succeed him. John Molson was the senior family member with more than thirty years service in the brewery. Tom, the largest shareholder, had served almost as long and was equally knowledgeable of the brewing business. Additionally, he was a fine engineer, but was modest and retiring. Hartland, the second largest shareholder, though knowledgeable about the brewery was neither a brewer nor an engineer. But he was a good accountant who understood high finance.

Always considered a bit of a rebel, he had that flair of daring-do that set him apart from other mere mortals who had not soared on high. It was a touch of charisma that gave him the air of royalty, which caused his tall slender stature to stand out in any crowd. Though Herbert Molson believe him most suited for the aggressive plans about to unfold, he asked Walter Gordon (later finance minister of Canada) of Woods Gordon to council the family on the best suited to take over the reins.

Molson's was the largest brewery in Canada and tenth largest in

North America. Walter Gordon advised that Hartland be appointed president of the company and Tom appointed vice-president. But Hartland was without sons to follow him, and this generation gap concerned him as he stepped into the family leader role. Tom's two sons, Eric and Stephen, were still at school and would be too young for executive positions for another decade, as would John Molson's son David.

Hartland asked his cousin P. T. Molson, then executive assistant to Lester B. Pearson, to give up his government position and enter the brewery as his assistant. When he accepted, Hartland announced to the press that Molson's Brewery was expanding into Ontario. No indication was given that in lifting their sights thus, Molson's were actually aiming much farther west—the Pacific Coast to be exact.

The piece of property they selected was on Fleet Street and owned in part by their archrival Canadian Breweries. To twig E. P. Taylor's nose effectively and ensure he was aware of their arrival, they negotiated through an intermediary, had P. T. Molson sign the deed, then phoned Eddie Taylor and told him to remove his large mobile beer advertisement sign from their new property.

With this salvo, the gloves were off. Tom Molson was responsible for the design, and in 1955 this $12-million brewery, breaking with Molson's longtime tradition of producing ale, launched Crown and Anchor Lager beer, which immediately captured a large segment of both E. P. Taylor's and Labatt's Ontario market.

The speed with which Hartland broke this tradition shocked the aging Herbert Molson, and four months before this brewery opened its doors, Bert Molson died of a stroke. A month before Crown and Anchor beer hit the pubs, Hartland accepted an appointment from Prime Minister Louis St. Laurent to the Canadian senate and in November of that same year made his first speech in the Upper House.

In 1957, Hartland and Tom Molson bought Senator Donat Raymond's shares in the Canadian Arena Company. This company was formed in 1924 by a small group of subscribers, five of whom were senior Molsons members, and owned the Montreal Forum and the Montreal Canadiens hockey club. This position of controlling ownership allowed them to share television time with Imperial Oil Company on the CBC's *Hockey Night in Canada* show, and this gave them national advertising. With this realized, Tom Molson made a trip across Canada to assess the potential of purchasing existing breweries west of Toronto.

Molson's Capilano Brewery, note the new neon logo panel and rotating tower sign.
Credit: A. G. Pugh collection

His first stop was Winnipeg and the Fort Garry Brewery, where he introduced himself as Mr. Wilson—an alias he continued for the remainder of his trip. In Calgary he met the Cross family to negotiate for Calgary Brewing and Malting, then he met Emil Sick in Seattle, but their talks came to a stalemate. The following year, after Jack McGillis a trusted adviser to the Molson family had conversation with Emil's son-in-law Nick McPhee, Hartland Molson made a trip to Seattle to talk again with this West Coast beer baron.

This effort failed, as did two more attempts, before Tom Molson suggested that perhaps a form of redeemable preferred shares, which would have the effect of deferring tax payments, might sit better with Emil's corporate background. Surprisingly, it did. The formal offer to the Sick shareholders was made in October, 1958, $27 million, of which $9 million in Molson shares were redeemable in 1963, was accepted for the Sick Brewery holdings. Molson's now owned two American breweries, one in Seattle and another in Spokane. In Canada, they owned a brewery in B.C., two more in Alberta and another pair in Saskatchewan.

In 1960, Molson secured the Fort Garry Brewery from the Hoeschen family of Winnipeg. And finally in 1962, after difficult negotiations with both the O'Dea family and Premier Joey Smallwood, they purchased the Newfoundland Brewing Company. Thus, they realized a brewing empire, sea to sea.

CHAPTER SEVEN

Stretching Out

The first outward sign of the Capilano Brewery's new eastern connection was the addition of Molson's name to that of Sicks as co-owners of the brewery, in gold gothic letters on the administration office's front door. Few took notice, and even less was made of the slight change to the beer bottle labels. But later the renaming of the brewery from Sick's Capilano to Molson's Capilano Brewery and the replacement of the famous revolving large 6 on top of the weather tower, with an equally large but less renown M, drew snorts of disapproval and predictions of dire consequences from the staunch Sick brewery fans. Many of them viewed it as a sad loss of local heritage.

Yet, ten years hence in 1968, when Molson's eradicated the last signs of the Sick era by removing the name Capilano from the brewery's logo, few really took notice. The reason, Old Style beer sales had failed to recapture its former market share, even with the best performances Ben Valerie had to offer. Molson's Export Ale and Canadian, promoted through national advertising, had established these as "the" brands. And most beer drinkers boggled with high-powered, high-quality advertisement by the big three brewers vying for their patronage, favored a certain brew more by its catchy jingle than by its flavor or body. This would certainly be true of those who had just come of age to buy a cool glass of beer.

Within the brewery, the employee's lunchroom probably felt the first change of corporate policy. This friendly, cheerful spot had been Mecca to many who traveled in from all points throughout the city to enjoy the hospitality of a free beer or two. Originally intended to follow the old Powell Street Brewery practice of always having a keg on tap and a mug nearby for a visitor's taste of the brew, it had truly grown grossly out of hand.

While a number of grand seniors regularly visited the brewery lunchroom during the quiet of the afternoon and quaffed a complimentary beer while reminiscing about the days of yore, a large numbers of trades people, truck drivers and city workers who had business at, or near, the brewery during the busier hours of the day crowded the small facility to the inconvenience of anyone trying to take a lunch or coffee break. This was even more evident at the end of the work day, when lengthy discussions with a great cross section of both brewery worker and townspeople was lubricated with Old Style brew.

While the administration building to the south of the brewery housed a large hospitality room for invited guests, tour groups and VIPs, and the brew master had a small taste lounge off his office on the top floor of the brewery for his more critical guests, the beer tap and coffee facilities in the employee's lunchroom was the unofficial goodwill welcome center. Tap man Archie Bird often had his wife join him to make toast or sandwiches for the boys. From the time the gates were opened in the morning until they were closed at night, people dropped in. Even the train crews putting away their locomotives for the night came over for a beer. It was often jocularly asserted that the employee's lunchroom tap at Capilano actually dispensed more free beer than some of our hotel accounts sold.

Molson's initiated a policy to reduce this obvious misuse of good intentions by controlling the number of complimentary beers a visitor could enjoy through a chit system and limiting visiting hours. While Sick's had really never attempted to curtail the consumption of beer by their employees (at Powell Street each man had his own copper mug and could fill it as often as he wished), they did have an iron-clad house rule that made no exceptions: any employee unable to carry out his work due to over indulgences in the product would be instantly dismissed. Molson's new policy, while retaining this stipulation, went a step further by limiting the number of beers each employee could consume while on the job, and defining the maximum amount of time they could remain on the premises after their hours of work—possibly the strangest regulations ever imposed upon a work force. But they offered a much improved pension plan, one that ensured their retirees could enjoy many of those nice things other pensioners apparently could not. And that has proved of a far greater value than the odd purloined glass of beer.

Probably the most noteworthy event of public notice at this time was the production of Molson's Export Ale. Art Pugh, with the help

The carbon dioxide collection system in the B block fermenting cellar. *Photo: Molsons*

of Eric Molson, designed and built the first experimental ale cellar using mostly all brewery labor. It was one of the last in-plant construction jobs carried out at Burrard Street. Henceforth, the demands placed on the brewery and its staff precluded carrying out such types of projects. It was farmed out on a cost-plus basis or bid upon by local contractors. For this small ale cellar, only the large steel ale tank, brine piping and tile setting were jobbed out.

For weeks the brewery crew worked diligently in a confined area off the mezzanine cooking floor adjacent to the cold area of the fermenting cellar. They broke out concrete, placed in new forms and rebar, then finally poured cement to realize a low ceiling cellar to house the special open-topped ale fermenting tank and its small yeast culture room.

Unlike lager beers, such as Old Style and Canadian, whose bottom-activating yeast is retained by internal standpipes (remember the weir pipe in the hot wort tank?), ale yeast ferments on the top surface of the wort. Thus, the yeasty crud that quickly grows over the ales surfaces has to be continuously removed to encourage fermentation, and this requires an open-topped tank with facilities for skimming.

While some of this yeast must be collected, washed and cultured for the next brew, because of its high air content none of the carbon dioxide gas is collected and it must be evacuated by exhaust fans. Because this gas is life threatening, the cellar had its own alarm warning and fresh air purge system, and it was capable of being sealed off from all the other cellar areas.

B block cellar was the second advancement and was more noticeable to the man on the street. Molson's had created a western division office in Calgary with Grant Allen heading an engineering team based there to assist each brewery with its new construction. Bruno Sobchuck, his one and only draftsman, drew up the construction plans for B block. And Art Pugh, donning his high-topped project engineer boots and with Eric Molson still at his side, superintended its construction.

Located between the south end of the existing three-storied A block cellars and the administration office building, its one-story concrete construction was well hidden behind a high cement wall that faced Burrard Street. Often referred to as the Burns and Dutton cellar after the contractors who built it, eight 15,500-gallon, glass-lined steel horizontal finishing tanks were housed in its brine-chilled refrigeration area, while the smaller working area containing the tank valves and gauges in a hose aisle were not. This first attempt at a two-temperature cellar pointed up much that could be done to improve on the theory.

Later construction on this plan of cellaring saw heavily insulated tanks with internal chilling ability, mounted completely within uninsulated cellar blocks at ambient temperature. In the final form, discussed later, these tanks were designed for vertical installation and insulated and weather proofed for exterior erection with suitable piping, etc., taken into sterile pumping and control areas. This design was much like the modern oil refinery tank farms utilize.

Len Jones arrived to take over as brewmaster and Grant Waddell moved to Winnipeg to become brewmaster of the newly acquired Fort Garry Brewery. Len's serious countenance, sharp eye and direct questions unnerved the older hands, and many sadly missed Grant's jovial approach to the brewing business. This was unfortunate for Len was known to smile at times and even show a humorous aside once in a while, but he was always serious when it came to running the brewery.

His dedication improved production, and belatedly most of the employees came to appreciate him not only as an outstanding brewmaster, but also as a fair and reasonable man. Through his short tenure at Capilano, production of beer was outstandingly improved. The following is just one incident of many he was responsible for, and though it was highly experimental, it required very little modifications to realize.

Contact with other brewers had always been maintained through the Master Brewers Association, which organized seminars, lectures, meetings, plant visits and conventions. But Molson's, now becoming a national brewer, felt there was also a need to bring all their own senior brewers and engineers together once a year to review and discuss company problems, procedures and policies. On attending Molson's first national engineering conference in Montreal, Art Pugh was twigged by a story from one of his eastern counterparts. It concerned a pipe welding error that appeared to have produced a surprising improvement in the separation of brewing trube within the hot wort tank.

As noted earlier, hot wort from the kettle contained a certain percentage of carried-over solids from the cooking and lautering process, hop particles and slippery little strings of gelatinized protein, all of which the brewers referred to as trube. Two major requirements for a clear and sparkling beer is the removal of all these cooking solids and the complete absence of any yeast spores from the fermenting process that followed.

While John Molson, the elder, had resorted to a gelatine recovered from fish viscera, called isinglass, to clarify his ale back in the 1800s when river ice was unavailable, chilling, settling and filtering had historically been the accepted method used to remove solids and yeast spores after fermentation. Modern-day pasteurizing can ensure bottled beers up to ninety days normal shelf life. Thus, the more trube removed before fermentation, the more efficient the final removal of yeast through chilling and filtering.

Art Pugh discussed this welding incident with both Grant Allen and Len Jones before getting the nod to try it out. The results were spectacular. They welded to the pipe that discharged through the top wall into the hot wort tank, an internal steel elbow cast on a downward angle off the vertical of approximately forty degrees, sufficient to create a swirling action within the tank when tested with plain water. Fortunately, Art decided to fit a taller removable standpipe of door height, in the outlet through the tank's sloped bottom, before trying out the effects with a hot brew. After the wort had been drawn off to the height of the standpipe and the door could be opened for inspection, they were amazed at the tall pile of solids that rested in the center of the tank bottom.

The height and angle of repose of this rather slippery cone of trube, indicated that the swirling action of the wort upon entering the tank from the tangentially directed nozzle near the top had created a vortex, or quiet zone, in the center of the tank, which allowed much of the solids to settle out and drop to the tank bottom. The swirling hot wort acted like a compactor, forcing each grain husk to remain where it dropped on top of those below it.

But another phenomenon actually took place as the depth of hot wort in the tank increased during filling, which really put the icing on the cake so to speak, and one that in later years would be used to create a cold boil in the tall unitanks. This was a thermal chimney in which the hot wort (180-plus°F) came in contact with the relatively cold bronze tank sides during the swirling action and gave up some of its heat, thus becoming slightly cooler and more dense than the wort which swirled around closer to the center where such thermal conduction was not as great. The hotter, and therefore lighter, wort near the center was displaced upwards by the cooler and slightly heavier wort that had come in contact with the tank sides, and this caused some of the lighter trube to also be carried upwards (much the same quiet phenomenon as is found in the eye of a hurricane or in the upsurging center of a cyclone or twister's spout).

When coupled with the reduction in swirl action near the center of the tank as filling progressed, this fine light sediment settled over the trube pile like chocolate on a fat ice cream cone and, more amazingly, stayed there as the wort was withdrawn from around it. Naturally, there were improvements to this method over the years, better draw-off piping, better tank-bottom configuration to retain the trube, and finally a new and larger hot wort tank incorporating all these improvements.

When this was reported in the fall at the next convention, it certainly became a topic for much discussion and experimentation by the other brewers. For Capilano, the immediate results from this method were very gratifying. Their centrifuges, which were not continuous cleaning types, often allowed trube to slip over into the starter tanks. After installation of the tangential nozzle and the startling reduction in this trube carryover, starter tanks became available on much faster turn around or not needed at all. In fact, as the months went by even the ruhing (aging) time was reduced. Altogether, and of course other process improvements also contributed to this statement, the brewery reduced the time between boiling the brew and racking or bottling the beer from more than forty days to under four weeks.

This realized almost a fifty percent increase in brewing production capabilities and prompted Len Jones to experiment with a top draw-off arrangement from the lauter tun that decreased the time to fill the kettle and boil a brew of beer thus increasing the number of brews produced each day. While increasing production with the same equipment reduced the unit cost, it also had a far greater saving in staving off that costly period when money would have to be spent to actually enlarge the brewery. No wonder Molson's quickly modified their other breweries in a similar manner. And it was only fitting that Art was sent there to guide them. This was the beginning of Art Pugh's rise to Engineering Superintendent of the Western Division.

As stated earlier, these were trying times. The population of the lower mainland was on an increase, and property taxes reflecting their demand for services to new housing development rose dramatically. Industries abandoned their highly taxed city locations and located more modern facilities farther out into the rural areas of the Fraser River delta areas, thus enjoying both a lower tax burden and a less confining location for expansion. Their migration away from the city enticed the commercial industries supplying them to promptly follow, freeing up large areas of city property for housing development, and many of these new neighbors enjoyed a glass of Molson's suds.

Through an active campaign of improved marketable beers and national advertisement, Capilano had managed to recover much of the market share that had been lost earlier to the competition, but the volume of even this modest (22–24 percent) market share had increased the numbers to where it was challenging the brewery's production capabilities to hold on to it. This was most noticeable with the packaged beers, even though the bottle shop had increased its staff and had begun to work two full shifts a day.

To accommodate greater output and provide sufficient storage of used and new bottles, a new warehouse area across the north end of the bottle shop was designed that departed from the brewery's standard of reinforced concrete. A huge hollow slab was built as a foundation, then walls of hollow concrete bricks framed in windows on the west side and large roller shipping doors on the north and east sides. Roofed over with corrugated steel carried on steel box girder joist, it was suitably weatherproofed with an overlay of felt, tar and gravel.

This construction plus the building of a small slab and concrete block building adjacent to the rail spur, east of the employee's building, for filtering and treating the water supply, were really the first noticeable signs of the brewery stretching outward. To service the new warehouse a double spur of rail was brought in from the east fence and laid along the north wall, and the parking area between this spur and the original one serving the train shed area was blacktopped.

Bob Henry now began to plan how he could install a new and larger packaging line, while maintaining current levels of bottling with the old line, even though both commitments would have to be realized in much the same area. How this was accomplished is a credit not only to Bob and Art who were on the front line, and Grant Allen and Bruno who guided them from Western Division in Calgary, but to the people on the bottle shop floor who cheerfully carried on production while equipment and conveyors were shuffled around them in a most intimidating manner.

One of the first items that arrived in late 1962 was one of the biggest—a two-deck pasteurizer with four times the capacity of the existing Barry-Waynemiller unit. Less than ten years before, Moon Cameron who moved over from the Powell Street brewery where he daily lifted heavy trays of bottle beer into a tall circular pasteurizer, had thought the Barry-Waynemiller unit the greatest cure for a sore back he had ever seen.

No one would have faulted the original nice new packaging center at Capilano Brewery on Burrard Street. Its satisfying, but modest, eighty-five bottles a minute output created a melodious chorus of tinkling clinking glass, staccato click-clack of labeler fingers and the heavier base thud of the drop packer, which timed the orchestration of brown bottles like soldiers on parade from washer all the way through to the carton gluer. But the bottle shop's continued expansion through the next quarter century, until it reached the unbelievable output of 2,000 bottles a minute was the real test of the workers' metal. Though they staggered at times from the physical demands it made upon them, and yes, some even perished along the way, they never gave up. Though it was a bloody battle, it was wonderful to experience that camaraderie of youth showing up in the new hands who took over as the senior hands retired.

The new pasteurizer, the relocated filler and crowner, and the connecting conveyors and inspection stations were all sandwich in between the bottling cellar to the west and an equally large cold room storing hotel bottle beer to the east along the south wall. Then the old Barry-Waynemiller pasteurizer unit was ripped out, as was Bob's office and the uncasing saws, so the huge new hydro jet bottle washer could be dragged in and erected for service.

This monster grew until it dominated the northwest corner of the bottle shop, even the old bottle washer, which continued to carry on its valiant struggle, seemed to shrink into insignificance. A gang of World Tandem labelers and two drop-packers, plus inspectors and two large carton sealers took up the remaining floor space as the old equipment was slowly phased out. Art Pugh built Bob Henry a small hanging office, like a birdcage on the wall above his new soaker, then installed a Mathew's palletizer in the warehouse and connected the carton sealers with it through an overhead conveyor from the compression belt.

Cases of beer tiered five high on pallet boards were whisked from the palletizer by powered forklift trucks and stored in the new warehouse. Trucks backing up to the east end of this building, where an overhead canopy sheltered the doors, were loaded with full pallets by bridging the gap to the warehouse floor with a steel plate so that battery-powered pallet movers could trundle right aboard the truck, and stow them without further handling. Each brewery truck was supplied with a manual pallet mover for discharging.

Boxcars were spotted opposite the doors in the north wall, and pallet loads of beer were tightly hand stowed into their interior to reduce shifting. This was further improved upon when an inflatable cushion was sandwiched between the pallet boards set on edge in the center of the boxcar doorway, which when inflated pressed heavily against the cases of beer in each end of the box car, reducing their ability to move.

But so violent were the gyrations of the boxcars when they were being switched in the yards on their way to our interior customers, that even this failed to prevent costly bottle breakage and product damage. Such rough handling could not be tolerated for long, and within a couple years as Phil Gaglardi improved the roads into the interior, Capilano changed to trailer truck delivery. Thus, the railroad's pursuit of efficiency in promoting flying switching (each boxcar is shook loose of its coupler and bashes like a demon of hell into any other rail car parked down grade of it), lost them business and left the brewery with two redundant rusting rail spurs.

Both new and used (recycled) bottles were received by Maurice Turcott at the two most western doors on the north side of this warehouse. And here Art Pugh installed an innovative approach to uncasing bottles, which lent itself to further improvement, yet never quite realized a fully automatic approach to what must be considered the most horrendous handling problem in the brewery. He designed a series of revolving disc saws that cut off the top portion of the cardboard carton, then built a twelve-point ganged bottle picker which lifted the bottles up by their necks onto the soaker in-feed conveyor, while the two portions of the cut carton dropped down a chute to a baler. This was later improved upon by running the cartons of bottles across the blade of a high-speed band saw that deftly cut away the bottom leaving the bottles unscathed to continue down the conveyor to the bottle washer, while the upper carton part was whisked by belt to the baler. With these improvements, Bob Henry was able to realize bottle runs of 400 to 500 bottles per minute, quite an improvement over the 85 bpm of the old line. This allowed, for a short time at least, the return to a single-shift operation.

In the brew house, Len Jones made one last improvement before he left for Calgary. The boil rings in the 200-barrel kettle left much to be desired. Like two large donuts, the top one slightly smaller than the lower one and joined together by a series of vertical riser, they were slow to create a rolling boil and, because of their large capacity, slow to reduce the action when the boil became too active. Len Jones replaced this affair with a vertical percolator type, having three twenty-four-inch phosphor bronze tubes. These double-walled steam tubes reacted quickly to the brewer's demands, and their violent ebullition was something to behold. The boiling kettle could be made to look like a giant fountain with rather serious overtones if great care was not exercised. This possibility quickly realized the installation of a temperature-sensitive boil over probe, which activated an air-to-close valve on kettle steam.

Vic Brachat, longtime brewmaster at Labatts in New Westminster, called this type of percolator built by Ellett Copper and Brass a very valued addition to his brewery over on Brunette Street. While his recollections of Grant Waddell and Len Jones were very pleasant, of John Britnell he was unstinting in his accolades.

"A wonderful person, we all liked John," he chuckled. "You know it was really he who got the B.C. group of Western Canada Master Brewers going. His easy going nature infected us all."

As Len Jones' successor, John came into Capilano Brewery like a breath of spring. An extremely talented old country brewer with a lot of new ideas, he soon had all infected with the urge to follow. (Playing on the Diefenbaker election slogan of the 1960s "Follow John," some wag took it a step farther and painted large white footprints all over our blacktop driveways that led to the brew house.) John Britnell was a large man in all ways, able to spare a moment to listen to a gripe, a suggestion or a joke with equal appreciation—cocking his head like an attentive robin to the former, nodding it in understanding for the latter or tossing it back to give a rich chuckle as the punch line allowed him to continue on his way.

John served the war years in the Royal Navy, and during the Norwegian campaign when Hitler was hiding some of his capital ships in the deep fjords of that coast, John commanded a small submarine that was sent to infiltrate their defenses and blow them up. He

John Britnell, longtime brewmaster, receiving a departing gift from fellow employees.
Photo: B. Meyers

recalled his greatest problems in these tiny submarines (being taller and more husky then most) was after his crew were squeezed into their assigned areas fore and aft of the conning tower, John had to fit his bulk into the remaining area under the hatch and periscope. As this was the only area big enough to swing a cat, John had to carry out the duty of cook for his crew by boiling water for prepackaged meals in a single electric hot plate between his legs. John made light of those harrowing patrols, where the weather was almost as hazardous as the antisubmarine defenses. This background experience made running a brewery seem like child's play, hence John could chuckle over minor setbacks and usually scheme up a better way to approach it. While John Britnell and his assistant brewmaster Ernie Dayton would herald in many new improvement and brewery additions, the era of their arrival seemed reminiscent of the earlier years.

Under this curtain of tranquility the brewery workers were able to rest on their laurels and allow their interests to spread out into other pursuits. Though only a few from Capilano really got involved with the preservation of the former wooden-hulled steam tug *Master*, the brewery quietly supported its role in many ways. This was especially true during the really difficult period of getting her through steamship inspection. A neglected three-year layup had allowed river pirates to steal or vandalize her vital parts and the weather to seep in and rust her steel parts or create dry rot within her wooden parts. Fortunately, both Art Pugh and Frank Edwards of the World Ship Society became interested in the project. In 1962, Frank and I signed the transfer papers and gave Gilley Bros. (the historic logging family for whom Gilley Ave. in Burnaby is named) the funds that had been raised before they could change their mind. The World Ship Society a group of ship lovers that preferred to limit their dreams to preserving pictures and stories not becoming a ship owner, generously agreed to give support to the tug project if the tug had its own identity. Thus the project was registered in 1962 as S.S. Master Preservation Society to limit financial responsibility.

Moored right behind the brewery at the fishermen's dock, the true scope of the work involved to get her seaworthy again evaporated away the rosy hue of euphoric ownership. It was Art Pugh who really took over the project and ensured success through his keen interest and great talents. Brewery manager Tom English, a member of the Royal Vancouver Yacht Club who later became their commodore, brought the project to Molson's attention and got their blessing to give limited assistance to the project's needs.

While Tom English had risen through the office ranks at Powell Street to become manager and later president of the Burrard Street brewery, his love of the sea had been nurtured more by his weekend yachting pursuits. So joining in with sweat and strain in the dirty bowels of this musty relic of the steam age was really a revelation that he attempted only under Art's trusted guidance. Art Pugh on the

The A block cellar upper floor addition with 12,000-gallon fermenter being delivered.

Photo: A. G. Pugh collection

other hand was right at home anywhere aboard the tug, having served his last years at sea as chief engineer on a large CNR tug towing rail car barges from Port Mann in the Fraser River to Victoria on Vancouver Island.

Art Pugh hailed from central Australia and served his machinist apprenticeship at Fremantle before going to sea as an engineer on a coal-burning freighter plying the Indian Ocean. The Japanese invasion down through Indonesia isolated this distant realm of the empire and forced Art to sail to England, where he was re-assigned under the War Emergences Act to a high priority job repairing submarines' Kingston valves. A fortunate paper shuffle in 1943 allowed him to join the Canadian Merchant Navy and sail as second engineer.

Coming ashore in late 1948, he successfully wrote his B.C. provincial engineer's exams and was employed at the Marpole Box Company, when the opportunity to join Don McRoberts building the Burrard Street brewery presented itself. Thus, he was well aware that the local fleet of tugs, freighters and passengers ships were rapidly being consigned to the ship breaker's hammer or sold foreign as coastal industries relocated nearer to road or railway services. For Art it was a labor of love that centered on the fine little Beardmore triple expansion steam engine and its two-furnace Scotch Marine boiler. He cheerfully took on the lion's share of the real work required to realize this dream and convinced his longtime friend Al Kinsmen to join him.

Former wartime sailing buddies, Captain Kinsmen was a first-class rigger and an ardent Chippy Chap (nickname for a shipwright in wood construction) who quickly took over the removal and replacement of much of the damaged wooden parts of the ship.

By late March of 1963 we were able to raise steam, blow the whistle and prove out the steering gear. In mid-April, Art cautiously rocked the cranks back and forth, working out the condensate and warming up the cylinders, before rolling over the main engine. Taking a cautious strain on new mooring lines with the engine running slow ahead for an hour or two, he tested out the link driven air and feed pumps and their piping. In early May, and with a slight bit of trepidation, the *Master* let go her lines and eased out of the crowded berth. What an exciting moment for all those who had worked so hard to realize it.

That summer of 1963, the *Master* took part in Vancouver's first

Sea Festival, became mother ship for the B.C. Salmon Derby, and in December became the port's official carol ship. The next summer, Mayor Frank Ney of Naniamo invited the tug to act as mother ship in a publicity stunt he and his city would become world famous for—the Nanaimo Bathtub Race. Vancouver City, not to be upstage by this small island metropolis, officially commemorated the tug by placing a picture of it on their vehicle safety stickers. Thus, every motorist on the lower mainland eventually had a tiny picture of the *Master* plastered on the lower right hand corner of his or her windshields.

While all this was going on, events at the brewery were becoming equally exciting. First, a wort-holding tank was installed below the brew kettle, and this allowed sparging off from the lauter tun while the kettle was still boiling off the previous brew, thus reducing the time between brews. By installing heating jackets in this tank, the wort was kept hot and quickly brought up to a boil when pumped up into the kettle. John Britnall also experimented with malt extract to speed up the brewing time. Overall, he improved it sufficiently to warrant installing more fermenters to handle the additional brews.

To improve the overall capacity of the brewery, it was decided that a whole new fermenting cellar was the answer. The existing fermenting cellar would be converted into a ruhing (aging) cellar. The new fermenting cellar was of all-steel construction overlaid with a felted tar and gravel roof, and rose for another two floors above the existing three levels of A block. The total area within this new structure would be left at ambient temperature (unchilled) and unfinished, with just the work areas and hose aisle sealed off by easily cleaned bake enamel steel paneling.

Only twenty of the thirty-two 300-barrel stainless steel fermenters planned for were installed at this time. Built by Ellett Copper and Brass with dimpled side jackets for brine chilling, they were delivered to the rear storage area of the brewery where polyurethane insulation was gunited, sprayed thickly over their exteriors using an extra large paint sprayer, before they were lifted up by cranes and slid into place. All this took place during one of the Lower Mainland's worst winters, requiring large plastic tents to protect this temperature sensitive operation from the elements, which added even more cost to this difficult project.

With the completion of a small yeast culture cellar off the pent-

The A block fermenting cellar.

Photo: A. G. Pugh collection

house tank room and the former fermenting cellar of A3 insulated to maintain the lower ruhing temperatures of 32–34°F, a new ale cellar holding a pair of open top tanks was built into the former yeast culture room area. The new fermenters, being higher than our existing brine system service lines, required a vertical extension fitted to the return line that reached up to the mill room tower roof and the balance tank relocated there. Perhaps a word on this chilling system would be appropriate.

The brewery's refrigeration system used NH_3 (liquid ammonia) to chill a water and calcium chloride solution (brine), and this chilled brine was pumped to cooling jackets and air chillers throughout the brewery as a secondary refrigerant. To ensure an air-free system with a constant head (i.e., pressure), return brine (i.e., warm) was pumped through brine chillers in the engine room to a standpipe that rose up through the brewery. This was valved off at each floor to supply refrigeration needs; it terminated at a pressure-activated relief valve on the A3 roof, which discharged into the return loop.

The returning warm brine from each floor was discharged into a standpipe that rose up to a loop fitted with a balance tank before flowing back to the engine room through a return pipe. It was this loop and balance tank that had to be relocated up higher under the tower sign to maintain an air free system, and the pressure gauge in the engine room recalibrated to indicate the status of the brine level in the balance tank. A float-activated switch in the balance tank indicated a low level to the engineer through a flashing red indicator light warning him to add brine to the system.

To service the increased demands on this system, a third brine chiller, a larger brine pump and a larger ammonia receiver were added, and then a six-cylinder Hall ammonia compressor and a new Linde NH_3 evaporative condenser were installed. These improvements increased refrigeration capacity from 220 tons to 425 tons per day. Adding a 300 cfm (cubic ft./min.) two-stage Broom & Wade compressor with larger piping and a new desiccant dryer increased air to 400 cfm. These improvements allowed us to package 500 bottles per minute and brew almost a quarter of a million barrels of beer a year (at twenty-five gallons per barrel) or approximately 6,000,000 gallons a year.

But it was the fleet of large new trucks that gained the most notice from the man on the street. Painted in the distinctive Molson's colors of royal blue and bright gold, they sported a cab-over design, which boasted a fully enclosed cargo deck with pull down roller doors and a battery-powered pallet mover.

In November, 1964, at the age of three score and ten, Emil George Sick passed quietly away in Seattle. Through a lifetime he had forged together a dozen companies all allied to the family business of brewing beer. Through the years ahead, Molson's would elect a much different thrust, one which John Molson Sr. had pioneered 180 years earlier—diversification into one of Canada's first large conglomerates.

An event worthy of note that depicts the community spirit of the people who worked for this brewery was the creation of a rollover bed for Jean McLeod. Gordie McLeod was a lead hand in shipping and noted for his cheerful disposition and outspoken ways. Gordie and his wife Jean were avid bowlers. And because the engineer's team had such a limited group to draw from, Gordie McLeod volunteered to bowl with the engineers, while Jean joined the ladies team. All were shocked upon learning that Jean had broken her back in a bad fall, which would require many months of intense hospital care if she were to recover at all. Gordie began spending most of his hours away from the brewery at the hospital, catching what sleep he could in a chair at her side. On one of their many visits to the hospital, Alf Humphries and his wife Elsie learned that Jean had recovered sufficiently to actually be moved into her own home if a means could be found to rotate her in a rigid bed every four to six hours. A home nurse would even be provided during those hours Gordie had to be away at work if the condition could be realized.

The doctor explained the type of bed that was required. It had to have two sets of spring frames that could be fitted to a rotating member at the foot and head. Thus, when Jean was laying on her back, the second spring frame could be bolted down across her chest and legs with the complete unit rotating until she was laying on her stomach. The other spring could then be removed and her back washed and massaged and she could lay or sleep like this until it was time to roll her onto her back again.

Alf took away some measurements and the doctor's advice and then looked through the bits and pieces in his basement while he schemed out a plan. To get permission to weld these up into a bed at the brewery, he approached Art Pugh with his plan, and this got Art involved in the construction design. Harry (HMS *Repulse*) Payne, our machinist/engineer from the Royal Navy, volunteered to turn out the pins and casters. Bob Berger, and others, ground down the welds and made all the surfaces smooth and uniform. Then our master painter Gordon McVean began applying the numerous coats of special paint that brought the finish up to hospital standards.

Approved by Vancouver General Hospital, Jean was discharged to its care for the remaining six to eight months of her convalescence, while enjoying the comforts and privacy of her home. When the rollover bed was no longer required, it was cleaned, repainted and donated to Vancouver General Hospital for others who might require similar treatment.

CHAPTER EIGHT

Fire Sale

Gus Fortier had joined the Molson Brewery in 1965 as plant electrician during the latter stages of Hume and Rumbles upgrading of the packaging center's electrics and the installation of a new field transformer. Though one of the newer employees, he had impressed many with his capabilities both in electrical and engineering problems. Art Pugh recommended he should be considered for the vacant position created by the unfortunate loss of engineer Bob Henry in an airplane crash.

To replace Gus as plant electrician, a likeable fellow named Nick Boons joined the maintenance team and a little later, as electrical demands increased, Dick Niven joined the team, too. Both Gus and Dick had worked several years as electrical foremen with Hume and Rumble. Dick had been in charge of the electrical installation at the O'Keefe Brewery project and had just made the decision to stay on as their plant electrician, when Gus invited him to join the electrical crew at Burrard Street. Promoted later to staff, Dick advanced steadily up to maintenance superintendent, before finally taking charge of the engineering department during the mid-1980s as the old guard retired.

With some of those events still well in the future, the brewery was presently undergoing a period of great upheavals in the brewing business. Buying up used equipment surreptitiously to bottle soda pop in 1966, entrepreneur Ben Ginter built the Uncle Ben's Brewery in Prince George and began to flood the market with his Blue Moose lager beer. Princeton Breweries, further south in British Columbia and known locally for its fine quality beers, also endeavored to break into the Lower Mainland market, but they stretched their production capabilities so far that their quality suffered. By the 1970s, Princeton Brewery had lost much of its regular market due to inferior quality and closed down.

E. P. Taylor's nice new O'Keefe Brewery on Boundary at

Some of the people involved in the successful running of the brew house, 1972. Left to right: author, Dick Niven, Gerhard Schulz, Nick Boons. *Photo: Molsons*

Lougheed closed its doors due to low market sales, and a bakery rose from its empty remains. Other small local breweries in B.C. had amalgamated under Interior Brewery's banner to stay alive and watched from the side lines as the big three suds makers, Carling, Labatt and Molson, rolled up their sleeves to battled it out on the coast.

As intimated earlier, Gus Fortier was a rugged outdoorsman. Below zero weather, living in a canvas tent and crawling up mountain logging roads in his old truck on the trail of a big moose were taken as standard fare. He and Art Pugh had welded a strong bond of comradeship on these sorties, for Art was also of the same kin, often taking his sons on river exploration trips that sometimes required long portages to finally reach their pickup point. It was fortunate they were both of this sturdy nature, for the next twenty years were to demand all the stamina each could muster.

The first test came shortly after Gus took over the bottle shop, when the brewing industry changed from long neck bottles to short stubby bottles. This demanded immediate problem solving at every step of the way in packaging. Bob Henry had often been chided that he no sooner got the packaging line running smooth as silk and could stay home on weekends, then he made a change in cartons or labels that caused breakage and confusion until he had worked enough weekends to get it all running smoothly again. Bob had snorted that he was creating work to make the millwrights wealthy, before explaining that the company had to hone production costs at every opportunity to stay competitive. If Molson accepted an improved carton or label that had greater sales appeal or reduced the unit cost of each bottle of beer, then Bob had to modify the machines and the packaging system to take full advantage of this savings, even if it meant they had to work extra hours to realize it.

The change over from long neck bottles to the short stubbies had both market appeal and production efficiency appeal, thus all energies were directed to realizing it in the shortest possible time. While most of us know little about market appeal, we can appreciate that many beer drinkers are attracted to their favorite brew just as much by colorful packaging and catchy jingles as by their supposed keenness of taste and bouquet. Thus, the stubby bottle, highly publicized as being the latest thing, could not be ignored for long by the great in-crowd. So Gus had to ensure a Molson stubby bottle was on LCB's shelf when they came to buy.

Production efficiency, while more easily defined, was much harder to realize. A shorter bottle required a shorter carton, thus less glass was needed to make the bottle and less cardboard was needed to make the carton. These were real dollar savers. The point that a stubby did not require a neck label also saved dollars. But, the real reason the breweries rushed to convert to the stubbies was its compactness that reduced warehousing, shipping and even marketing space. Six tiers of stubby cartons could be stored in the same space as five tiers of long necks. This represented a 20 percent increase in warehousing and shipping areas without any construction costs.

To realize such a radical changeover while maintaining sufficient market production, taxed the ingenuity of those responsible for the project and demanded the keenest cooperation and greatest fortitude from those who operated the packaging equipment while bottles exploded and smashed all around them. This was the second major battle fought and won in the packaging center, yet many more had to be fought during the years that followed to finally realize the awesome 2,000-plus bottles a minute output by the year 1985 (my final year as chief engineer). It was understandable that many senior people would become battle weary in the process. But the success with which they overcame the problems to realize it ensured Molson would again become a profit-making company, and thus they would be entitled to a well-earned retirement with benefits far exceeding earlier expectations.

Fortunately, the new hydro jet bottle washer, which relied on hundreds of high-pressure jet sprays to clean both the inside and outside of each bottle, did not have the hundreds of long brushes that had plagued the old soaker carrying out the same job. But modifying the hundreds of pockets that held each bottle as it wend its way through the soaking tanks and washing sprays, plus retiming the in feed and discharge gates, created a certain amount of bedevilment. The bottle filler was more difficult to modify than the labelers and packers, yet any difficulty within the packaging line instantly created bottle jam-ups with considerable glass breakage and loss of product resulting.

The prime requisite when transferring a beer (like the racking or decanting of a wine) is to eliminate any possible air contact with the product. This is usually accomplished by moving the beer under a protective carbon dioxide blanket (an overlay of heavy gas which displaces the air atmosphere well above the surface of the beer) and by minimizing any cascade effect that might release the gas already injected to carbonate the beer (those tiny little effervescent bubbles that rise off your glass of fresh beer or crackling rose wines to tantalizes your nostrils). When one tilts a glass either at the beer tap or when pouring in a bottle of beer, this allows the beer to run down the inside of the chilled clean glass without cascading. This not only reduces its tendency to foam away the carbonating gas, but also creates a carbon dioxide atmosphere in the glass that rises as an overlay above the surface of the beer, displacing the air that had been there. Beer coming in contact with air oxidizes rapidly and often is most noticeable to the palate as a bitter aftertaste, for which drinkers blame the brewer rather than themselves.

Racking (filling) of both kegs and barrels is accomplished by laying the keg or barrel on its side and inserting a tube through a side opening until it almost touches the bottom. Carbon dioxide gas is injected to force out some of the air in the barrel and create a gas blanket under which the beer is allowed to flow in. As the level of

The bottle filler and crowner, 1975. *Photo: Molsons*

beer in the keg rises, the tube also slowly rises and maintains the discharge just below the surface of the beer displacing any air in the keg out through the bunghole. When the keg is full, the racking sleeve with its retracted filling tube is quickly removed from the hole, and a wooden bung plug is hammered in to seal the opening. The total process takes just minutes, and with three or four racking arms in production, a keg of beer rolls out on the floor every minute, or about 400 per working shift.

Over in the bottle shop at this same time, the old fillers handling a ten-ounce bottle accomplished all this at the breathtaking pace of more than four bottles a second! Twenty years later, almost 2,000 bottles a minute is accepted as standard production. Here is how it was done then and really almost the same today. A large round carousel (merry-go-round) type of table is fitted into the bottling conveyor line and fed sterile bottles from the washer through a timing gate. Small liftable platforms fitted around the perimeter of the carousel table, each receive a bottle as the revolving carousel lines up with the timing gate. Above each platform is a filling tube fitted with a sliding neck cover and a cam-operated cock to supply beer from a pressurized tank on top of the carousel. As the table revolves, a roller finger fitted to the platform travels along a circumferential track under the carousel, and the ramps on this track quickly pushes the platform holding the bottle upward until the sliding cover seals the neck and the filling tube almost reaches the bottom inside the bottle. At that moment, a cam-operated push rod snaps open the beer cock, which fills the bottle as the table whirls around.

The platform roller finger, following the downward slope of the circumferential ramp lowers the platform until at the completion of its wild ride, the beer cock is shut off and the filling tube is clear of the bottle. With the platform again at conveyor height, the bottle is whisked through the discharge gate and thence into the crowner—a smaller drum-type revolving carousel where the cap (crown) is pressure sealed by crimping on top of the bottle.

On the bottle filler of those days, the perimeter of the carousel wheel had to be approximately 180 inches, about five feet, in diameter to accommodate all sixty of the three-inch platforms. And each platform had to rotate at a peripheral speed of approximately one foot per second. The crowner, being one-quarter the diameter, spun in excess of four times this speed. (In later editions of high-speed fillers, the carousels were more than eight feet in diameter with up to twice the number of filling spouts.) Before being conveyed away to the double-deck pasteurizer, all full bottles pass through banks of visual and later electronic inspectors that check both bottle and crown condition as well as the level of beer in each bottle, rejecting swiftly those that do not measure up.

Some of the stubby bottles, with their more pronounced shoulders, suffered undue thermal stresses or even thin or weak sections, causing them to fail during their initial run through the bottling line. Unfortunately, often even the good ones were quickly broken in their thousands, when modified equipment failed to perform in anything less than perfect alignment and timing.

By the time this was all behind them and the brewery was enjoying the benefits of the twenty percent increase in storage, Art Pugh's promotion to Calgary as engineering superintendent for the western division was realized. Fred Kirby moved up to chief engineer at Burrard Street. One of his first jobs was to utilize the now-redundant covered shipping bays across the tracks from the boiler room, for offices and workshop. Alf Humphries finally got his own welding shop, the engineers a maintenance shop and Nick Boons and Dick Niven got their own electrical bench. Bruce Patrick with the company as machinist charge hand of packaging maintenance and joined by Eddy Morison and Wally Schultz took over a major portion of the workshop to fit in a thumping big shaping machine and our fifteen-inch Wilson lathe for their heavy machine jobs. Not forgotten was the brewery's doughty master painter Gordon McVean, who exchanged his drafty wooden paint shed in the parking lot, for a warm, centrally located paint shop within this new facility.

Above this workshop area, and below the high ceiling of the original shipping bay, Fred designed and built a set of offices. This included a nice airy office for Gus Fortier, who quickly donated his former birdcage office above the steaming soaker to his foremen. With new furniture in a large drawing office, Fred with equal magnanimity bequeathed his old office in the now noisy engineroom to us. This still left room for one more office, and the new stores clerk Ron Gates moved in there.

Christmas 1966 was hoving into view as this was being completed and, as was established custom, the brewery was decorated for the occasion. Each year there was a large Christmas tree erected, often on the roof of the administration building, once on the packaging roof and this time on the highest spot available, the tank room roof above the brewing offices.

Snow came early to the Lower Mainland that winter and this caused an accident that, though most sad, was most miraculous considering the circumstances. Late Friday afternoon before leaving for the weekend, Cecil Graham took a box of light bulbs up to the roof to replace those burnt out or broken on the Christmas tree. Alf, Harry and Frank, busy with their own jobs, only noted his long absence when they began to put away their tools and write up their reports prior to changing their clothes and heading out into the storm.

A casual look around turned into a worried search. When Cec could not be located within the usual areas, Harry Payne climbed up on the roof to check the tree. Finding no sign of him there, he returned to the warmth of the brew house to thaw out and ponder what to do next. Then a horrible thought crossed his mind, he had only been looking upwards for Cec. What if he were somewhere below him? He rushed back to the exterior fire escape landing and looked down onto the snow covered engine room roof. No sign of him there, and no footprints, he just had to be inside somewhere.

Before stepping back into the bright warmness, Harry's eyes glanced down through the late afternoon gloom, noting the familiar roof protuberances such as fans, pipes and pumps, now no more than large humps of snow. There seemed to be one more lump of snow than he could account for. Praying he was mistaken, he quickly shuffled down the slippery snow covered steps, climbed over the railings and ploughed across the roof to reach the extra mound of snow and brush some away.

There was Cec cold and still—the snowflakes unmelted on his face and hands. Harry's calls for help got quick response, and by the time an ambulance arrived the fire department had strapped Cec into a stretcher and carried him down to the train shed area. At the hospital they managed to revive him and began sorting out all his injuries. But what was surprising, though they were many, none of the injuries proved fatal.

Somehow, as he fell from the roof he had bounced off the railing and steel landings leading below with glancing blows. Then, miraculously, he missed all the hard and pointy things that rose out of the engineroom roof that would have punctured or maimed him. His

The area where the fire started in block A cellar.   *Photo: A. G. Pugh collection*

forty-foot fall had been slightly cushioned by the thick layer of snow. It was the snow and cold that really saved his life, for it delayed his return to consciousness and the shock that might have killed him before he was discovered and hospitalized.

Cec Graham was brought up on the prairies, where he learned the skills of a farmer, even firing and running his father's large Case steam tractor. Hard work had never frightened Cec, and he grew up to become fireman on the railroad, shoveling coal on both work trains and freight trains, while he slowly qualified for a job on the right side of the cab. Arriving out on the coast during the hungry thirties, when his spare board status on the prairie division no longer earned him a livelihood, he got a part time job at Fritz Sick's Powell Street brewery shoveling hog fuel into the boiler's Dutch oven furnace, as relief shift engineer. Cec required all the optimism and fortitude his long years of struggle could muster to pull himself out of

Black smoke pours from the roof during the cellar block fire.　　*Photo: A. G. Pugh*

this accident. Yet, just over a year later, still limping a bit and having to flex a hand that suffered a cold numbness, he returned to his workbench at the brewery to carry out light duty jobs.

The year 1967 was of significance for several reasons—for Canada, it was our one hundredth birthday, and the full-sized replica of the SS *Beaver* was created by the Royal Canadian Navy to cele-

168

Brewery work stops as firemen fight the stubborn blaze.   *Photo: A. G. Pugh*

brate the centennial out here on the West Coast. In Montreal, the birthplace of Molson's Brewery, the world's fair Expo 67 on St. Helen's Island opened its doors to millions of visitors. For Molsons it was a year of decisions.

The death of Percival Talbot Molson a few months after becoming president of Molson Breweries Ltd in 1966 and the good fortunes of the company, which realized surplus funds on hand by the following year, made it imperative to invest these funds profitably. David M. Chenoweth, appointed to fill P. T.'s void as president, was the first nonfamily member to hold this office. And he spearheaded a diversification program that would lead Molsons to become one of the great conglomerates of the era in Canada.

Small outward damage conceals bent beams below.   *Photo: A. G. Pugh*

The new insulated fermenting tanks for the south end of A4 and A5 cellars began arriving from Ellett Copper and Brass. A tall crane lifted them up over the keg house, where exterior panels had been removed, and slid them in on the heavy steel beams that would carry their weight when in service. After the exterior panels had been replaced and the service pipes fitted, the enameled interior walls were erected, completely enclosing the dark, cramped service area away from the brightly lit, sparkling clean wide cellar aisles.

All this had been successfully concluded and only minor work and clean up was in progress when the cry of "Fire!" echoed down to the engine room. A glance to the roof top gave little indication of the magnitude of the fire, and after placing a call to the fire department and stationing a man out in the driveway to guide them in, in my role of temp chief , I raced up the stairs to get a closer look at what problems the firemen faced for access and the status of evacuation from the fire zone.

Upon opening the door into the wort cooling room, which was common to all levels of the fermenting cellar block, I stopped dead. The doorway was solid black, as though a black wall had been created in the opening, then very slowly the wall began to slide downward and flow around my legs and feet and into the brew house. Slamming the door shut, I stationed a brewery worker there to ensure it remained shut, then ran down one floor in the brew house, and around to the cellar staircase to where heavy black smoke was already beginning to seep downward.

Here I found Harry Lambert, the newly appointed brewing foreman, directing people out of the building and attempting to account for all who were in that area before the fire started. With no way into the black void, which hid the tank and cellar room, I continued down the staircase to get an air breathing backpack and a portable lamp from the engineroom. The firemen arriving there elected to scale up the outside with their ladders and cut through the roof to fight the fire from above, while others with air packs and lamps enter the area from the fire exit and tank room.

By this time the intense heat had buckled the metal roofing, and the overlay of felt and tar melting down to feed the blaze caused a huge column of black smoke to rise high above the brewery, stopping traffic over the bridge and attracting hundreds of people and the news media. The unheard of was happening—a large brewery was burning up. Everyone who recalled events over in Scotland a few years before, when a distillery went up in smoke, remembered the horrifying stories of premium aged Scotch whiskey running like water down the gutters of the street. Like the thrifty townspeople over there who had gleefully scooped it up with cup and bucket, many of the swiftly gathering onlookers hopefully considered this delightful possibility and kept an eagle eye open for any undue rush of amber liquid away from the brewery.

The tremendous heat under the heavy steel roof girders caused even them to sag, and melted tar poured down to fuel the combustion of more urethane insulation. By this time all brewery and trades people were out of the buildings and accounted for. Black smoke oozed out of every door and window of the cellar block and brew house to join the huge column of smoke rising from the roof, and it certainly appeared at that moment that the brewery was lost. However, with yeoman effort, the firemen ripped up sections of the roof with porta-power jaws and bars to cool the blaze with water, fully aware it might collapse under them at any moment. Inside, even hardier souls burdened with heavy air packs and limited vision from within their face-masks attacked the blaze with fog and spray nozzles.

Lifting in the bottle shop's beer tanks.

Their tenacity began to show telling signs that a change was being enacted. More white smoke than black began to rise from the brewery; then, even this was slowly reduced. Two hours after the firemen arrived, steam vapor, dirty water and black soot were all that remained to indicate the harrowing experience. By evening, there were few outside indicators to draw anyone's attention to the mishap—a few soot or smoke marks about the doorways and windows, which crews were cleaning up, and a section of torn-up roof that was mostly hidden by the parapet.

The actual cause of the fire was subject to certain speculation; Maybe it was started by a welding or burning spark that the fire watchers might have overlooked or an exposed light bulb that might have melted and then ignited some roofing tar or other combustible waste. This could have fuelled a more fearsome heat as the polyurethane began to burn within the very confined and crowded area. The dense toxic smoke of the polyurethane hid the true source of the fire, when skillful use of the fire extinguishers kept close at hand could have been used to put out the blaze. After that only the cooling effect of fog nozzles from inside, and the deluge from openings in the roof, reduced the heat of the chemical fire below its combustion temperature.

While Molsons spent a considerable amount of their budget on national and regional advertising, expounding the merits of their brews, they frowned on media coverage that might distract from the sound business image projected by this corporate policy. Fortunately, the media was in a tolerant mood and most comments were offered with tongue-in-cheek jest, which actually acknowledged Molsons' increased acceptance in the marketplace as the cursor that prompted the expansion in the fire area. One local newscaster suggested his listeners should be on the alert for a fire sale of beer at the brewery.

Senator Hartland Molson stayed at the helm through these tumultuous years as chairman of the board, and thus made the deci-

The block B cellar addition.   *Photo: Molsons*

sion not to relocate the Burrard Street brewery away from the residential sprawl, which was spreading swiftly over the former industrial sites of False Creek. This was really no joy for many of the new neighbors, for brewing odors, vapors and sometimes smoke from various activities were sometime waft into their areas when easterly winds and misfortunes coincided.

To eliminate this possibility as plans to increase the size of the brewery were undertaken, antipollution equipment was designed to be installed that would ensure clean air for neighbors and less pollutants for the sewers. By early 1968, four floors of unrefrigerated cellars had been built on top of B block, but the start on a new brew house was delayed as city clearances were tardy in being realized.

One of the reasons for this tardiness was the upgrading of the downtown city sewer system, which would pass by the front door just ten feet underground after being carried across False Creek below the deck of Burrard Street Bridge. Thus the removal of No. 1 boiler and the installation of a new 50,000-pound per hour gas-fired packaged boiler preceded the brew house construction.

Gus Fortier, satisfied with the stubby bottle changeover, installed the brewery's first beer-canning machine with its conveyors and inspectors. By the end of 1968, it was turning out 600 cans a minute of Old Style and Molson Canadian lager beer. Upgrading the filter room with diatomaceous earth primary filters and five micron finishing sleeve filters dispensed with the huge pulp filters and pulp washing tanks and allowed a much larger stainless steel beer chiller to be added. Most of the long white hoses that had transported the beer through the old system were replaced with shining, quick-coupled stainless steel piping.

The handling of ever-increasing quantities of malted barley as our brewery became larger, strained the storage capability and required trying logistics to keep a flow of railway grain cars ever in transit to the brewery. Hoping to alleviate this growing problem, the railways began to ship it in large new grain tank cars developed for the wheat trade, which could carry up to 150,000 pounds of malt or corn. Twice that which the former boxcars could handle, with about the same labor cost.

These tank cars were huge, built to maximum railway clearances of their day with dumping gates for each of the four sections a few inches above the railhead. But, therein lay another problem for the brewery. In theory, these gates were to be spotted over the grains receiving hoppers and the plate valve dragged open by a gear-driven rack. In practice, there was only a rail side hopper, which required an extension chute to unload. Extending the rail spur westward into the train shed area, until it conflicted with the spent grains unloading system, still did not allow the last compartment in the grain car to be spotted beside the hopper.

To overcome this, a low-level conveyor was built to slide under the car and carry the grains on a continuous belt to a receiving hopper. But only one car could be unloaded before the yarding locomotive had to get back to shift in another full car from the yard track. Unlike the smaller boxcars, which had often been shifted with a dump truck that had been fitted with a coupler on its front frame for that purpose, these larger tank cars required a special inching lever, lots of muscle power and even the old truck, though this still did not allow exchange for a loaded car.

When the problem was coupled with the feast or famine delivery of these grain cars from all over the continent, it pointed out the need for something better. John Britnell, satisfied with the improvements he had accomplished, decided to leave Molsons and return to England where he could pursue a plan to create a brewing malt extract that would eliminate this problem. He hoped to create an extract (syrup) that could be stored in a much more concentrated and readily usable form in large tanks within each brewery, thereby doing away with delays and hazards of grain shipment on almost a daily basis and alleviating the need for shunting in and out the huge grain cars where trackage and storage were at a premium.

Molsons decided on a different route to follow, at least till John got his malt extract system perfected, and John Pickering came to Burrard Street as brewmaster to oversee its installation and bring our new brew house into production. John Britnell's departure from the brewery was a sad occasion for his likable nature had endeared him to many. With the monies donated by the crew at the brewery, John and his wife were presented with Cowichan Indian wool sweaters. On a later visit back to the brewery, John reported these created quite a stir when they landed in England wearing them.

The new boiler was to be fired with natural gas bought from BC Hydro on a low, interruptible rate, making it more economical to burn than the heavy bunker oil used at the time for the older 18,000 pound per hour B & W boilers. But—and it was a big "but"—this cheaper rate could only be enjoyed during low demand periods. When heavy usage was experienced during extreme cold weather and this fuel became in short supply, the bargain price would shoot up to fifty times that cost. Thus, it behooved the brewery to keep on hand a supply of fuel oil and the equipment to burn it should this happen. There would be at least two hours' notice to change over to fuel oil, but, hopefully, weather conditions would also alert them to this probability.

To provide fuel oil burning capability on such short notice, meant that the heavy No. 5 (bunker C) fuel oil tank had to be filled and heated, ready to use at any hour of the day or night during the months of winter's chill when heavy domestic demands could and often did rise both in Canada and the U.S. The high pressure, six-inch gas line came in from First Avenue, paralleling the new water main under the yard, to a pressure reducing station before entering the east side of the boiler room at a modest 5 psi burner pressure. Its usage required fail-safe combustion controls fitted with automatic purging and timed sequencing relays monitored by an oxygen-analyzing system, all electrically interlocked to prevent furnace explosions.

Before this new boiler project was completed and a start on the new brew house project was still many months away, John Pickering arrived at the brewery with his new assistant brewmaster Tom Buckley. This marked another great turning point in the company's history. The brewery was about to be introduced to vacuum grains unloading, pneumatic spent grains handling, below ground level production handling, and automated brewing.

Automated brewing sounded pretty hi-tech in those days, but it was nothing like the automation finally realized when the world entered the realm of the PLC/LED and computer control era ten years hence. Back in 1969, electrical timers, relays and sequential switching were relied upon to control pneumatic actuators and electrical drives. And parts of this system could be run in parallel, so that one, two or even three brews could come down through the system one behind the other.

It was mind boggling, and sometimes a little frightening, so a large graphics panel overhead in the brewing control station monitored the various events with color lights identifying when processes were underway or completed. But things were not always as the panel lights indicated. Sensors or microswitches could, and did, lie when the mechanics failed or partially failed. Thus the brewers had to be constantly alert in order to avert mishaps by switching into a manual mode to hold up the various processes until the problem could be eradicated.

The new brew house, with the exception of the original bottle shop, was the first of many of the new brewery buildings to be built over a full basement where vital operating equipment and vessels would be installed below grade level and require pumps to keep the areas dry. The same conditions that caused this also caused one of the equipment floors within the new brew house to have limited headroom. Both were to tax mechanical maintenance greatly through the years ahead.

To supply the new brew house with its much larger water usage, as well as the new bottling line that was in planning and the additional cellars that were under construction, a new water main was brought in from First Avenue. The original water supply that had paralleled the train shed rail line after coming through the main gate, with a bypass into the sand filters and chlorinating station, had handled the increase demands to date but not without mishap and great concern. Major problems had been caused by the increased weight of trucks crossing it behind the boiler room and the rail line that ran alongside it carrying the huge grain cars. Numerous leaks from sprung or broken joints had flooded the 20,000-gallon fuel storage area and created leaks into sumps and electrical vaults. While Vancouver's water supply is touted as the cleanest in the world, repairs to the city's system and disturbances at the reservoirs sometimes allowed sediment to get into the pipes. As a heavy end user, whatever the sand and gravel filters could not remove often migrated through and settled in the underground distribution mains. Weekend flushing of the system removed much of this, while super chlorinating attempted to control any bacteria that might incubate in the sediment. But there was always the concern that any increased velocity could bring it into the processes; so the brewery opted for bigger water mains.

Breweries consider their water supply quality so highly, they designate it as brewing liquor, and quality control chemists daily monitor and test not only the main supply point but also most of the distribution points through the brewery. Breweries are usually built beside or near a good supply of clean brewing water, like the Burton

River in England where famous brews such as Burton's Ale were created. The failure of many breweries can often be linked to a supply of water that has deteriorated in quality or quantity, as much as any economical changes.

To enhance Vancouver's supply of crystal clear, soft rain and snow melt waters, Sick's Capilano Brewery had hardened their sparging water by adding mineral salts from the Burton River. Carling O'Keefe trucked in tanker loads of hard spring water from Shannon Falls, which they claimed enhanced their special beers. While down in the States, Olympia Brewing and Hamns touted their deep artesian well water with creating their beers' distinctive appeal.

The new twelve-inch water main from First Avenue entered under the main gate before angling toward the brewery, where it rose up from four feet underground to ceiling height at the southeast corner of the boiler room. Passing through to the northwest corner of the engineroom, it divided into three systems to supply packaging, brew house and cellar block. The chlorine injection system was relocated to the gatehouse area, providing the chlorine a longer dwell time in the water mains to hopefully eradicate any bacteria.

Because evaporation in the boilers will concentrate the chlorine into an acidic agent heavy in hydrogen ions that can damage the boiler, a two-inch pipe of unchlorinated water for boiler feed was led in underground from upstream of the chlorinating station. Later, after replacing the gas chlorinator with a hypochlorinator located in the engineroom to treat just the cellar and packaging water lines, the above two-inch pipeline became redundant and was used as a convenient way to bring in a new seventy pair telephone cable without digging up all the black top and lawns.

While the new brew house was being constructed, the grains handling system was upgraded. A new Buhler mill was installed in the mill room, and larger cereal and malt hoppers were installed on the existing kettle floor that automatically weighed themselves (through pressure gauges) on their oil-filled dashpot supports. In the tower's upper room, the same tall crane that lifted in the heavy Buhler mill and a dust separator one floor lower lifted in a huge vacuum pump up to this top-most part of the brewery.

A rotary valve on the bottom of the dust separator allowed the grains lifted up from the malt car hoppers to the top of the separator by the vacuum pump to exit this negative pressure area without an

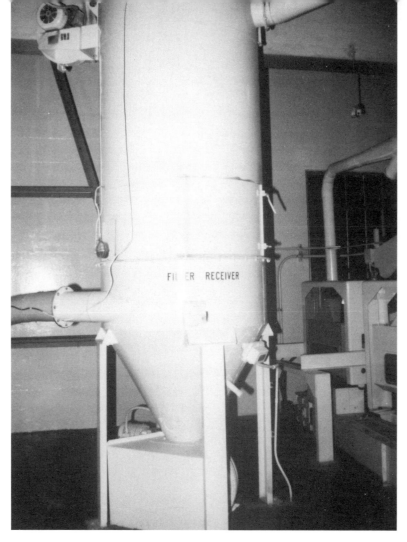

The vacuum grains unloading system. Vacuum pump is in upper right with inspiriting grain in lower left. The back blower in the upper left continuously cleans the filter sleeves. The shaker that removes foreign objects can be seen in the right background.

Photo: Molsons

inrush of air. Filter bags protected the vacuum pump from dust and grain parts while an automatic back-blowing system ensured these filter bags did not become unduly burdened with dust. The dust-free grains were conveyed to tall silo storage within the tower building.

When required for brewing, these grains were dumped through a motorized plate valve onto the existing below ground level cross-belt conveyor feeding the existing bucket elevator, which lifted them

The pipe in the foreground comes from bottom collection of lautre tun. *Photo: Molsons*

back up again to the tower area. Here they went through a magnetic shaker that removed any metal particles or dust before directing the grains down to the next level, where the heavy rollers of the mills cracked open the hard shells, allowing sparging to leech out the starchy sugars.

For this new system of grains receiving, an external ten-inch steel pipe led up from the train shed area to the top of dust separator in the tower. Flexible pipe connected this to one or two grain cars shunted in beside the engineroom and boiler room. By carefully adjusting a flow of grain and air into this pipe, the vacuum pump could lift it up the hundred odd feet to the tower. To protect against excessive negative pressure in the system a vacuum breaker was installed, and to reduce grain breakage a small overair vent was fitted that ensured a steady flow of grain being swept up the pipe.

Automated back blowing of the filter sleeves discharged the dust collected into a cyclone separator, where it was bagged and sold. This was a far cry from the old Powell Street Brewery where malt from Calgary Malting came in eighty-five-pound sacks and black or roasted barley in one hundred-pound bags. Every bag of which had

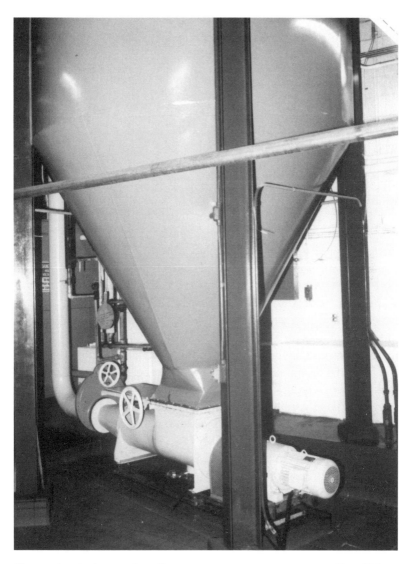

The spent grains hopper above the screw auger. *Photo: Molsons*

be unloaded from trucks or railcar in the yard and stowed in piles on the upper floor of the brewery by strong brewery workers.

All the crew had helped carry out this monthly chore, and even Moon Cameron, a massive former weightlifter, claimed it was sweaty hard work. The yearly delivery of hops in 200-pound bales was even more strenuous, requiring each man's copper mug of beer to be kept close at hand. It certainly was easier at Burrard Street.

In the original grains removal system, which had just been replaced, the lautre tun discharge had been located high enough above the smaller truck loading mash tank to allow the spent grains to be swept from the lautre tun plates down through a chute into the tank. As brewing increased, so did the amount of spent grain. Joe Wolzon, who had just been awarded the contract to remove it, kept increasing the number of trucks on the job, but the farms wanting this waste product were farther and farther out of town, thus increasing the length of time required for each truck to be away from the brewery.

The new spent grain tank, being much larger and taller than the original one, required a screw auger to lift the mash from below the lautre tun to the top of the round silotype vessel. But it held more than double the spent grains as the former, which gave Joe a much greater time span for his trucks to be on the road. This, plus the fact that the tank dump valve was higher off the base, allowed Joe to put a much larger truck in this service, which ensured him the freedom to offer this material to dairy and cattle farmers much farther out of town and thereby gain a much better price for this once unwanted product.

With the design of the new brew house being twenty feet lower (ten feet below grade) this system would not be practical, so an even larger and taller spent grains tank was erected on the driveway behind the boiler room, and the spent grains were pneumatically ponndorfed (blown) up into it. To supplement his two large trucks in this service and also supply the much larger U.S. dairy system along the border, Joe entered the field of piggyback trailers, becoming one of the first on the Lower Mainland to do so. The spent grains from the new twenty-five-foot diameter lautre tun dropped down to a ponndorfing system in the brew house basement, which propelled it upward and eastward via a twelve-inch pipe over the engineroom and boiler room roofs before dumping into the top of the spent grains tank.

Joe was a remarkable fellow. A few years previous, when the brewery's first spent grain trucking company complained they were losing money on the deal and wanted the brewery to pay more towards its cartage, Joe appeared and offered to pay Molsons for the troublesome waste product. He did this by establishing a clientele of dairy farmers both up the Fraser Valley and across the line, who valued it highly as a supplementary cattle feed. As noted, he was able to implement a piggyback trailer truck system for the brewery. To load, the smaller box was slid off its trailer rails into the truck's larger dump box. The truck then backed under the spent grains dump valve, and when the trailer box was full, the truck returned to its four-wheeled trailer and slid the smaller loaded box back onto the trailer's rails. Backing again under the hopper, the truck then fills its own empty dump box, before coupling up to the trailer. This half-hour operation proved so cost effective, he began paying Molsons twenty dollars a ton for the privilege of hauling it away.

Though the system lent itself to speedy loading and unloading in confined areas, the long run of pipe and the extreme height of the spent grains tank needed to provide clearance for the truck created problems that were both spectacular and difficult to eliminate. During extreme cold weather freeze-ups were common, and at other times when the mash was too wet, the air blew right through the grain, creating blockages that were extremely difficult to clear. While new to the brewery, ponndorfing systems were widely used elsewhere to transport product. The new unit was located in the brew house basement under the spent grains hopper. A large motor-driven auger forced the mash into the ponndorfing chamber through a round plate valve, where a peripheral nozzle (a narrow circular slot downstream of the plate valve) pressurized the chamber after the auger had pushed sufficient grain into the discharge pipe to seal off its opening. Trapped, the air pressure quickly increased until it became sufficient to blow the plug of grain down the pipe. This created a pressure drop in the ponndorfing chamber, allowing the auger to again push in another plug of grain to seal the pipe, when the process would be repeated.

While these plugs of grain were relatively small, approximately twenty-five pounds, the pulses created by their passage (about one to two a second) could easily be felt. When coupled with water carry-over or blockage, these mild pulses became violent surges that often broke the large clamping bolts where changes of direction were necessary. A heavy ten-inch steel pipe rose fifty feet from the brew house basement, then after skirting the buildings it angled across the boiler room roof before rising another twenty or so feet to discharge into the spent grain tank near the top.

Every plug of mash in the pipe, if it could be seen in slow motion, moved ahead about one to two feet each time pressure rose and fell in the ponndorfing chamber. The plug driven out of the ponndorfing chamber was moved directly by the air pressure in the chamber, all the other plugs throughout the entire length of the pipe, each separated by a sealed bubble of pressurized air, were moved by the hydraulic action of the plug driven out of the ponndorfing chamber.

The action was akin to a train of boxcars, where the locomotive pulls the first car with its coupler, and the coupler on the other end of that car pulls the one behind it, and so on. If a coupler breaks, the train behind comes to a stop or, worse, is free to run away. In the ponndorfing system if a coupler (air bubble) is lost, the plugs slide together and become too heavy to move causing the whole system to come to a stop.

The wetness of the mash determines the sealing capability of the air bubble—too little and each plug shifts closer to its neighbor until the pipe is plugged solidly, too much and the plug falls apart and the air blows right through it allowing the water to collect in the low points and the air escapes leaving the mash behind. When those conditions arose, the whole system jerked and banged so violently that the tall spent-grain tank swayed and rocked in a most terrifying manner. Learning to maintain the proper standard of grain wetness and ensuring adequate drainage after usage improved the performance of the system. Winter cold was overcome through steam tracing, while a large expansion loop well anchored at either end reduced the gyrations of the tank.

The innovations during this time were many and just a few are noted in this history. The brewery was expanding and progress was irreversible, so if something didn't work out as planned we worked longer and harder until it did for if we yielded to a compromise it would surely come back to haunt us. We didn't want to "lose the battle for want of a nail."

CHAPTER NINE

The New Image

Getting permits to build the new brew house and clearances to excavate up to the property line bordering Burrard Street, especially with the city sewer department planning their own excavation for the five-foot force sewer line down the east side of this street next to our property line, took considerable time. Then heavy rains saturated the ground after this deep excavation had begun and pumps were required to keep the footings and hardpan free of water until the forms were finally placed and concrete pumped in. The forms climbed ever higher casting the shape of the new large structure that frowned down through windowless openings on the bridge traffic detouring around the hoarding that hid these twin projects.

By the winter of 1970 most of this area had returned to a semblance of normalcy, though tall cranes still had to be spotted on the road at times to lift in large cooking and brewing vessels or heavy machinery. Inside the brewery, a beehive of activity located the various parts and pieces, and interconnected the pipes and ducts. Three-phase electrical power was run in from the new field transformers out by the gate, bypassing the engineroom panel by skirting along the exterior of the train shed wall in three-inch steel conduits before dipping down to the brew house basement switch panel.

For those who had time to peek in as they whisked by on the bridge approach, the tall amber-tinted windows provided a view of the large shiny stainless steel cooking vessels and brightly tiled walls. Even the three huge neon-lighted logos on A block's west wall seemed to compliment this gleaming new tall structure.

Within the brew house's upper floor, the brewmaster's staff relocated themselves into spacious new offices that afforded each a panoramic view of the city, such as the busy waterway of False Creek, the sparkling blue expanse of English Bay or the mountains and islands that bordered it. Generous airy hallways and sound-

The No. 1 kettle looking west onto Burrard Street. The exhaust vent is in the center of the dome, with hop intake on the left and boilover probe on the right.   *Photo: Molson*

absorbing construction isolated this sanctuary of management from the bedlam of noises below them. A large library that doubled as a conference room housed a ten-foot polished teak table and a dozen padded teak chairs, a long counter with coffee maker and sink and a refrigerator well stocked with Molson's finest for visitors and guests, while a wall-length set of shelves for trade books and catalogue gave the room its required purpose.

The former quality control laboratory and the brewmaster's office were bequeathed by John Pickering to his brew house and cellar supervisors, and divided into three small offices. The Copper Room (referred to by some as the snakepit), officially the brewmaster's tap and taste room, was ripped asunder to provide location for a huge new hot wort tank, which extended up through the roof into a penthouse. The quality control chemists, who more than anyone had suffered from the new construction and its invasion of their sterile environment, now enjoyed a large airy work area overlooking the packaging center to nurture their cultures, count their bacteria and test the beers.

Below these offices were two partial floors extending halfway out into the brew house. The top one carried the lautre tun, a large flat-bottomed, stainless steel domed vessel from which the wort was sparged out of the mash. This floor terminated at a balcony that looked down thirty feet to the huge stainless steel dome of the kettle. The floor directly below the lautre tun was sealed in behind windowless walls of decorative tile that overlooked the kettle. It housed the drive units for cookers and lautre tun, the run off valves and pipes for the latter and drag and screw conveyors for all three.

The kettle floor was the show place of the brewery; its fifty-foot windowed walls flanking Burrard Street gave an eye-catching view to passersby of the huge gleaming cookers and kettle. Large windows opening into the main entrance foyer gave visitors a hint of the vast room they were about to enter, though nothing could prepare them for the vaulted ceiling that rose up to the underside of the office floor on top of the brewery or the glistening multicolored glass-tiled walls highlighted through flood lights that caused the whole area to sparkle.

The gleaming kettle and cookers with the smell of brewing grains and hops accentuated the sight of the colorfully lit control center with its twinkling graphics panel and attentive white clad brewer. This was the futuristic sight of a brewery. It awed the uninitiated and impressed even more those who understood what they were seeing.

What most did not see unless they were special guests, such as those from the brewing industry within the brewmaster's association, was the complex piping and pumping arrangement below in the brew house basement. Here the spherical bottoms of the huge vessels showing only their topmost portions on the kettle floor, descended through the floor to rest on steel columns above massive stainless steel pumps, which transferred the brewing products through their cycle.

All the cookers were jacketed with multisteam zones, suitably serviced by large pipes with pneumatically operated steam valves. All dumped to the pumps through pneumatic disc valves fitted with electrical position indicators that registered on the brewing graphic panel. Upward of 10,000 gallons of product rushed through these pipe every three-hour cycle. Supplying all this water (brewing liquor) was a tall sparge tank standing in the northeast corner of the basement. And above it, off the mezzanine equipment floor level, was a 10,000-gallon brewing hot water tank. A spent grains (mash) hopper rose from above the ponndorfing equipment behind the basement switch panel, while a long stainless steel hop jack glistened within a tiled pit below the kettle, where a fifty-horsepower pump pushed the product up to the large new hot wort tank residing in the former Copper Room area on the second floor.

The evolution of both the spent grains and new grains handling equipment during this period was significant. However the creation of a fine beer still depended on the brewer's choice of barleys and the quality of the crops. Some comment should be made about the grains and cereals that are needed to produce a quality brew, particularly the brewer's yeasts (ale/lager) which ferment it, the meld of bitter hops which give it flavor and tang, and the types of barley (whether malted, roasted or black) that determine the character and body of the ales or beers so created.

While barley is grown worldwide to produce a thickener or starch base for foodstuffs such as soups and stews or flour dough for bread and pastry, transportation and storage of the milled product has always posed a problem. Indeed, in wilderness locales such as the Klondike, where a year's supply of staples had to be packed in at one time, sacks of flours were often sealed tight by momentarily being submerged in water. This created a near stonelike outer layer when it dried, which protected the contents from air and rodents alike.

Historically, grains like rice, wheat and barley were the basic sources of flour and starch long before Mayan maze (corn) or the humble potato were ever brought back to the European table by Sir Walter Raleigh. The type of barley found most suited to the brewer's needs was that close at hand and economical to acquire. Certain cultivated barleys rejected by the bakers and cooks of those early years, plus those grains that grew wild, were readily available to the brewers of yore and, when properly malted, gave beer its distinct amber hues.

There are essentially two types of barley—two-row and six-row. In the latter, three kernels of grain are produced at each node resulting in six vertical rows; in the former, only one grain develops on each node on alternate sides of the head producing two vertical rows. Six-row barley is predominately grown in Canada and United States, while two-row barley preferred by most European brewers is grown in the old world. Molsons use a blend of barley consisting of 55 percent six row and 45 percent two-row malted barley. As noted by brewmaster Victor Brachat, this is available as malted, roasted (caramel) or black barley. Milled corn is another basic food starch from the new world, though now grown almost universally, that is processed for cereals, flours and brewing needs.

Moisture is the greatest hazard in handling most grains. Even the durable northern hard wheat suffers reduced value when left moist for any time, and treated or milled grains are even more vulnerable. Transporting of these products, especially to the wet West Coast, puts them at their greatest risk. Temperatures can range all the way from boiling hot on the prairies to freezing cold through the mountain passes. Humidity, especially when grains arrive out on the rain coast, can cause heavy condensation within the freezing contents of the modern steel grain-handling rail car. Rough handling of these commodities, especially malted barley that is very friable or crunchy, can create excessive breakage of the kernels with a resultant loss of starch in the form of flour dust.

While the new grain handling system reduced this loss and speeded up the unloading, delivery of the malt cars was subject to weather and circumstance, and at times resulted in a feast or famine inventory for the brewer. John Britnell's aspirations to supply commercial qualities of malted barley as a liquid or syrup, much as malt extract is now available for medicinal and hobby brewing needs, created a significant interest in the hop industry.

Both Len Jones and John Britnell had experimented with corn and sugar beet syrup from the U.S., as well as cane sugar syrup from Rogers (B.C.) Sugar. All had been discontinued by the time the new brew house came on stream. While John pondered the problems of producing commercial volumes of malt extract for brewers' needs, he was keenly aware that hop storage also suffered similar problems, and experimented with an extract of this ingredient that had the consistency of road tar until heated with steam. Perhaps, if it were offered in a cartridge mode, such as stick glue is now offered for the electrically heated glue guns, they could become feasible for brewers.

But the hop man's problems had more dire need of a solution for the following reason. Hop storage required considerable volume under controlled conditions. Hops were harvested and processed once a year, thus breweries had a vital need to replenish their inventory annually. Larger brews created a larger problem of hop leaf (blossom) carryover, resulting in lost product, contaminating of the environment and the plugging of vents and drains.

The extract solution appeared to answer all these problems, plus it required a much smaller volume of storage, which could allow the brewery to hold a much larger inventory of hop extract in the same volume of storage allocated to the baled hops. Historically, the dried blossoms of the female hop plant gained their popularity as a brewing flavor because of their bacterostatic effects. Their inclusion prevented the growth of many types of bacteria that could quickly spoil any unhopped beers, and they provided remarkable flavor stability and foam retention. The resins and essential oils of the hops, which contribute to the distinctive flavor and aroma of most beers, are most pronounced in the seedless variety. Only the female plant produces hop blossoms, and only the female plant grown away from the male vines will produce seedless hops. Sick's Breweries grew this type exclusively at their Kamloops hop farm.

Hop vines are perennial and propagated from rootstock cuttings. In early May the hop vines are trained onto hanging strings from overhead trellises six feet high, and harvesting continues from mid-August through to late September. Cut loose both top and bottom, the string-grown vine enters a hop-picking machine, which removes the hop cones. Loaded into a drying kiln that removes 80 percent of their moisture, the cones are packed into 200-pound bales wrapped in heavy burlap (approximately two feet by three feet by five feet tall) and shipped to the breweries in the fall each year.

The year's supply of hops usually comprises two different types of hops. One type is heavy in bittering resins and added first to the sweet wort in the kettle; the other type is heavy in aromatic oils and added last to the kettle's brew for flavor. The brewers had from the beginning at the Burrard Street Brewery slowed down the boil and the exhaust fan before adding the hops to the brew through the top door of the kettle. This was very convenient because the kettle door and hop room were on the same floor level and less than fifty feet away from each other, and the tubs of various hops, suitable broken up and weighed, were easily rolled out to the very edge of the kettle.

The new kettle was in another building, one floor lower and at least another fifty feet farther away. To convey the hops to this kettle, they were dumped into a large hopper near the hop room, where they were fan blown down into the top of the kettle. Descending like a snowstorm of light flakes and heavier clumps into the highly turbulent atmosphere of the boiling kettle, the exhaust fan dutifully inspirated many of the hop leaves into the rooftop air scrubbing system, and these quickly settled in the fiberglass ducting or plugged the water sprays in the air scrubber.

Fortunately, the hop producers were able to offer a pelletized product, which eased this carry-over problem and improved hop storage capability. By shredding and milling the dried hops, the hop producers were able to compact them within a heated press to a very hard cylindrical (pellet) form that proved more durable for kettle handling. Vacuum packaging ensured against deterioration of flavor over a much longer storage period.

Putting the new brew house into production caused many other problems, though none proved insurmountable to the engineering crew's combined talents. During most of the construction Gerhard Schulz and Nick Thun had continued their brewing magic in the now windowless cell that once had been the showplace of gleaming copper and brass. Yet, each managed to get hands-on experience in the new brew house as trial brews were run and systems proved out, usually with Nick Boons or Dick Niven hovering nearby to jump circuits or perform other electrical wizardry.

Finally, John Pickering decided it was time to swim or sink. The new brew house came on stream and the old one began to gather dust. No sooner had congratulations been offered, than the next new project hove into sight. This was a new and larger packaging center—a wraparound building that would enclose the west and north sides of the existing bottle shop and warehouse.

It was during 1971 that the old steam tug *Master* got into trouble. She had put in an active year of goodwill sailing for local marine events and was tied up at the Evans Coleman dock at the foot of Columbia Street between events. During the darkened hours of the quiet night, vandals cut her loose from her mooring, allowing her to drift forward onto the rocks at the head of the pier.

Fortunately, the watchman at Kingcome Navigation over on the North Vancouver Ferry dock next door noticed her predicament and alerted Vancouver Tug (now part of Sea Span) and they dispatched a tug and pumps to prevent flooding of the *Master*'s vital parts. She had drifted up almost parallel with the rock-filled shoreline, but as the tide receded she settled with her starboard side listing away from the shore and in danger of tipping over. Several anxious hours passed as the flood tide rose above her deck and lower house before the tug shuddered tiredly and began to rise from her near grave. Surprisingly, hull damage was almost nil, but it took weeks of volunteer labor to clean up the paintwork and put everything back in order.

While Molsons appeared to be doing well with its conglomerate interests (retail hardware, chemicals, stationary, steel and machinery), within its brewing interest things were becoming quite bleak with Capilano Brewery actually running in the red. The unit cost of product had to be reduced by supplying more of it to the market place. The new packaging center became a top priority.

The demands of this new construction would tax all to the limit. Gus Fortier came close to a nervous breakdown before he finally succeeded in reaching the designed output, then surprisingly he left the brewery to start a conveyor business of his own. Art Pugh rushed back to take up the role of engineering manager and hold control over the many facets of endeavors. John Pickering faced more and more militant labor disagreements that threatened production stoppages. As each major brewer on the West Coast (Labatt, Carling and Molson) vied more keenly for the beer drinker's favor, the LCB, policing their methods of gaining such patronage, created media headlines with their dire warnings to rein in their aggressive marketing strategies or face the maximum penalty.

In a kaleidoscope of colorful events, well organized by engineering standards and management policy, the brewery began to change its outward appearance. First, the name was changed from Molson Capilano Brewery to Molson Brewery B.C. Ltd. This created a small howl of protest from the staunch Old Style beer drinkers, who were quickly becoming the minority as sales of their favored brew slipped from second to third place after the Molson Canadian Lager and Frontier Malt Liquor brands.

Secondly, Tom English, who had risen from acting manager to manager of the brewery and finally vice-president of Molson's Western Breweries, became president of the newly created Western Division formed within Molson Brewery B.C. Ltd. Tom's longtime marine interests were then directed to supporting the Molson Marine Patrol, a privately owned high speed craft, which advised on marine events, weather and fishing information through a daily VHF report over local broadcasting stations. It also provided assistance or sea rescue when required.

But most visual of the changes occurring were those in front of the brewery where earthmovers and diggers returned to that majestic sweep of Burrard Street and began ripping up lawns, sidewalks and gardens. Within a short time hoarding skirted the carnage, hiding it from public view, as clay and glacial till were scraped out to reveal the true hardpan onto which deep footings were poured. Winter again descended as the crews labored in knee-high water and ankle-deep mud to erect the forms for massive abutments and basement walls to hold against the ever-increasing weight of traffic thundering by just fifty feet away.

By early spring, the basement walls stretched northward from a new tall concrete sewer sump at the junction at the brew house to march around the north end of the warehouse and terminated in the shipping area parking lot. By early summer, concrete floors level with those of the existing bottle shop and suitably provided with expansion joints were overshadowed by massive walls that continued to rise until they reached roof height of the existing bottling shop and warehouse.

The final floor was poured and graded after the western wall, which enclosed the new packaging office floor and the fire proof staircase that would interconnect the brew house, rose to its finished height. To the north and east of this rose two structures to house a fire escape and a special pallet elevator.

As Indian summer cast long shadows, the precast wall panels were lifted and bolted into place between these structures. When they had been welded and sealed, the deep roof girders were lift up and fitted and the panels of corrugated steel roofing quickly laid to cover the vast floor area. Before the chill of winter rains arrived, the roofers had overlaid their insulation with tarred felts and gravel.

After the larger pieces of equipment had been lifted in, the huge window openings received their metal-framed windows. By Christmas, what had appeared as a great void was now cluttered with staging, ladders and welding machines as the monstrous bottle washer and its equally large partner the pasteurizer spread out to occupy much of the central floor area. By early spring of 1972, the two seventy-two-spout Cinco bottle fillers and crowners had been placed between these two imposing machines and glistening red brewery floor tile had been laid around them.

The bolting down of the bottle labelers and end loaders in the northern section of the packaging center allowed the tile setters to complete the floor so the complicated array of conveyors and inspectors could be installed for a test run. The results proved the electrically driven conveyors were not flexible enough and the conveyors overfeeding the machines became bound tightly with bottles. Removal of these bottles either empty or full defied previous experience, and most often many of them had to be broken out with a steel bar or hammer just to gain that few thousandths of an inch clearance to lift out the remainder.

This was only one of the many teething problems Gus and Art faced in attempting to get production up to the designed 1,200 bottles a minute expectation. In this case, the installation of hydraulic drive motors with variable load sensing or detecting controls proved a workable answer. While bottle breakage and product loss were highly visible as packaging personnel struggled to carry on in this battlefield of exploding bottles and flying glass, the supply of bottles to the washer and the delivery of full goods to the shipping dock required equal heroic efforts.

Before looking at the supply and product flow through this new installation, keep in mind that the smaller and more compact packaging line below it had to continue working two shifts, and sometimes overtime hours, to maintain the output of beer to the marketplace. All efforts had to be directed so as to not interfere with them or their flow of goods.

The large main floor area under the new pasteurizer and packaging equipment was slated for a shipping and receiving warehouse role. During much of the construction period, it had been used as a receiving area to store the various parts and pieces required for the new bottling line. Possibly the most trying phase of any specialized production construction is the logistics of bringing on site the production equipment without interfering with the construction schedule. While much of the large items, such as pasteurizer, tanks and bottle washer have a manufacturer's completion and shipping date, few of these people can offer a holding area after the item comes off their production line, so it is shipped to the construction site. Thus it becomes mandatory that the construction schedule and the manufacturer's schedule be identified through a critical path schedule, ensuring major items arrive on site almost the same day on which they are

The third brine chiller and new NH₃ receiver begin to take up floor space in the engine-room. *Photo: Molson*

to be lifted or moved into their final position within the construction. Smaller items vital to the scheme of things like gear drives, motors and pumps, which usually can be ordered out of manufacturer's or supplier's inventory, are subject to the risk of supply and demand. Thus, they must be bought well in advance of their installation and stored on site. As these types of things were shifted upstairs and installed, the space they had occupied in the new warehouse area was quickly filled up with pallets of cased beer.

The reason for this was the need for floor space at the west end of the old warehouse to install uncasing equipment required for the new line above. To appreciate the juggling problem, it must be realize that the overall plan for the packaging center would not be complete until the existing bottle line was removed and all uncasing was carried out in the area it now occupied. To keep things going after construction had blocked off Maurice Turcott's bottle receiving dock on the north wall, temporary conveyors leap-frogged over existing conveyors and through holes blasted out of concrete walls to feed the old soaker.

The No. 2 case palletizer also had to be installed at this time in this same area, and floor space became a premium. Earl Hardy and his assistant Matt Stewart desperately looked about for places to hold beer as inventory. They even resorted to loading the trucks at night just to gain floor space to store the next day's production, and this created the enticement for the "great beer robbery."

Stories abound of the things people do to get a free case of beer. Broken bottles or, more often, chipped crowns were a hazard of a high-speed production, and though most regrettable in getting out to the public, they were speedily compensated for with a home delivery of our customer's favorite brew. There were many other claims and complaints whose validity was not only questionable but downright dishonest that were settled with a case or two of beer, just to silence a bad mouth.

While these people were knowingly blackmailing the brewery and getting away with it, they couldn't resist boasting about their exploit, and naturally their cupiditious listeners quickly attempted similar feats. Angus McSherry, who often delivered the complimentary beer, noted wryly that seldom was it the first or second bottle opened or consumed which heralded the indignant complaint. More often than not it was the last bottle in the case they returned to him that had caused their ire.

Without going into the details, there were others who made claim on the brewery for more tangible compensation such as dollars to repair or replace clothing or upholstery that had been damaged by leaking beer cases. Then there was the little old lady who dragged a case of our beer across her highly polished dining room table, and demanded we pay to have a deep scratch on its surface French polished. Unaware we no longer stapled the bottom of our cartons, she was crestfallen when shown it was glued and incapable of making such a scratch. But, here again, she was such a dear misguided soul, and there just might have been a tiny shard of glass in bedded in the carton, it was decided that the brewery would spend a hundred bucks and have the damage repaired. Better to have somebody's mother singing your praise on high, then sucking in her breath while intimating to her friends how heartless and uncaring the brewery was.

Perhaps the most unfortunate scam happened to Molson's competition—that of the mouse in the beer bottle. Labatt would have been far wiser to have quickly paid off its perpetrators than to have thrown down the glove and challenged its probability. The newspapers gleefully scooped up weeks of highly public interest stories for their front pages, and the mouse became a daily topic wherever beer drinkers gathered. Neither side won anything from the repulsive incident, but it did cause most breweries to look very inquiringly at their own bottling procedures. Molsons carried out a series of experiments that checked quality control and proved that such an incident was impossible.

But there were other ways to get free beer out of a brewery. Stealing a case of beer seems ludicrous—it is a bulky thing to purloin, heavy to pack and worth relatively little for the risks it involves. Yet, the quiet brewery shrouded in the gloom of night, entices those who dream of its liquid inventory to perform prodigious feats to ferret some of it to the other side of the high barb wire and, later on, razor-steel topped fence. People have dug under the fence, cut through it and even climbed over it to scamper away gleefully with a few cases of beer. Sometimes dropping and breaking more than they carried away and other times leaving behind their loot when discovered by security patrol.

An incident related to me by Ed Dahlby and Gordon McDonald gave great satisfaction to all but those who were caught. While not a real sting, it had all the thrills of one. Ed was engineer on graveyard shift and Gordie was night watchman. Doing his two o'clock rounds of the cellars, Ed spotted from the fire escape some furtive movement out at the fence near the tram barns. Calling down to Gordie on the intercom to phone the police, Ed cautiously climbed over the roof until he was almost above the thieves and accounted for their comings and goings. Gordie positioned himself near the main gate to give entry to the police, while other patrol cars swooped silently in from the east and west. In the melee that followed, half a dozen or more burglars were caught, including a young woman.

They had backed a truck up against the fence near the darkened tramcars, threw a mattress over the barbed wire, piled up pallets to form a few steps on the brewery's side, and then began lugging out beer from the shipping dock. Climbing up the pallet boards they tossed their load of beer cases over onto the truck roof where the girl lowered them down to the driver who stowed them in the box. I believe the truck was half loaded when the driver ran off and hid under a boxcar where a police dog sniffed him out.

All this was just a prelude to the great beer robbery, which centered around the loaded beer trucks being used for night storage when floor space during the new bottle shop construction was in such short supply. Withholding names to save any embarrassment, here are the facts. The driver of the truck in question, after getting his shipping orders, started his engine and then decided to go into the lunchroom for a hot coffee as the truck warmed up. Lo and behold, when he returned, his truck was gone!

Bemused more than worried, and believing one of the other drivers had shifted it for some reason, he made a quick circuit of the parking yard and driveways. No truck. It had vanished, disappeared. Gone certainly, but where? He reported back to shipping, and after all the chuckles and kidding had subsided, Matt Stewart, the assistant shipper, had to phone the police. They in turn were just as bemused until Matt disclosed it was loaded with more than a thousand cases of premium beer, and then he got their full attention.

Endeavoring to be serious, the desk sergeant took down all the particulars amid a background chortle of wisecracks and laughter as the facts became known within the police station. It was the case of a lifetime, and the radio dispatcher quickly alerted all of Vancouver's finest on patrol.

"All cars, be on the lookout for a stolen Molson brewery truck loaded with fresh cool beer. Apprehend occupant. Guard beer."

The police reporter on duty picked up the story. It flashed onto radio and television, and filled the front page of the evening's newspaper. It even made the national news, but no truck was seen.

Then, on the third or fourth day of its disappearance, a hesitant phone call came into the brewery asking if they were still looking for a truck loaded with beer. When that was affirmed, the caller said a Molson truck had backed up at the rear of a Burnaby hotel parking lot and was selling beer at half price. The RCMP was alerted and they caught the young fellows who had daringly driven it away from the brewery.

After three days of peddling beer in out-of-way parking lots, they got just a little too brazen and presumably felt a brewery truck parked behind a beer parlor would appear natural enough. They just might have made it if the anonymous caller had not alerted the brewery. While the Bentall Street warehouse/shipping center was still several years away, bonded warehouse space for beer and some supplies was rented to negate the need for further storage of beer in trucks.

Meanwhile new crews were being trained to fill in gaps as the senior, more skilled operators were shifted upstairs to bring the new line into production. Near bedlam resulted while the two uncasing lines were run one over top of the other, each temporarily positioned until the transition would realize the gangs of uncasers that would finally fulfill this function for just the new line.

The uncasing line with its high manual labor input and dirty and dusty working condition, coupled with the high speed whine of the cardboard cutting band saws, made it a prime area in which to initiate the new employees. Sweeping up and lugging away the broken glass from both lines was another job requiring more manual labor than technical skills. These two areas received more than their quota of casual labor, though those found unsuited were quickly weeded out.

While most hired on a casual work basis inherited this menial labor, those showing ability and willingness to learn more responsible jobs as machine operators were brought onto the permanent work force through a job posting system as openings came up. By the following year, when packaging was putting out more than 40,000 cases of beer per day, the work force had grown to an unbelievable 170 persons. Among them was the first female production worker, Donna Cholette, who learned to drive forklifts and operate packaging equipment as competently as any male employee.

Shortly after the new 1,200 bottle a minute packaging line began steady production, mostly dealing with Canadian and the old line handling Export Ale and Old Style, two more outward signs displayed the new status of the brewery. First was a large fleet of new trucks. Herb Wilmon, admired by all and affectionately referred to by most as Gramps, retired from the trucking business. And Molson's, electing to go the rental route, moved their company colors onto power tailgated, long-boxed Hertz lease units. The new shipping dock had hydraulic ramps that allowed new fast forklifts to double and triple deck the pallets in these trucks, as well as in the numerous trailer units that shipped product into the interior or to Vancouver Island. Upgrading the unloading areas at the LCB and hotels allowed similar forklifts to unload the trucks quickly.

The second event that came to public notice was the removal of

The rear of the brewery with employees' lunchroom and water filter plant in the foreground. Note the grains car and hop truck to the right.   *Photo: Molson*

the traditional tower sign above the mill room. A huge wraparound steel banner in the royal blue of Molsons, enclosed the whole top section of the tower and was faced east and west with the Molson logo outline in colorful neon lighting. A set of switches and relays flashed the time of day and weather forecast alternately through large panels of sealed beam lights on the north and south faces of the banner.

Within the brewery, as the new bottling line began to take over the bulk of production, Dick Niven accepted a position as bottling supervisor as did Garry Lane who had earlier joined the company as a quality control chemist. This eased somewhat the burden carried by Gus Fortier. The new packaging offices overlooked the in-feed of the soaker, where the fumes of caustic soda and the high humidity plagued the occupants. So Jim Crony was happy to turn his office over to Earl Hardy and move down to the shipping floor. This shuffle allowed the offices above the maintenance shop to be turned into a locker and change room for both maintenance and engineering staff. This eased the crowding of new employees over in the main employee's building. And by judiciously squeezing in more lockers over there, Molsons was able to buy time before deciding where to locate a newer and larger employee's facility.

Most favored placing it on top of the old bottle shop roof, thus readily accessible to both packaging and brew house people but not so convenient and certainly a more hazardous travel route to most everyone else. Finally, in 1976 a decision to make no decision was arrived at. Art bought some portable buildings for a temporary lunchroom and placed them off the southeast corner of the employee's building. Demolishing the pantry/tap room to create an interconnecting corridor, they installed showers and lockers in the old lunchroom, and for the next ten or more years this was home to the brewery workers.

John Pickering, a young and energetic brewmaster who had seen through most of these traumatic changes, left before the employee's lunchroom question had been settled. His next challenge was in distribution where a two-delivery system had persisted since pre-Molson days, one by Pacific Brewers Delivery (owned by the three breweries) and the other operated by each brewery. This finally resulted in the creation of a warehouse and distribution center at Bentall Street.

Moving up to take over the responsibility of brewmaster/plant manager was a pleasant, soft-spoken former flying officer of the Royal Air Force. Tom Buckley had served in the bomber command during the terrible days at Malta when Rommel's African Korps threatened to overwhelm Britain's control of the Suez Canal and the oil fields of Arabia. Only the battered aircraft he flew from the bombed airfields in Malta could plague Rommel's supply line of ships and denied him the fuel and supplies to press his advantage. Thus granting Monty time to mount the Allied offensive, which drove Rommel forever from this prized objective.

Squadron Leader Buckley had left the air force to enter brewing in England after the war, and had spent the last four years assisting John Pickering through the era of building the new brew house and packaging center. He felt strongly that the *esprit de corps* that had always been Molsons hallmark was flagging far behind those great developments, and he set about to rejuvenate this feeling of pride.

Visiting most parts of the brewery at least once each day, he stopped to chat with the fellows and hear their concerns or gripes. Often offering suggestions of his own to get their reaction, he then followed up with his staff to seek an improvement. While this appeared to be a nice gesture with some degree of communication, the noise of the work place and the demands on the workers, precluded any in-depth discussion. He tried holding small discussion meetings with the various departments, but work schedules, etc., often precluded some from attending, so he explored another channel.

Approaching Alex MacDonnell, whose skill with words had often been posted on the employee's notice board, to depict his humorous observations about life at the brewery, Tom invited him to write and publish a quarterly newsletter about events and development at the brewery. Alex was the perfect choice to do so, as a former head of Local 300 Brewery Workers Union and recently retired from Molson's delivery service. Alex had begun his working career with the old *Calgary Herald* before trying his hand as editor of a couple of small prairie weeklies before Black Friday closed them down.

Migrating to the coast during the Hungry Thirties, he got a job with Fritz Sick as a teamster delivering wooden kegs of beer to the hotels around Vancouver and never looked back. Alex was game to give it his best shot, and proposed they call it the *Eye Opener*, after Bob Edward's famous Calgary tabloid that had provided Albertans with deliciously scandalous exposés of political and economical events during the early years of this century.

While it became the first newsletter produced from this brewery, two other newsletters/magazines had been produced which had carried information about activities and development. Emil Sick had the *Enterpriser* published at Rainier Brewery in Seattle during the fifties, which gave good coverage of events within his huge brewing empire. Then, in the midsixties Beverly Meyers, granddaughter of Alfred Muntz, Fritz Sick's pioneer partner of Fort Steele/Fernie days, produced the *West Word* for Molson's western division out of Calgary.

Tom Buckley hoped to produce a more local interest newsletter than either of these had been and invited contributions from all. It grew slowly into a folded four-page monthly publication carried on by John Schoutsen during its final years, after Alex retire as its editor.

Tom wrote many informative articles on the various brewing processes and products, including those on hops, malt, water and yeast (which have been used freely in this story). Art Pugh contributed a monthly update on the various engineering projects underway or planned at the brewery. While Jim Heap provided information on sales promotion and Eric Barry contributed both historical articles and reports on employee activities.

A canning line capable of 500 tins a minute was installed shortly after the new bottling line was deemed a success, and after it had

The can filler with the bottling line to the left. The empty tins, inverted and washed, enter the counterclockwise-turning carousel to discharge on the opposite side from viewer. There are cartons of lids in the right background. *Photo: Molson*

been debugged and was running smoothly the old bottling line on the main floor was dismantled and removed. New uncasing saws, conveyors and dust collectors were installed in this area to supply bottles to the upstairs soaker via a long drop leg. The rest of the old bottling shop became storage for new and used bottles and this released floor space for more storage of full goods in the former warehouse.

For a couple years the brewery went into a make and mend mode as their share of the beer market fluctuated with the uncertainty of the times. Though a decision to install a new type of cellar system had been agreed upon as part of the brewery's upgrading, the unitank system was not undertaken until 1976, when site location plans had been finalize.

Traditionally, breweries have shifted beer from fermenter to ruh tanks then to finishing tank and finally into usage tanks for racking or bottling by settling or filtering between each cellar to remove yeast spores and improve clarity. The new system would realize most of this all within one special tank. The huge tanks, mounted vertically and chilled by ammonia jackets were designed for removal of the bot-

Eric Barry and author at an editorial luncheon for the *West Word*.

Photo: Beverly Meyers

tom yeast while retaining the freshly fermented beer, then aging it by inspirating carbon dioxide gas up through the beer before filtering and polishing, and placing in usage tanks for bottling or racking.

Fully insulated and weatherproofed, the system could be erected exterior of the existing brewery buildings, much like the cracking towers of an oil refinery. But no accord could be arrived at where to install them. The reason behind this indecision over the unitank cellar location was that future expansion plans had not yet been finalized. The First Avenue property Emil Sick unwittingly sold to Hoffar Diesels, and now owned by Osborne Propeller, was being negotiated upon as the site for a future shipping center. There were even thoughts of relocating the keg washing and racking to this area, thus reducing yard traffic to service trucks only. A second bottling line was also being considered along with a whole new concept of yeast removal and beer filtering.

In view of all these probables, the plan finally accepted was to dig another hole in front of the brewery in which to build the unitank cellar and then build two floors of office area on top of that for future relocation of the administration staff. This then left the area south of the brewery for future cellar expansion. By improving the keg han-

The unitank cellar with the beer transfer pump in the foreground. Note the CO_2 injection meter on the side of the vertical tanks.   *Photo: Molson*

The unitank cooling system with NH_3 pumps and accelerator in foreground and ponndorf air compressor at the back.   *Photo: Molson*

dling and racking, and installing the temporary employees lunchroom as already noted, the brewery would likely weather the next five years without having to expand outside its fence.

The creation by Steve Collinge of the Bentall Street distribution center precluded the need to use the property off First Avenue for more than a parking lot. It would remain thus as slowly and resolutely the events unfolded that would lead Molsons into the role of megabrewery.

CHAPTER TEN

Into the Electronic Age

The area south of the new brew house and west of the existing A block cellar fronting Burrard Street was the site selected for the new unitank cellar. Once more construction started as the fall rains turned the dirt to mud and much the same difficulties were experienced as during the previous construction. Through the fall and winter of 1976, amid snow, rain and freezing temperatures the forms and rebar followed the diggers down into the hardpan, while pumps kept the water level at workable height.

By spring, husky cement walls rose above ground level and the bases for the new tall stainless steel tanks were poured. The large size of these tanks necessitated their installation before further construction took place. And their movement from Ellett Copper and Brass on the Fraser River to the brewery site required some great feats of engineering just to get them there. Because of their great height, they could not be shipped in an upright position, and their large girth had to be reinforced by internal bracing to prevent collapse while being transported on their sides.

Barged around to the old Arrow Docks in False Creek, they were lifted onto trailers and trucked over to Burrard Street, where during early morning lulls in the traffic they were lifted over onto their bases within the brewery. By late fall, with the walls and roof completed and windows installed in the two floors of future offices above the cellar, the ammonia equipment that had been erected in the brew house basement was piped into the tank jackets and tested.

The unitank jacket cooling system was of the flooded ammonia type, requiring a large liquid ammonia receiver in the engineroom and a new ammonia condenser erected on the boiler room roof. But because brine chilling loads were expected to be reduced while the unitank system was operating, no increase in compressor capacity was deemed necessary.

The engineroom roof in the foreground and boiler room roof at the back with the NH$_3$ condensers in view.

Photo: Molson

To recap, the refrigeration system up to this time had used a secondary refrigerant to chill the product, a solution of chromate-treated calcium chloride in water referred to as brine. By controlling the pH level with caustic soda and ensuring air did not enter the system through the flooded loop and balance tank arrangement, erosion and corrosion of the heavy steel pipes and steel chillers in this system could be reduced to a minimum. If a leak developed, it could easily be diluted with water and washed to sewer while repairs were underway with little or no hazard to anyone.

With the exception of a few minor failures and a couple of piping modification, the new refrigeration system worked to perfection. Unfortunately, the brewer's aspirations of creating a finished beer within just one tank proved far more difficult and elusive to realize. First and foremost was the challenge of removing the yeast after the completion of fermentation. The second test was coming up with a satisfactory method of aging. Here a modification in the carbon dioxide injection methods made a certain improvement, while melding beers in the finishing tanks realized an acceptable product.

Possibly the greatest headache to engineering, was the problem of trying to collect the CO_2 gas offthe unitanks without the crud and foam from the active fermentation carrying over and contaminating this sterile process. Through the previous years, as more and more horizontal fermenting tanks were added, the gas collection system had grown only modestly. As more and more piping had been added to connect these extra fermenters to the foam tank, the original potassium permanganate-treated (deoxidizer) foam trap had been replaced with a larger water-sprayed foam trap, but basically little else had been done.

Consequently, this system was already running in a less than perfect condition, experiencing carry over, blockages and air entrainment (any air in the CO_2 gas collected reduces CO_2 condenser capacity and can oxidize beer it is injected into). Heavy losses required almost weekly truckloads of additional liquid carbon dioxide being brought into the brewery before the unitank project ever got the green light. Thus, included in the unitank project budget were also funds to update the CO_2 system.

A new two-stage compressor and rotary booster, a new gas condenser and liquid storage receiver, plus a larger foam trap, larger regenerative activated carbon deodorizers and re-evaporator were all approved. With floor space already made scarce in the engineroom due

The beer filter room with slurry tanks and pumps. Note the extensive use of stainless steel tanks and pipes. *Photo: Molson*

209

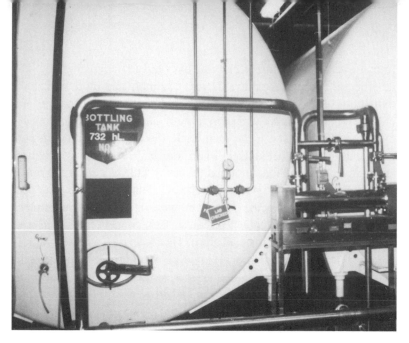

De-areated water tanks used during high-gravity brewing.   *Photo: Molson*

to an additional brine chiller, a third air compressor and new ammonia liquid dump trap, the new carbon dioxide liquid storage tank and its condensing equipment had to be located in the old brew house area. The new carbon deodorizers and filters were bricked into a gas-proof room, where Charlie Stannard had once pitched kegs and barrels and Dennis Johnson was forced to hang the CO_2 re-evaporators off the walls, above the new compressors.

While all of this improved production of the gas and the addition of an in-place cleaning system reduced foam carry over in the collection pipes, it was the introduction of de-aerated water to the foam tank sprays that really improved the quality of the usage gas. This was borrowed from the high-gravity beer system mentioned earlier (i.e., brewing and aging much stronger beers to conserve tankage by 15–25 percent, then diluting it down to normal strength for packaging).

But collection of CO_2 gas from the tall unitank system during fermentation was a different story entirely. Some simple arithmetic will point up the problem. A horizontal fermenter, approximately nine feet in diameter and twenty-five feet long, held about 500 barrels (12,000 gallons) of wort/beer and provided approximately 200 square feet of liquid surface through which the bubbles of CO_2 could escape. In a

The CO$_2$ compressors with NH$_3$ compressor in background.   *Photo: Molson*

unitank of approximately twenty foot diameter, only about 300 square feet of liquid surface (50 percent more) was provided to release the gas bubbles from three times as much (1,500 barrels) of actively fermenting wort/beer. Thus, more than twice the agitation of surface foam and crud took place to release the gas, and not all of these fast-rising bubbles of gas had released their coating of foam, etc., before they arrived at the foam trap. The carry over of foam often exceeded the ability of the sprays to disperse and was pulled into the booster stage of the collection system with rather nasty results that coated and plugged the equipment shutting down the system.

Putting in a larger liquid dump trap did not eradicate the problem, but a solution was found that, though simplicity itself, was far from satisfactory to the brewers. By reducing the amount of wort/beer put in the unitank, the gas space in the top of the vessel was increased, giving a greater dwell time for the rising gas bubble to shed its mantle of foam before entering the collection system.

Actually, these unitanks were then handled in much the same way as the horizontal ones down through A and B block cellars, with the beer being shifted from tank to tank as the yeast was removed and aging took place. The installation of yeast removal centrifuges with continuous cleaning in later years enhanced this process and took the heavy load off the beer filter room, so it could concentrate on final polishing and carbonating of the finished product.

From 1976 to 1979 while these events were taking place, a lager beer called Ryder and a heavy malt brew called Brador were introduced to the market. To promote more product support, Molson purchased the marketing rights for the new Pacific Coast (Triple A) baseball team, and bought the Montreal Canadiens Hockey Club for the second time after the Bronfman syndicate decided to sell it.

Thus Molson protected their national advertising through the *Hockey Night in Canada* television series and preserved their family honor within Canadian sport. With this regrettable matter finally put right, Senator Hartland Molson retired.

In 1979, Bob Weaver came out to Vancouver as plant manager, and Molson's World Cup was introduced as the first-ever men's downhill ski race in Canada. Scheduled to be held at Whistler Mountain in early March, it had to be cancelled due to hard ice and poor snow conditions. The following year it gained worldwide recognition for Canada, and has continued to be a featured sport event supported by Molson. The year 1979 also saw the reacquired Canadiens waltz off with the famed epitome of hockey—the Stanley Cup.

But less public events within the brewery had a far greater interest for many who were not involved in the marketing image. While Burrard Street brewery was justly proud to have almost stemmed its hemorrhage of red ink, the parent company had actually enjoyed total sales that exceeded $1 billion!

This record-high income enjoyed a dollar dividend earned by all shares in the company, which now included Beaver Lumber Company (hardware), Wilson Office Specialty (stationary) and the Diversey Corporation (chemicals). In the year following these rewarding events, Molsons reported even greater earnings, of which their brewing interests accounted for 66 percent, and in B.C. the brewery was credited with its first profit balance in many a year. That year, Eric Molson took over the reins as president of Molson Breweries of Canada.

During 1979–80 came the retirement of a number of longtime employees, most notable to all at Molson Brewery B.C. was that of Tom English, president of the western division. T. H. English in many eyes personified the role of gentleman—sober and strong in character, honorable and considerate of others. His long association with the brewing industry and its community support systems created many friends who would quickly echo those sentiments.

Many of the seniors from the Powell Street days also retired during this period. Included among those was Max Schmidbauer. Max did beautiful wood work; a former barrel maker over at the old Capilano Brewery, he built a miniature oak barrel to replace the large tin can they had used to collect funds for the Cripple Children's Hospital. It drew gasps of admiration from all who saw it. Unfortunately, one of the brewery's many visitors must have coveted it, or its contents, for it disappeared one Christmas just before its contents were to be donated to the hospital. Max quickly produced a second one and an emergency funding drive filled it. Max had also served his time in barrel making at Silver Spring Brewery in Victoria when Vic Brachat was there.

Les Chiswick, whose father Bob Chiswick had joined Fritz Sick in 1905 at Lethbridge, also retired from western division during this time. Les had always made it a point to drop in and chat whenever his footsteps brought him near the boiler room. A tall gentle man, he was always very interested in employee activities and the brewery history. To commemorate the company's fifty years of brewing, Emil Sick had presented a diamond ring to his father. Because Mister Sick had also presented Les with a similar ring, he felt his father's ring should be presented to a noteworthy employee and he gave it to me.

Walter Weisner and Cec Graham also retired about this time. They carried on their goodwill efforts after retirement by organizing activities for the retirees. Karl Mueller, the former bottle shop superintendent from Powell Street and nephew of Fritz Sick, had always made it a point to come down to the new brewery and visit with the boys after he retired. He had a nut farm out in the Fraser Valley, and he packed hazel nuts up in one-pint brown paper bags, which he presented to each of us. His annual visit started the tradition of the old timers showing up at Christmas time for a drink and chat with the boys.

Gerhard Schulz was probably the most active man I knew at the brewery, before and after his retirement. Like Walter Weisner, he was one of Fritz Sick's original employees at Powell Street and quickly got involved in the brewing end, serving all his years at Burrard Street as kettle man on the nightshift.

Reminiscing about these long-service employees brings to mind the Service Award Dinners Tom English initiated. The retirees were always invited and most all attended. Tom presented silver beer mugs to those attaining fifteen years of service and gold watches to those achieving twenty-five years service. He always assured there was a lovely meal, lots to drink and nice surrounding in which to enjoy them.

Gus Fortier left packaging to start up his own business, but he was soon back at the brewery installing the new conveying equipment his company was supplying. By the time the second bottling line was coming on stream, Gus was spending almost as much time at the brewery as when he had been packaging manager. Gary Lane took over Gus' job for a few years, and Dick Niven took over packaging maintenance bringing Bruce Patrick on staff as his foreman. Eddy Morison left maintenance to become a foreman in packaging, and Nick Boons left the brewery to open a motel up in Penticton. Many new faces appeared in the workshop as the pace quickened, and the brewery went back to double shifts with graveyard clean ups.

By 1980 with Hal Moran as president, another mighty expansion was about to shake the old brewery, a new 1,000 bottle a minute bottling line was to be installed and programmable logic controllers (PLCs) were going to run it. The goal was the capability of producing more than 2,000 bottles a minute with both lines—over thirty bottles a second—and Art Pugh moved over into packaging to take charge.

Rick Killan moved up to engineering manager, and Dennis Johnson joined him as project engineer. With the threat of more upheaval as the brewery became more computerized, the allure of restful retirement enticed both Tom Buckley and Fred Kirby to join the retirees. Giff Robb and Dave Lethwaite split Tom's job, and I stepped into Fred's position. Bob Chambers was enlisted from the Calgary office to be project supervisor of the new bottling line construction, but couldn't arrive on site until later in the year.

The summer of 1980 marked the brewery's entry in the electronic world. The silicone chip and the diode were going to bring electronics into the boiler room and computers into the offices.

CHAPTER ELEVEN

Changing of the Guard

Back in 1971 Molsons established an American marketing arm called Martlet Importing Co. Ltd., located in Great Neck, New Jersey. Its purpose was to improve beer sales to the United States, and it succeeded so well that by the early 1980s Molson was the second largest importer of foreign beer into the U.S.A. During this same period Eric Molson, following the example of Tom Molson before his death, carefully arranged for the family to reacquire large holdings of voting shares in the company. Splitting the shares to finance their conglomerate holdings had diluted that control. But by November, 1981, Eric had succeeded in putting control of the company back in the Molson family hands by holding more than 55 percent of the voting shares. These two events point toward the reason Molson was spending millions of dollars to expand the production of both their Ontario brewery at Barrie and their British Columbia brewery at Vancouver.

The American beer market loomed high in their forecast sales. And by brewing and packaging popular American brands on the Canadian side of the border, it appeared they could enjoy the best of both worlds. This philosophy had emerged after the Supreme Court of United States of America had ruled against Molson's application to purchase outright Hamm's Brewing Company, under a conflict of interest clause. Eric Molson, like his great-great-great-grandfather John the Elder, knew that what ever other interests Molson might have, brewing of good quality beers was still the family's prime interest, and that this philosophy had kept the family viable through a tumultuous two centuries of Canadian business.

The recession had caused sales of its chemicals, its office supplies, its steel products and its petroleum equipment to plummet until they burdened the brewery's income with their deficit. But as old Fritz Sick found out through the great depression, recessions usually

Photo 85: The carton end loader formed and dropped cartons onto rollers the beer bottles would be pushed into cartons and the end flaps would be glued and sealed in the center area. *Photo: Molson*

caused the number of beer drinkers to grow. Eric Molson wanted to be ready to capitalize on this fact, so he pushed for greater production capability and greater sales promotion. The brewery struggled to comply, though the cost was heavy both in dollars and stamina, and some with failing health had to step aside before the final act was over. The manner of this struggle now unfolds.

The latest expansion, which the planners hoped to realize within a three-year building budget, was by far the greatest and most ardu-

216

ous any at the brewery were to ever experience. Upgrading the services to supply the new equipment began first, and paced the construction/installation projects. This involved more electrical power, installing a new dual fired boiler with microelectronic controls, plus converting No. 1 boiler to the same parameters.

A huge new rotary ammonia compressor and a large rotary air compressor both had to be fitted into the already crowded engine-room, while their allied equipment like condensers, driers and receivers had to be fitted in extraneous of these areas. The carbon dioxide collection and re-evaporation system was to double its former capacity within the former brew house main floor.

The new packaging line which would be installed on the ground floor below the present bottling floor, required a building extension out to the north property line, and displaced the warehousing and storage area. A new warehouse and shipping facility had to be acquired, and this eventually became the Bentall Street shipping center. More tankage was required in the bottling cellar to supply this new line, and a new sewer and glass collecting system had also to be realized within the basement area under this floor. To complicate things more, the caustic cleaning system had to be increased and some of these tanks were also placed in the basement area.

In A block cellar building, a new yeast collection system was to be installed, designed around two large, continuous, self-clean centrifuges and two huge ammonia-chilled beer coolers, displacing the ale cellar's open fermenters. The complete system would be automated, and the cellar tanks converted to a train system. Though brewing would be automated first using Allen Bradley's 1771 series PLCs, it was really the new automated bottle line with its soaker and pasteurizer that required the installation of a second 50,000-lb./hr. boiler and its larger ancillary equipment.

The master plan had a critical path for each phase. Only that material, equipment and labor scheduled by this plan could arrive on site, and each phase was sequenced to compliment the next one that followed. A labor strike almost threw all plans to the four winds. Fortunately, the recent enlarging of the engineering staff allowed the brewery to maintain basic services and hold a million or so gallons of product at optimum level of quality, until the labor negotiators parleyed a deal to get the machinery running and beer trucks rolling out again.

Labor strikes had troubled the brewery at an ever-increasing frequency, since those earlier tranquil days when Alex MacDonnell had been president of Local 300 Brewery and Cereal Workers Union. The International Union of Operating Engineers working under a separate contract, were to some degree isolated from this turmoil, but the affiliation with the labor movement precluded any thought of crossing a picket line, unless cleared to do so by the union involved in the dispute.

During the brewery worker's strike in the early sixties, with labor relations less strained, IUOE members were able to maintain vital services and keep steam on the plant. In the labor disputes that followed, this privilege was not repeated, and unable to peacefully pass through the Brewery Worker's picket line, the IUOE engineers at Molsons voluntarily became unemployed. Thus, they were not eligible for any form of assistance, strike pay or unemployment benefits and had to find what temporary work they could elsewhere to feed the family and pay the mortgage.

Both Sick Capilano Brewery and Molson's B.C. Ltd had enjoyed good employee relations through the earlier years. Ironically, the labor disputes that plagued the brewery in the later years were seldom of its own making. Management had a commitment of togetherness through their Pacific Brewers Association, and labor's stance of solidarity came from its "one big brewery workers union" philosophy. One or the other of these two powerful bodies, depending where the dispute originated (in all fairness I don't believe either the management team or the labor work force at the Burrard Street brewery ever initiated a dispute), dictated whether the brewery made a brew or not.

Employees at Burrard Street enjoyed benefits that were second to none in the brewing industry as can be noted by this book's descriptions of the great *esprit de corps* that existed through those tumultuous periods of expansions. Without such cooperation, the job would have been much more difficult and the results less satisfying. On a personal note, in my last years at this brewery, when tempers threatened to flare up and spirits sometimes flagged, I could often see little examples of this spirit. For example, when I requested extra help for clean up and painting chores, brewery workers with the least amount of brewery talent would show up at the engineroom stores. Supplied with scrapers, brushes, paint and rags they cheerfully took on all the nasty corners, difficult places and only moved away when the areas sparkled with bright cleanliness. On more than one occasion, these people worked through their lunch break or after hours to complete a job at no extra charge, because they didn't wish to leave it unfinished yet had to return to their production job on the morrow!

Unfortunately, the brewery's latest labor strike in 1980 left the LCB shelves bare of the public's favorite brews, giving opportunity to the smaller nonunion breweries in the province to enter the marketplace or, worse still, allow the large American breweries to import their highly advertised product to stock the LCB shelves. Realizing the need for better communication and relations between labor and management to forestall such calamities, Molsons elected to create a personnel manager and appointed Butch LaRoue, to carry it out.

During the strike, while these plans were being adopted, most other staff members were delegated to keep the brewery clean and maintain cellar beer quality ready for the market that the brewery hoped would be there when labor returned to package and ship it. It was strange to see managers and sales reps donning work clothes and gumboots to clean tanks, lug hoses and wash floors, but it sure did gave them a better idea of the product they normally tried to sell.

Rick Killan was able to assign several production staff people to help maintain engineering services around the clock, and it was ensured they had the minimum of equipment to monitor and sufficient training to carry out the procedures. With only the NH_3, CO_2 and O_2 equipment operating, the brewery was not required by government regulations to have a certified engineer on hourly duty, and this arrangement fulfilled both the brewery's needs and insurance requirements during this period of nonproduction.

Once the dispute had been settled and Molsons was again supplying the market place, the plant manager and Butch LaRoue began holding production meetings with both staff and union workers in attendance. The militant feeling took time to erase. Tempers on both sides were tried to the limit to breach the gap and discover workable and amenable arrangements. But it did go away and credit has to be shared to some degree with the rank and file, who worked just as diligently and unsparingly to make it do so.

When Bob Chambers arrived in early fall to supervise the excavation and create the foundations for the north packaging extension, the boiler removal project was well under way and Rick Killan, keeping well versed in its progress, was himself supervising the

The new 50,000-lb./hr. duel fuel boiler, 1983.

brewing automation project. All this work had to be keyed to production, yet the next five years would produce more causes to shut down the flow of product than any other period in the brewery's history. A boiler room fire, though it did not shut down production, was more an embarrassment than a threat to the brewery. And it certainly proved that Murphy was alive and well.

The No. 2 boiler was being prepared for removal, and a section of the north wall of the boiler room (twenty feet wide by twenty feet high) was cut free by masonry saws and lifted out. This facilitated removal of the old boiler's larger pieces and provided entry for the new 50,000-lb./hr.package boiler. This opening alongside the train shed rail line was draped over with plastic sheeting to keep the weather out, while still allowing for removal of sections of the old boiler as they were cut loose.

The steam, condensate and fuel oil pipes that had serviced this boiler were in a shallow trench between the wall opening and the boiler front. These had all been cut and capped off with compression fittings, checked off by both the contractor's foreman and the shift engineer before being covered over with scrap steel pipe and plate awaiting removal. Winter arrived early that year, and for the first time the shift engineer had to wear coat, gloves and hat to keep warm in that drafty boiler room.

Then, the unheard of happened. The main steam sensing line froze—this up near the ceiling of the normally hot boiler room! Naturally, the problem was a little elusive to realize and production came to a halt. Fortunately, packaging had not yet started up for the day, so only a few people were put out of work until the problem was fixed by the simple procedure of closing a window that the crew cutting up No. 2 boiler had left open.

Unfortunately, the heavy snows that had begun to fall that early morning also delayed the demolition contractor's truck and crane arriving to remove the scrap steel piling up in front of the old boiler. To compound troubles even more, the brewery had to swing over to alternate fuel as quickly as possible, as the unusual arctic cold front was taxing the gas company's ability to supply vital services.

Normally, with two hours notice to get off the gas service, it would have posed little concern with the company's duel fuel firing method. The smaller (18,000-lb./hr.) boiler would have been fired up and put on the line, burning oil. Then the larger (50,000-lb./hr.) gas-fired boiler would be changed over to oil firing and put back on line. If the changeover were slated during a light load period, the smaller boiler would have no problem maintaining line pressure.

Unfortunately, the back up boiler was all laying around in pieces in everyone's way, and the only low steam usage period during that day was less than an hour away. But, advising the various departments, workers got everything ready to take advantage of this lull.

Though most would be away at lunch, I was not unduly concerned. The fuel oil equipment was circulating on standby, the fuel tank was warmed up, and the best engineers were on hand.

Like a team, the gas fuel was tripped off, the oil fuel valve was latched up, there was ignition and then the firing rate began to increase. It looked like a win-win proposition until the atomizing steam valve was spun wide open. Right then the loud crack of doom signaled otherwise—Murphy's second trick. Steam roared up from among the steel scrap piled over the trench, and it didn't take an Einstein to realize the steam pipe had come uncapped. There was nothing for it but to go back onto gas firing and pay the surcharge until the pipe was repaired.

I called all the help we could muster, even the contractors crews jumped in to help. The scrap steel was literally thrown outside in the haste to get down into the trench. Fifteen minutes before the two-hour notice would have run out, a more promising cap had been put on the steam pipe and tested. I looked at the clock as I called the gas distribution center. We were ten minutes into the penalty time but were making steam on the oil burner. I was satisfied, but it was only momentary bliss. The next instant all hell broke loose.

That's when Murphy taught us another law from the land of the four-leaf clover—expect the unexpected. Above the din of ringing bells and hooting hooters, I could here the cry of "Fire, Fire!" Flames were licking around the doorway between the engineroom and the boiler room where the carnage of No. 2 boiler still lay scattered about the floor.

Dodging through the flames, I ran into the boiler room where Bill was pointing up at the wall that divided the two equipment areas. Black smoke and orange flames coated the entire wall. The supply lockers built into the area were on fire, most of the oily packing and gasket material providing the tinder to provoke even more flames and heat. Compressed between the still-standing parts of the boiler and the reinforced concrete wall, the fire lacked sufficient oxygen and room to grow into a major fire.

Fortunately, there was a new hose point piped in between the boilers, and it took just minutes to lay out the hose, turn on the water and put the fire out. The mess it created would take considerable greater effort to eradicate. That was when I heard the sirens and realized the firemen, alerted by our new automatic alarm, were risking

The Seitz filler that could handle 1,000 bottles a minute. *Photo: Molson*

life and limb to rush through the treacherous snow-clogged streets to come to what amounted to a garbage fire!

Hastily I phoned in to cancel their hazardous commitment but, needless to say, I could not deter the firemen from their duty, and one fire engine continued on alone to check the fire scene. That was the apparatus vehicle that my youngest son was driving. I was very embarrassed trying to explain away to his captain how burning sparks from the oxyacetylene torch had not been spotted and put out by the fire watcher because he was too busy trying to hastily move a bunch of scrap steel outdoors because someone else had been sloppy in their plumbing.

No sooner had the fire truck departed when another huge piece of equipment panted up to the boiler room door its whistle roaring with indignation because the tracks over which the empty grain car was to be removed was covered over with steel pipes and plates. Jim Crony came to my aid then, sending over a half dozen of his lads and their big Bull Moose forklift truck. The early winter darkness had settled in by the time all was finish, and I was quite happy to brush the snow off my car and follow the evening rush home to peaceful Burnaby.

By late January the new packaged boiler had been slid in through the wall opening, the slab bolted back in place, and fitters were busy installing the up-takes and stack. In the engineroom, a steel platform had been erected above the main switch panel to carry much of the new electrical service. On the boiler room roof in March, a large NH_3 condenser was lifted into place to serve the new 425-ton Mycom screw ammonia compressor being installed in the engineroom where the eight-inch Linde compressor from Powell Street had stood for almost thirty years.

Through the late spring, a second 25,000-pound CO_2 liquid storage tank was installed west of the elevator, which required a large opening jack hammered into the train shed. And to keep the year's work exciting, the Linde NH_3 compressor in the engineroom was replaced with a large 1,000 cubic foot per minute air compressor complete with a new header underground through the tunnel to the packaging basement, where it supplied a pair of regenerative air driers.

While this was sorted out and tied it into the existing systems without interrupting any of the vital services, Rick Killan had cut a hole in the north wall of A block on the third-floor cellar level to install large ammonia-chilled beer coolers and centrifuges. Over in packaging, Art Pugh and Bob Chambers were desperately storing the components of their new $9.5-million bottling project where free space on site or at Bentall Street allowed. When this could not be had, they cajoled the shipper to hold it in his yard. These included items like the 900 bottle a minute soaker, a 110 valve head Seitz filler, three Jagenburg labeling machines, two end loaders, a drop pack machine and an ABC sealer. All this expensive equipment would take months to replace and was very vulnerable to damage while in storage. A colossal two-deck pasteurizer and three more

The six-cylinder ammonia compressor in foreground and air screw compressor in the back.   *Photo: Molson*

automatic palletizing machines were also due from the builder's production line, hopefully their arrival in Vancouver would not be before Bob Chambers had created the floor space for them. This required completing a fifty-foot extension on both floor levels of the existing packaging building and the creation of new walls complete with doors and windows.

The beer filter control room; temperature gauges are below panel clock and the graphic and flow recorders are above consul selector switches.   *Photo: Molson*

A new workshop area was planned at the east end of the existing No. 1 line, and a mezzanine floor level above it was slated for equipment stores and maintenance offices. Steve Collinge and Matt Stewart vacated the shipping area below this to Jim Crony for his bottle receiving/full goods transfer and moved over to a 52,000 square foot warehouse on Bentall Street, where it became our shipping and warehousing center. This allowed the floor of the warehouse they had vacated to be cut with masonry saws and removed for the in placing of pasteurizer footings, larger sewer lines and a glass trap.

The existing conveyor system feeding No. 1 bottle washer had to be modified to also supply the new No. 2 bottle washer being assembled just north of the uncasing area. Within months this corner of the brewery became the most confused battlefield any had witnessed. Its successful completion was due as much to the dedication of those who worked around and on it as to the planning that went into it.

When completed both bottling lines (No. 1 above and No. 2 on ground level) would receive old and new glass through the six uncasing saw lines in the original bottle shop. Both would discharge full cartons to the five palletizers in the original shipping and warehouse building, where each pallet of cased beer would be Saran wrapped and immediately loaded into trucks for transfer to Bentall Street.

Over in the brew house, the new PLC system required thousands of feet of wiring to run between the Allen Bradley control room and the brew house console. These wires interconnected all the valves, switches and sensors that initiated or monitored the brewing procedure. The relays, timers and microswitches allowed workers to direct processes, just like a road's intersection signal light or sign directs vehicular traffic to flow a certain way. A programmable logic controller (PLC) not only directs but also monitors to ensure the function is carried out. It can also redirect, just like a policeman standing under a traffic signal can redirect traffic regardless of the signal's shape or color. And PLCs can blow a whistle, ring a bell, flash a light or shut down a process.

While many stand in awe of how programmable electronics manage control systems, they are not infallible and are subject to malfunctions that require special skills to trouble shoot and repair. Colin Park, and later several of the newer electricians went to the Allen Bradley school to familiarize themselves with these systems. It was not an easy transition, even for those having great electrical skills, for microcircuitry is even more elusive than most electrical system, regardless of what type switching or relaying controls are considered. Fortunately, the control people supplied video training films, and a video camera was employed to record troubleshooting and repair of many of the mechanical and electrical systems. Art Pugh supervised a in-plant video to safety orient all Molson employees with the new equipment, especial all the safety interlocks and lockout procedures.

Doug Pearson, installing Bailey Meter's highly transistorize combustion control system on the new packaged boiler, fortified their massive user manuals with such a film. Bailey's controls utilized silicone chips, thermistors, LEDs and many other space age components that could make the engineer's job either a dream or a nightmare. To ensure the former rather than the latter, Doug made a video training film that not only described the removal and replacement procedure of its dozen or so microcircuit boards, but how to trouble shoot and locate a problem area. (For many of the other older engineers of that day, this film just augmented the deep feeling in our gut that we had a tiger by the tail, and only by the last few hairs of that appendage.)

The full goods palletizers automatically load and lower pallets of cased beer, which are then wrapped in a protective film before going to the shipping center. *Photo: Molson*

Though few of us mastered the finer points of this analog/digital control, we could all operate it with some degree of finesse, and often many problems could be traced back to the equipment it monitored— those with which we were familiar and could repair.

Dick Niven began to schedule plant electricians around the clock on each shift, and they were much more knowledgeable than the engineers with electronics. Only when they could not correct a problem in the time available to them, did we call in Bailey Meter's service man at a $500 fee. However, plant electricians proved capable of fixing more than 50 percent of the control problems.

With the installation of the big new rotary ammonia compressor and its 700-horsepower motor, the screaming rotary air compressor and the roomful of other machines, the engineroom could be a fearful place to the uninitiated. So, through this period with so much construction underway in both the boiler room and engineroom and scaffolding and pipe work going on overhead, these areas were closed off to all except those actually working there.

This also became true in many areas in packaging, and such restrictions made the job of getting to the production areas difficult for everyone. This pointed up the need to find a new route not only into the brewery, but a new more central location for the lunchroom and change areas. Even then the roof of the old packaging building seemed an ideal place to locate these, but to move people safely back and forth from it defied all.

That production went ahead and went well was certainly a big plus in job attitude for those brewery workers who had to work under, over and around all this confusion. It was great credit to all that both the boiler and the brewing automation project came on stream with the minimum of disconcerting misadventures. It certainly required great dedication by the uncasing crew to maintain a steady flow of bottles up to the bottling line, when all around havoc was rampant.

Over in A block, where Rick's project of yeast removal and the train system seemingly required miles of new stainless steel pipe, they began installing a huge network of light weight stainless steel sewer pipes hung from the cellar ceilings. Thus, the cellar crews had to work under the most trying of conditions. It was like a scene from Dante's *Inferno*, the howl of cut-off saws, the clatter and banging of tools against metal, echoing forth from the smoke of welding and burning; the damp cold atmosphere where heli-arc flashes reflected on the sweat-streaked white tanks and white walls gave everything a hellish hue.

Through this came the leather jacketed welders and fitters, lugging heavy welding equipment and subassemblies of gleaming stainless steel pipes. Around and over them came the gum-booted cellar men, their white clothing clinging wetly to their limbs and body, pulling their heavy white hoses like draft horses, until the tangle of hoses, pipes and wires on the yeast and water flooded floors almost defied a safe place to put one's foot, while lifting the other out an equally hazardous location.

As Bob Chambers closed in his work area on the north side of the packaging center and began installing bottling equipment, the tile setters and painters followed closely behind, thus allowing the conveyor installations to proceed almost on their heels. Workers had to rush to complete services installation to stay apace of their rapid progress. The huge Micom ammonia screw compressor gave several surprises before it was tamed. First its 700-horsepower motor blew the expensive switch gear installed on the mezzanine platform into

The author with ammonia compressors.   *Photo: Molson*

near junk, much to the chagrin of the supplier who quickly tried to shift the blame and its rebuilding cost over to the brewery.

The switch unfortunately did not shift under load conditions, but through time sequencing, and it attempted to do this before the compressor had come up to speed. To ensure this would not happen again, we installed an unloader that dumped head pressure till safe rpms were attained. Next, there were terrifying freeze ups as this huge machine literally sucked the system dry and produced so little super heat that it froze almost up to the condensers. This called for a rethinking of the piping and required a number of pump-downs of the ammonia (evacuate all NH_3 from the pipes) on weekends and weld in new pipes before it was alleviated.

Problems with upgrading the CO_2 system were many; the brewery created some and others were due to the supplier's questionable design. Many took years to finally solve, others took thousands of dollars of material and supplies to eradicate. Of equal exasperation, though not quite as long-termed, were the problems uncovered in upgrading the plant's air system. The system had been taxed to above maximum flows to maintain production, until the new and larger units were received and installed. Both could trace many of their later problems back to those periods when design capacities were exceeded. With the older compressors, a replaceable desiccant drier

230

was used to remove moisture that had not precipitated out of the air going through the separator. As demands increased, this desiccant drier was sorely pressed to prevent moisture being migrated over to the many sensitive controls and air users in the packaging department. When the desiccant became over saturated with moisture, it broke down into a dust, which could and did get carried by the swift flowing air into the process piping. This highly corrosive material could build up and plug small orifices or corrode mild steel piping, especially in the unprotected area of threaded joints.

All atmospheric air contains a certain amount of moisture in it. Surprisingly, on nice dry days the air carries more moisture than on cool, wet days when the moisture is precipitated out as rain. In compressing this air, its temperature is raised far above the ambient (room) temperature, vaporizing any moisture into a gas (steam). If this can be chilled quickly, the moisture will precipitate out in droplets (rain), which with proper baffling can be separated out of the air stream, and drained off. To ensure dry instrument air, the air from this moisture separator is then led through a drier where any remaining moisture in it is absorbed by either a disposable drying desiccant (calcium chloride base) or by a desiccant that can be removed from service and regenerated.

In the new drying system, two driers were installed, which allowed one to be on the regenerative cycle while the other was in service. Packaging had added many new air users during the latter years, especially in the uncasing area blowing dust and cardboard, and up on the line where pneumatic muscles (air cylinders) pushed bottles and cartons together. This had created a high in-line velocity of air speeding toward these users, especially after the brewery added the larger compressors and pressure drop no longer was a problem. But, therein lay the greatest problem. The old desiccant dust that had been migrating slowly up the various headers and pipes during those earlier days, now was being swept up like a dust storm that began to plug orifices, filters and score micro finished cylinder walls in actuators.

Weekend after weekend, people worked to remove pipes and fittings and clean out the accumulated desiccant dust, some of which had solidified in rock hard lumps and scale. What couldn't be remove, was by-passed with new runs of larger pipe. Eventually, most of the complaints from the packaging air system were laid to rest.

By late 1982, many of the trying moments were over; Rick was getting his system on line, Bob was looking forward to a bottling run after Christmas, and I had a large crew of novice but enthusiastic painters busy making everything look pretty again. It was at this time the old steam tug *Master* got into trouble. This time there was no knowing watchman to alert help to her dire circumstance, nor was there much immediate help when she was found submerged to her funnel at the local shipyard. In fact, callous disregard for her perilous position almost doomed her future as an operating marine artifact.

Fred Kirby had carried out the role of ship's husband before he retired, a quaint old country terminology that pointed up the reason why ships are often referred to as she. The ship's husband was the manager for all the ships needs and insured she was not liable to debt nor wanting in seaworthiness. It was during this time that she was visited by a heavy set, husky young fellow more knowledgeable in rebuilding old classic cars than tugboats. He would become her most noteworthy husband. Jim Macdonald was appalled at her sad condition and made a decision that through the next four years would try him to the limit.

He decided to volunteer his services rebuilding the old tug in its entirety. And his goal was to show her at Expo 86, so all the world could see how beautiful a sight a boat under a full head of steam really was. He called on Dick Smith, a retired marine engineer who had served his time on the CPR's pre-war Empress shipping line to the Orient, to help him.

To secure help and funding for repairs to the tug, they restructured the group into the SS *Master* Society, with Jim as treasurer and restoration coordinator, and Dick as chief engineer. Duly registered under the Provincial Societies Act, these two began a restoration on the tug that would finally realize a seaworthiness almost equal to that created by Arthur Moscrop when he built her, the *RFM* and the *Sea Swell* all at the same time on the north shore of False Creek, right behind the brewery in 1922.

By early summer the following year, the *Master* was cleaned and patched up enough to honor a flag waving commitment to Vancouver City by leading a parade of ships through the harbor, before commencing a mother ship role during the city's three-day Sea Fair Festivities. By early fall she was deemed unable to carry on any longer and her long overdue restoration was begun. Dick began stripping the boiler ready for retubing and replacing the breechings. Jim got the services of several volunteer shipwrights to rebuild the house-work, decks and gunwales; others volunteered to lug ashore the debris of their efforts. Then the first of several little miracles happened.

Jim got an offer from the developers of a waterfront housing and shopping center in New Westminster wanting a nautical theme, who offered the use of the redundant Public Works dock and its workshop and equipment, for the tugs refit. Sea Span moved her over there so quickly, the plastic covering protecting the open parts of the ship, flapped wildly like the sails of the old wreck of the *Hesperus*. There she joined the former public works snag puller *Samson V.*

With the *Master* enjoying her first real home, Jim began to look at the more long-term needs. An offer from the Federal Winter Works Program provided skilled shipwrights and carpenters. And a donation of logs and rough lumber from Macmillan and Bloedel, encouraged Jim to begin pulling the tug apart, rebuilding as they went. The government welding school (PVI) offered to fabricate tanks, funnel and boiler breechings, and a supplier miraculously came forward to supply the necessary steel.

Back at the brewery Bob Chambers was enjoying a certain degree of success with his new bottling line, and Rick Killan's project went on stream with a minimum of misadventures. However, 1983 had one harrowing prospect loom up—the industry wide decision to change back from the stubby beer bottle to the long neck. It was a slightly different configuration of bottle than that of former years under the Sick flag. It was a marketing ploy; people like a change and the stubby, though ideal for storage and handling, did not have the consumer appeal that a tall, lean bottle of beer suggested.

The bottle change was not ideal for Molsons; they had put millions of dollars into equipment to package the stubby bottle, and several million more into creating spare parts stores in Edmonton and Toronto. The new equipment already installed, top of the line though it was, suffered from expensive and time-consuming spare parts delivery. Molsons had created their own stores of spare parts. That almost proved their undoing, for the change required they modify them as well as the parts on our machines, and this taxed most to the limit.

An elaborate plan was devised so that dual parts were on hand near each machine. Fortunately, the brewery's two-line operation allowed the opportunity to continue packaging while making the change over, though it could not help avoid the horrendous bottle breakage experienced until all the parts and all the machines were again working together.

During this period Hal Moran, president of Molsons B.C. Ltd., having weathered such a tumultuous period in the brewery's growth was rewarded by an executive position in head office. After a farewell party, which resolved itself into a roast depicting some of the lighter moments of his tenure at Burrard Street, Hal left for Montreal. A few months after Jack Beach had returned to Burrard Street to take over Hal Moran's office, Art Pugh gave notice of his intentions to retire in the spring.

He planned to celebrate that moment by driving north in his truck until he could roll the front wheels into the Arctic Ocean. Despite being born in Australia and spending many of his earlier years at sea, Art Pugh had probably traveled over more back roads, trails and rivers in B.C. than most native born sons of this wilderness province. His trip north with his family was to be his grand finale. It almost was denied him.

Art was finding the mounting demands required to manage his department were exacting their toll on his stamina. He was spending more time resting up for the next day's or the next week's onslaught, and less time enjoying the fruits of his labors. With thirty-five years of service to this brewery, he decided it was time for a real rest. Unfortunately, the stress of the change over from stubbies to long necks with its long hours of overtime, had wearied his body until one evening he collapsed in agony on his livingroom floor.

The frightening diagnosis of cancer of the bowel would have driven most men to despair, but Art, when I visited him the evening before his operation, was already planning out his trip north for early September instead of early June. He was confident the extra three months for convalescence would regain the vigor and stamina he required for the trip.

His great optimism carried him through his ordeal, and true to his convictions, he did make the arduous truck trip to the Arctic Ocean. He even came back to the brewery on short intervals as a consultant, but enjoyed life as a gentleman farmer out in south Langley until the end. This incident caused me to rethink my own vulnerability. I, too, found the demands of the job creating a weariness that only longer hours of rest and afternoon naps on the weekend fortified me to carry on.

Approaching the magic company service number of ninety, composed of service years and age, I was pleased to learn that I would be eligible for a full pension the following year. Molsons agreed to a retirement date of June 1, 1985, and that gave them a whole year to find a replacement, but it gave me just twelve short months to get my department in order.

While I managed to accomplish most of the necessary tidying-up tasks, Molsons failed to entice a replacement for my job. Few who looked over the lengthy three pages of job responsibilities or visited me for an on the job inspection, thought it a desirable position. Even Fred Bogden, transferring here from his superintendent's job at Prince Albert Brewery, decided at the last moment against taking it. It was left to our new plant manager Ian Stanner and our personnel manager Glen Swartz to solve my retirement problem.

Just over a week before my glorious hour was to arrive, Ian and Glen resolved the predicament by giving the exterior building maintenance responsibility to Bob Chambers, whose own workload had lightened considerable with completion of the packaging project. They shifted over to Dick Niven the yard and building interior maintenance; and then Fred Bogden, reconsidering the new terms of reference, accepted the role of chief engineer.

Spending my last week with Molsons, gifting my knowledge and hiding places to Fred, I enjoyed several nice luncheons feted by the various departmental staff groups. The company's official dinner bash saw several government officials and contractors there to present me with gifts and tokens of appreciation, but it took many months before the real feeling of retirement was realized.

For six months I rested a lot, going on short vacation trips with our camper van or putting in a few hours a week down helping rebuild the steam tug *Master*. One day, the phone rang and Captain Cy Andrews invited my son Rod and I, to come over to Allied Shipyards and meet Don Christie, the new owner of the SS *Beaver*, a replica of the Hudson's Bay ship.

Don had a skilled shipwright and crew of volunteer's working day and night to get the *Beaver* ready for Expo 86, and Cy hoped I would join them to look after the rigging and gear and then sail as his mate and relief skipper when that was realized. Rod worked four days on and four days off with the Burnaby Fire Department and had considerable experience rebuilding several other old boats. Duly impressed, Don invited Rod to join him rebuilding the *Beaver*.

235

Making it conditional with my son's off hours of work with the BFD, we both agreed to become a father and son team.

It was pretty nasty work at first, especially during those late winter and early spring days. Because of illness, Cy Andrews recommended I become the ship's captain, promising to return when and if he could after suitable convalescence. Then one sunny warm day in early May, the steamship inspector signed all the papers registering the old girl as a class-four passenger vessel and I as her master. The next day, after extracting ourselves from the confusion of the shipyard's basin and waving off our helpful tug, we cleared Second Narrows and sailed for Expo 86.

A month later the *Master* was ready to join us, and I gratefully accepted the honor to command her on the latter part of her voyage to Expo 86. My cup indeed runneth over with joy. Over the next ten years, the SS *Beaver* and I made 1,265 voyages and performed 62 weddings before I returned her to Victoria in March, 1995.

Epilogue

After buying out Carlings O'Keefe, Fosters of Australia announced during late 1990 that they were merging their interest with Molson and would be augmenting some of their existing breweries to brew Molson's beers, while shutting down others and brewing their beers at Molsons. The amalgamation of these three great brewing interests under the name of Molson Breweries Ltd. would enjoy well over 60 percent of the Canadian beer market, leaving the balance for John Labatt, Interior Breweries at Creston (amalgamation of Nelson, Trail and Cranbrook Breweries) plus the import beer makers to fight over. British Columbia's megabrewing center would be the brewery on Burrard Street.

In the United States, Martlet and Century Importing would then be marketing about twenty-four brands of imported beers plus the well-known Molson products. These include Foster's Lager from Australia, Kirin from Japan, John Courage brews from United Kingdom, Kronenberg from France, Caribe from Trinidad and Steinlager from New Zealand. More than 20 million cases of beer would be sold through these two outlets during the first year of the merger. Helping to create the awesome marketing numbers that place Molson as the oldest established business in Canada and one of its most successful, is Molson's longtime support of sports. While the National Hockey League and international skiing come quickly to mind, their support of the Winter Olympic Games and figure skating are constantly acknowledged on local television.

The vitality of the Molson organization and the aggressiveness of the people who man the Burrard Street brewery will ensure the continued growth of this imposing giant. Unfortunately, growth often causes remoteness between the many parts that form the whole. During the period of this story the company managed to work together as a team, not always in accord but at least dedicated to the singularity of the endeavor. Thus, Molson overcame many obstacles and its workers earned a modest reward for the success of their pursuits.

Only time will tell how well the new team handles their problems. The megabrewery on Burrard Street today is the amalgamation of many breweries that did not survive the problems of their times. But, as has been noted, they all played a part, or at least complimented the story, of this great seaport brewery.

After my retirement, the engineering team under Rick Killan completed three big jobs before they, too, took their leave. Bob Chambers installed another huge 500-barrel kettle before he left. He had already determined where the tall vent duct would rise up to the roof, and pointed out with some glee to me a hole drilled through the floor under the desk in his office. It was evident he realized his office would be no more. But Bob couldn't have cared less as his retirement home on the Sunshine Coast was near completion and he would soon vacate his office.

Dennis Johnson, the young and upcoming professional engineer, would leave Molsons for more challenging fields. He had been a great help to me during my trials and tribulations of the power plant expansion. His last job was to move the administration office people into new offices above the unitank cellar and prepare the site south of B block for the eight outdoor unitanks that replaced the administration building.

Rick Killan completed the unitank installation, then upgraded the carbon dioxide collection system and deaerated water system before he too left for more rewarding fields. Dick Niven moved up to engineering superintendent and remained there until Molson, Foster and Carlings amalgamated, then he too retired to start his own company building and supplying conveying equipment.

For the others, they were sorted out by age, ambition and skills. Many elected to stay on but an equal number did not. Those who elected early retirement packages enjoy much better pension benefits than we who had retired earlier. People, who still looked forward to many more working years, accepted a generous separation package and went to new employers.

Across Canada alone, sixteen breweries were involved in the merger; almost half of them would close their doors. Thousands of people who thought they had a secure job lost them when the deal was signed. Some took early retirement while others received generous separation payments and decided to look elsewhere for new employment opportunties. For many of the others whose talents and age were viable to the brewery's needs, positions were offered in production and marketing which promised attractive rewards for ambitious endeavors. Unfortunately, there were some who did not fit in to any of these categories; hopefully they found other vocations that were equally as rewarding.

Fred Bogden was one of those that elected an early retirement package, then accepted a rewarding position with the government as boiler inspector; while John Morris of Carling O'Keefe was equally happy to take Fred's place as chief engineer at Molsons. Tom Saunders, taking over Dick Niven's job as engineering manager, finally built the new employee's facilities on the roof of the old bottle shop before trashing the portable buildings that had housed the employee's lunchroom three times longer than Art Pugh planned. Rob Campbell took over employee relations at Molsons from Glen Swartz, who along with Dave Lewthwaite joined Fraser Valley Milk Producer's Dairyland division.

A new department was created to handle Molson's public affairs. Bruce W. Pearce, who started his career twenty years before with Carlings at their Etobicoke plant, became manager of this department in late 1990. His support of my efforts to write this story, and his contribution of the many graphics that accompany it, has ensured this book will be a presentation worthy of all those people who dedicated much if not all their lives in the brewing industry, and thus ensured that the huge mega brewerey that sits so imposingly at Cornwall and Burrard Streets, will be a viable legacy to all who follow in our footsteps. —W.A.H.

A Historic List of B.C. Breweries

Atlin Brewing Company, Atlin (1903–10)
Bavaria Brewery, 138 Fort St., Victoria (1872–92)
Breed Brewery, New Westminster (1868–74)
Canadian Brewing And Malting, Vancouver (1910–18)
Capilano Brewery Ltd., Powell St., Vancouver (1934–58)
Carlings Brewery Ltd., Vancouver (1957–89)
Castle Brewery, Nelson (1899–1904)
City Brewery, Seaton St., Vancouver (1887–89)
City Brewery, Agnes/Douglas St., New Westminster (1880–89)
Columbia Bottling Wks., Rossland (1898–1904)
Columbia Brewery, Powell and Victory St., Vancouver (1889–1910)
Columbia Brewery, Grand Forks (1898–1910)
Colonial Brewery, Douglas/Blanshard, Victoria (1860–68)
Cranbrook Brewing & Malting, Cranbrook (1868–71)
Cunio Brewery, Barkerville (1868–71)
Doering & Marstrand Brewing Co., Vancouver (1892–1902)
Elk Valley Brewing Co., Natal (1910–19)
Elkhorn Brewery, Greenwood (1899–1905)
Enterprise Brewery Ltd., Revelstoke (1898–1918)
Esquimalt Brewery Co., Victoria (1890–1901)
Fairall's Brewery (Excelsior), Victoria (1880–88)
Fernie/Fort Steele Brewing Co., Fernie (1915–37)
Fort Steele Brewery, Fort Steele (1878–1915)
Excelsior Brewing (Fairall's Brewery), Victoria (1888–95)
Imperial Brewing Co. (Rainier), Kamloops (1880–1921)
James Bay Brewery, Victoria (1862–66)
Kaslo Brewing Co., Kaslo (1897–1903)
Kerr Brewery, Barkerville (1868–69)
Kootenay Breweries Ltd., Trail (1897–1937)
Labatt's Brewery, New Westminster (1958–)

Lansdown Brewery, Nanaimo (1885–1921)
Le Roi Brewery, Rossland (1897–1918)
Lion Brewery, Rossland (1897–1904)
Lucky Lager Brewing Co., New Westminster (1941–58)
Nanaimo Brewing Co., Nanaimo (1889–91)
Mainland Brewery Ltd., Vancouver (1888–92)
Merritt Brewery, Merritt (1910–16)
Millstream Brewery, Nanaimo (1863–65)
Milwaukee Brewery, Gulch Trail (1899–1910)
Molson's Capilano Brewery, Vancouver(1958–)
Moyie Brewery , Moyie (1899–1910)
Nelson Brewery, Nelson (1898–1915)
New York Brewery, Sandon (1892–1905)
Ofsnher Brewery (see VBL), Vernon (1892–97)
O'Keefe Brewery, Vancouver (1958–74)
Old English Brewing Co., Victoria (1923–25)
Phoenix Brewery, Yates St., Victoria (1859–1924)
Phoenix Brewing Co., Phoenix (1899–1910)
Pilsener Brewing Co., Cumberland (1909–16)
Quesnel Brewery, Quesnel (1865–69)
Rainier Brewing Co., Kamloops (1921–28)
Red Lion Brewery, Nanaimo (1884–89)
Red Star Brewery, Brewery Creek, Vancouver (1890–91)
Revelstoke Brewery, Revelstoke (1898–1900)
Rossland Spring Brewery, Rossland (1896–1901)
Royal Brewing Co., Chilco St., Vancouver (1902–10)
Salt Spring Brewery, Nanaimo (1874–75)
San Francisco Brewery, Brewery Creek, Vancouver (1889–90)
Silver Spring Brewery, Victoria (1897–1957)
Stanley Park Brewery, Vancouver (1897–1902)
Union Brewing Co., Nanaimo (1891–1918)
Vancouver Breweries Ltd., Vancouver (1912–57)
Vernon Brewery Ltd., Vernon (1897–1910)
Victoria Brewing Co., Victoria (1859–1954)
Westminster Brewing Co., New Westminster (1882–41)
William's Brewery, Fort Steele Street, Victoria (1877–78)
Ymir Brewery Ltd., Ymir (1899–1905)
Yuengling Brewing Co., Trail (1899–1900)

Cooking with Beer

There are many ways to use beer in cooking. These are a few tried-and-true old time classics. Boiling the mundane weiner in beer enhances it to gourmet quality and using beer in place of wine in an English trifle makes for an interesting dessert.

Beer-Glazed Ham

1 can (3-4 lbs) ham
1 tbsp dry mustard
1 tsp ground cloves
2 tbsp vinegar
½ cup brown sugar, packed
1 can beer

Remove ham from can. Place ham fat side up on rack in shallow baking pan. Combine cloves, sugar, mustard and vinegar and spread over ham. Pour beer in bottom of pan. Bake in slow oven (325°F) for one hour, basting with beer every five minutes.

Luncheon Meat Bake

1 (12 oz.) can luncheon meat, sliced
1 (20 oz.) can pineapple tidbits, drained
1 (23 oz.) can sweet potatoes
¼ cup brown sugar
½ tsp salt
½ tsp cinnamon
¾ cup beer

In 2-quart baking dish, arrange alternate layers of luncheon meat, pineapple and sweet potatoes, slicing large potatoes in half length-wise. Sprinkle with brown sugar, salt and cinnamon. Pour beer over all. Bake in moderate oven (375°F) for 35 minutes.
Makes 4 servings.

Beer-Rabbit with Sausage

1 lb. Cheddar cheese, grated
3 fresh egg yolks
2 slices of toast
12 oz. beer
2 tbsp butter or margarine
2 (8 oz.) cans breakfast sausages

Place cheese and butter (or margarine) in double boiler. Heat slowly over simmering water until partially melted. Add 4 oz. (½ cup) beer and blend until smooth. Beat egg yolks slightly, add 4 oz. (½ cup) of beer and blend with cheese mixture. Cook slowly, stirring constantly, until thick and smooth. Simmer sausages in remaining 4 oz. (½ cup) of beer in frying pan until beer has evaporated and sausages are browned. Spoon sauce over toast and top with sausages. *Makes 6 servings.*

Quick Chicken and Beer

1 can condensed cream of mushroom or chicken soup
¼ to ½ tsp curry powder
2 tbsp catsup chili sauce
1 (6 oz.) can boned chicken, diced
1/3 cup of beer

In a saucepan, blend soup, curry powder, beer and catsup and add chicken; heat thoroughly. Serve over hot seasoned rice, toast or heated chow mein noodles. *Makes 4 servings.*

Beer Nog

3 eggs
2 cans beer, chilled
¼ cup light cream
Grated nutmeg or lemon rind
2 tbsp sugar

Combine eggs, cream and sugar; beat until well blended. Add chilled beer, beating constantly. Serve at once, sprinkle with nutmeg or lemon rind. *Makes approximately 1 quart.*

Beer Spice Cake

½ cup shortening	¼ tsp ginger
1 cup brown sugar, packed	½ tsp nutmeg
1 egg	1 tsp baking powder
1 ½ cups sifted flour	¼ tsp baking soda
½ tsp salt	½ cup chopped nuts
¾ tsp cinnamon	1 cup beer

Cream shortening and sugar until light and fluffy. Add egg and mix until thoroughly blended. Sift together dry ingredients; add nuts. Add alternately with beer to creamed mixture, blending well after each addition. Pour into greased and floured 8 x 8 x 2 inch baking pan. Bake in moderate over (350°F) for 50 minutes or until cake tests done. Cool and frost with chocolate beer frosting.

Chocolate Beer Frosting

3 tbsp butter or margarine
2 squares unsweetened chocolate, melted
2 cups sifted icing sugar
2 to 3 tbsp beer

Cream butter or margarine; add sugar gradually, beating well after each addition. Add chocolate and beer; beat until smooth and of spreading consistency.

Bibliography

American Can Company. *Cooking with Beer*, New York, 1950.

Berton, Pierre. *The Great Railway*, Toronto: McClelland and Stewart, 1972.

Brewers Association of Canada. *Brewing information in Canada*, 1980.

Brewers Journal. "Fritz Sick," Aug. 1952, Vol. 107, No. 2, Chicago, U.S.A.

Denison, Merrill. *The Barley and the Stream*, Toronto: McClelland and Stewart, 1975.

Master Brewers Association. *History of Brewing,* Vol. 7, No. 1, New York, 1946.

Ormsby, Margaret A. *British Columbia: A History,* The MacMillan Co. of Canada, 1958.

Schoutsen, John. Molson newsletter, *The Eye Opener*, Vancouver, 1981.

Sicks' Brewery. Monthly magazine, *Enterpriser*, Aug. 1950, Seattle, U.S.A.

Woods, Shirley E. Jr. *The Molson Saga, 1763-1983*, Toronto: Doubleday Canada Ltd., 1983.

Index

More Great HANCOCK HOUSE History Titles

Alaska Bound
Michael Dixon
ISBN 0-9639981-0-2
5.5 x 8.5 • sc • 190 pp.

Big Timber Big Men
Carol Lind
ISBN 0-88839-020-3
8.5 x 11 • hc • 153 pp.

Border Bank Bandits
Frank Anderson
ISBN 0-88839-255-9
5.5 x 8.5 • sc • 88 pp.

B.C.'s Own Railroad
Lorraine Harris
ISBN 0-88839-125-0
5.5 x 8.5 • sc • 64 pp.

Buckskins, Blades, and Biscuits
Allen Kent Johnston
ISBN 0-88839-363-6
5.5 x 8.5 • sc • 176 pp.

Buffalo People
Mildred Valley Thornton
ISBN 0-88839-479-9
5.5 x 8.5 • sc • 208 pp.

Captain McNeill and His Wife the Nishga Chief
Robin Percival Smith
ISBN 0-88839-472-1
5.5 x 8.5 • sc • 256 pp.

Crooked River Rats
Bernard McKay
ISBN 0-88839-451-9
5.5 x 8.5 • sc • 176 pp.

The Dowager Queen
William A. Hagelund
ISBN 0-88839-486-1
5.5 x 8.5 • sc • 168 pp.

Fraser Valley Story
Don Waite
ISBN 0-88839-203-6
5.5 x 8.5 • sc • 96 pp.

Gold Creeks & Ghost Towns (WA)
Bill Barlee
ISBN 0-88839-452-7
8.5 x 11 • sc • 224 pp.

Gold! Gold!
Joseph Petralia
ISBN 0-88839-118-8
5.5 x 8.5 • sc • 112 pp.

Great Western Train Robberies
Don DeNevi
ISBN 0-88839-287-7
5.5 x 8.5 • sc • 202 pp.

Harbour Burning
William A. Hagelund
ISBN 0-88839-488-8
5.5 x 8.5 • sc • 208 pp.

JailBirds & Stool Pigeons
Norman Davis
ISBN 0-88839-431-4
5.5 x 8.5 • sc • 144 pp.

Mackenzie Yesterday & Beyond
Alfred Aquilina
ISBN 0-88839-083-1
5.5 x 8.5 • sc • 202 pp.

Mining in B.C.
Geoffrey Taylor
ISBN 0-919654-87-8
8.5 x 11 • sc • 195 pp.

New Exploration of the Canadian Arctic
Ronald E. Seavoy
ISBN 0-88839-522-1
5.5 x 8.5 • sc • 192 pp.

Potlatch People
Mildred Valley Thornton
ISBN 0-88839-491-8
5.5 x 8.5 • sc • 320 pp.

Quest for Empire
Kyra Wayne
ISBN 0-88839-191-9
5.5 x 8.5 • sc • 415 pp.

Timeless Trails of the Yukon
Dolores Cline Brown
ISBN 0-88839-484-5
5.5 x 8.5 • sc • 184 pp.

Walhachin
Joan Weir
ISBN 0-88839-982-0
5.5 x 8.5 • sc • 104 pp.

Warplanes to Alaska
Blake Smith
ISBN 0-88839-401-2
8.5 x 11 • hc • 256 pp.

Yukon Gold
James/Susan Preyde
ISBN 0-88839-362-8
5.5 x 8.5 • sc • 96 pp.

View all HANCOCK HOUSE titles at **www.hancockhouse.com**